NEW AND EXPANDED EDITION

WHAT YOUR CHILD NEEDS TO KNOW WHEN

ACCORDING TO THE BIBLE / ACCORDING TO THE STATE

WITH EVALUATION CHECK LISTS FOR GRADES K-8

ROBIN SAMPSON

HEART OF WISDOM PUBLISHING

WHAT YOUR CHILD NEEDS TO KNOW WHEN:
ACCORDING TO THE BIBLE / ACCORDING TO THE STATE

FIRST EDITION:
© 1993 BY ROBIN SAMPSON

NEW AND EXPANDED EDITION:
© 1996 BY ROBIN SAMPSON

REVISED 2001 EDITION
© JULY 2001 REPRINT MAY 2003
Heart of Wisdom Publishing, Woodbridge, VA

Web site: http://HeartofWisdom.com

E-mail: info@Heartofwisdom.com

ISBN: 0-9701816-1-2

ACKNOWLEDGEMENTS

Dedication

*And I thank Christ Jesus our Lord, who hath
enabled me, for that he counted me faithful, putting
me into the ministry;…This is a faithful saying, and
worthy of all acceptation, that Christ Jesus came
into the world to save sinners; of whom I am chief.
Howbeit for this cause I obtained mercy, that in me
first Jesus Christ might shew forth all longsuffering,
for a pattern to them which should hereafter believe
on him to life everlasting.*

—1 TIMOTHY 1:12-:15-16

To my children, and grandchildren,
born and unborn,
may they all meditate on the book of the law
day and night, and observe to do
according to all that is written therein.

Thank you all for your many words of encouragement.

I feel I must share this and pass on what has been a blessing to me. After much contemplation and reasoning (excuses) children are older (5th & 7th), already have resources of this nature, do I really need another book like this, etc., I listened to my heart (and confessed again all the money I had wasted on curriculum out of fear) and bought the book - *What Your Child Needs to Know When.*

The main reason it appealed to me was because of all the descriptions telling how it included not so much what the state expects, but first and foremost what and how the Lord wants our families focused on and the biblical model of learning and the education of our children. This book is great!!! The bibliography is excellent-- I had already read some of the books and found more I would like to read, but Mrs. Sampson has pulled all these resources together for a convicting, mind-renewing read that leaves one not only informed, but challenged and focused on the Lord for His perfect direction for our children-- their hearts and mind and education.

If you've not yet been exposed to this kind of thinking, then this is an excellent resource to read. If you have already been exposed to this kind of thinking and the renewing and growing is ongoing, then this is an excellent book to read.

I am blessed that I live in a state where achievement testing is not mandatory, but I still will have use and value for the evaluation lists. But even if you never use any of this information, the first half of the book which is what I have thus described is worth every cent. If you keep a list of items you either want to purchase or look at book fairs, etc., this is one to put on that list!

....

I'm currently reading your book *What Your Child Needs to Know When* and it is EXCELLENT!!, and I can't wait to begin the Heart of Wisdom teaching approach. I felt like it was an answer to prayer when I read about it. Keep up the great work and may God bless you!!

....

I recently bought and received your book *What Your Child Needs to Know When.* I have to tell you that it is much more than the catalogs describe it as.I have been wanting to run our school days in a different way (with more emphasis on scripture), but didn't really know how to change my rigid-schedule-ways, and didn't have the courage to do so for a long time. Even though most of our curriculum (if not all of it) is Biblically-based, it just wasn't the way that I wanted things.

It has seemed to me in the past that if I didn't run a tightly scheduled ship, that things would run amuck, get out of hand, and that the kids just didn't seem to get their things done by the end of the day when left to work at their own pace. To avoid seeing some child aimlessly walking around, or wasting time, I decided long ago that we would have a

schedule to go by to keep them focused. However, I have never really liked it! I want to be Spirit-led in my schooling. I have read some things that started me thinking of how I could get going in the direction I so desired. The thing that helped me do it was your book!

....

I love the philosophy of teaching and the example of what a typical day might be like for you. God must have really got a hold of me then and things have been really different in our house! If we weren't done with Bible by 8:30 before, I would announce it was time for math! (Sad, Huh?) Now, we start Bible maybe by 8 or 8:30 and sometimes go until 10 or 10:30! And the most exciting thing about it is that after Bible (worship, and memory verses, and much discussion), the kids seem to go on their way and get their work done better and more quickly than before. It has been astounding to me that they get done sooner than before! Thank you for being obedient to the Lord and for being an example to me.

....

I purchased *What Your Child Needs to Know When.* after discovering *A Family Guide to the Biblical Holidays.* This book was such an inspiration to me and helped me to re-evaluate my curriculum choices. For fans of Charlotte Mason and Ruth Beechick, this is a must read! For everyone else considering homeschooling, this book will introduce you to a God-centered method of educating your children, while ensuring you have guidelines to meet state educational standards at the same time. It is a neccesary resource for home-schooling!

....

After reading about the Heart of Wisdom appraoch in *What Your Child Needs to Know When,* my life was changed. We dropped everything and began one of our best years ever. We just used the bible and other living books I had on hand, all three children (16,11,3) working together enjoying the Bible just from what you outlined in the book.(no extra money) Just implementing what we already had, never having had time to use before...I have Homeschooled for 15 years. I really have enjoyed using Ancient History: Adam to Messiah, I absolutely love it. (I am new to computers) But the links from the books are definitely worth it. Thanks again.

....

I bought your *What Your Child Needs to Know When* years ago. I appreciate your admitting to stepping down from earlier conceptions of what is acceptable,grade level,even Biblical or Greek in reference to those timetables we all have whirling in our heads.One confirmation God often gives me that I am plodding along the path intended for my family is continued revelation to just how faulty my conception of education is was and continues to be and how HE continues to encourage my enlightenment despite my relentless insistence on using the compass rose of others.

TABLE OF CONTENTS

This is a letter to my Great, Great Grandfather from my Great, Great Grandmother in 1887 (original spelling).
She wrote this letter as she lay at death's door. She died before it was completed.
What a joy it was to find the thing she desired most for her children was the needful thing Jesus spoke about to Martha.
I hope it touches you in as emotionally powerful a way as it has me.

This you shall find some day. Dear John, when I shall have past away forever, and the cold white stone will be keeping its lonely watch over the lips you have so often pressed, and the sod will be growing green that shall hid forever from your sight the form of one who has so often nestled close to your bossom.

For many long and sleepless nights when all beside my thoughts was at rest. I have wrestled with the consciousness of approching death, until at last it has forced itself upon my mind, and although to you and to my dear children it might seem but nervous imagination, yet Dear John it is so.

Many weary hours have I passed in trying to reconcile myself to leaving you whom I love so well, and the darling children. God has given us, that need a mothers care and prayers.

Oh, how hard to struggle on silently and alone with the sure conviction that I am about to leave all forever and go alone unto the dark valley of death.

But, I know in whom I have trusted and leaning upon his arm, I fear no evil.

I could wish to live if only to watch over you when in pain, sickness and death, but it is not to be so and I submit, you shall share my last thought and prayer on earth.

When I am gone, try and find comfort in Jesus. Never close your eyes to sleep without each reading a verse in the Bible and as my little ones grow up teach them to love the Bible and the church of God.

But, amidst all let memory carry them back to a home where the law of kindness reighed, where the mothers reproving eyes was moistened with tears, and the father frouned more in sorrow than in anger.

I know the spot where you will lay me, often have we stood there together. I loved to visit the place and I know you will love it not the less when I lay there.

WHY THIS BOOK WAS WRITTEN

Each year approaching testing time, homeschool parents panic and wonder "How do I know if we are prepared for the achievement tests?" "When do I teach double digit multiplication?" "What kind of words are on the spelling test?" "When do I teach homophones?" "What are homophones?" etc.

To answer these questions, apprehensions, and fears, I authored the first edition of *What Your Child Needs to Know When,* consisting of the Basic Checklist of Skills (pages 173-310). It rapidly became a homeschool bestseller.

WHY THIS BOOK WAS EXPANDED 1996

Sadly, most homeschoolers that bought the first edition of this book did so out of fear—fear of the state requirements. The check list in the first edition helped homeschoolers meet the standards, but it did not explain how important it is to evaluate why and what we are teaching our children.

Most home educators begin their homeschool journey with a strong desire to teach their children God's Word and the necessary academics to prepare them for life. But somewhere along the way they drift off course. The original goal of teaching their children "God's ways" mysteriously transforms into teaching what the "state" or "world" requires.

This new edition includes 200 pages (explained on pages 9 and 10) to help you put the achievement test and the National standards in the proper perspective.

True wisdom is having the ability to judge correctly and follow the best course of action, based on knowledge and understanding. Knowing the facts (economical, mathematical, scientific, etc.) is not enough to make a godly decision. To make a wise decision one must know what God says about the situation. Almost anyone can gain the necessary scholastic achievement to become a doctor or a businessman, etc. But is it truly achievement if they become a crooked doctor or businessman? What good is it to know five foreign languages if one does not have tongue control? What good is it to read Greek literature if one does not know the Proverbs of Solomon? What good is it to be proficient in accounting if one cheats on income taxes? What good is it to know the names of every bone in the human body if one does not know how to give a kind word?

God gave us directions to reach His divine appointed destination. Our first goal must be to teach our children God's ways and paths. We claim a wonderful promise in Mal. 4:6a: *And he shall turn the heart of the fathers to the children, and the heart of the children to their fathers.* But we often forget verse 4 telling us that the promise happens when we remember

God's ways. Are you aiming your children to have a heart of wisdom, true wisdom, from God? When we remember to acknowledge Him in all our ways, He will direct our paths. I pray this book will give you a glimpse of the true and righteous standards our Lord has for your children. His yoke is easy, His burden is light.

WHY THIS BOOK WAS EXPANDED

The 1996 version of this book included an introduction to the Heart of Wisdom approach (a combination of several formal and informal educational methods.) Since that time this approach has developed and progressed. Chapter 8 "Aiming for a Heart of Wisdom" and Chapter 9 "Implementing a Heart of Wisdom Approach" have been rewritten to reflect the growth. Other chapters have been slightly changed and new resources have been added.

WHAT THIS BOOK IS NOT

This book was not written to make achievement tests the focus of home education. Americans are already concerned too much with academic success and too little with the whole child. Many elements of learning and development are not captured by standardized tests.

The National Education Association's agenda is an aggressive, socialist, anti-life, anti-family policy. Consider the philosophies studied: Plato and Greek thought, Islam, Marxism, Rationalism/Humanism, Buddhism and Eastern mysticism, and Evolution.

Home-school parents can tell their children's strengths and weaknesses from working with them daily. They do not really need achievement tests. First of all, the achievement tests do not test a child's relationship with God. God's spiritual requirements are so much more significant than any academic requirements defined by man. Secondly, home-schooling parents generally have higher standards than the school. Children are all unique with individual God-given talents that cannot be measured by a test. Man's teachings, programs, and standards only evaluate a small portion of a large picture. They do not evaluate wisdom for living a prudent and righteous life. Your most important accomplishment will be to teach your child God's holy Word, true wisdom, to prepare him or her for a life of service.

This is not a book that requires you to start at the top of the Table of Contents and linearly work your way through to the end; although that may not be a bad idea. Read the chapters with an open mind (and a highlighter). Pray about ideas which are new to you, and ideas which seem familiar. Give yourself a chance to see things from a point of view other than what you are accustomed to. This book is divided into four major sections:

SECTION I: PHILOSOPHY OF EDUCATION

Section I explains how we have been conditioned to believe that the state is competent to assess our children's intelligence. This section looks at America's two main world views—Christian and secular, then goes on to clarify the difference between state education and biblical education, taking a brief look at each major time period to see how public education arrived at where it is today, and how important it is to return to a Bible-centered education.

SECTION II: STATE ACHIEVEMENT TESTS

This section explains what achievement tests are, explains test terms, test scores, testing limitations, and how to avoid test anxiety, and answers the most frequently asked test questions. It also critiques testing evaluations and explains better methods of evaluation which you can implement with the information and Check Lists in this book.

SECTION III: TEACHING WISDOM

Section III is an introduction to the Heart of Wisdom teaching approach based on the philosophy described in this book. It explains how to use the Bible as the core of the curriculum. It includes ideas and resources for implementing this approach with any curriculum. For more about this approach visit our Internet site at HomeschoolUnitStudies.com.

SECTION IV: EVALUATION CHECK LISTS

The first two chapters in Section IV include two very important Check Lists—a Bible Reading Check List and a Character Quality Check List. The rest of the check lists in Section IV include basic skills from the main achievement tests. You will fill out the check list of skills at either your child's grade level or a level below. The results will help you in several areas.

USING THE CHECKLISTS

CHECK LISTS AS DIAGNOSTIC TOOLS

The Check Lists are divided by school subjects and then by grade. Each subject division includes teaching advice on that subject and a check list to keep track of your children's skills. These Check Lists are more effective diagnostic tools than achievement tests, which measure knowledge of subjects taught and how well a child can take a test.

Each Check List measures a broad range of abilities or skills that are considered important to success in school. Check Lists show you what to look for when checking the basic skills your child should know in each grade. Check Lists enhance the process of observation, make it more reliable, and help ensure consistency by providing an explanation and illustrations for each performance indicator.

CHECK LISTS AS PLANNING TOOLS TO DEVELOP OR CHOOSE CURRICULUM

If you are using this book to plan your curriculum, simply use the appropriate Check List to make a list of things your child has not mastered, make your own modifications to include or emphasize what you consider high priority, and add special items central to your own philosophy. Once you have determined the goals you want to accomplish, schedule and plan your time. Be sure you master the basics in this book.

Studies show that combining the check list with a cumulation of the child's work, such as a portfolio, will give a great deal of information and evidence about children's activities and development that can be used to enhance instruction and to plan future goals. (Meisels, Liaw, Dorfman, and Fails)

"TEACHING TO THE TEST"

If you invested in this book to "teach to the test," I recommend that you first read this book and reexamine your motives. If you simply teach to the test, the test results will be worthless. You won't know what your child really knows; the results will only reveal whether or not your child has the ability to remember specific information for a short period. Teaching to the test alters what you can interpret from test scores because it involves teaching specific content. It also weakens the direct judgment that can be reasonably drawn about students' knowledge. Rarely should you limit your inference about knowledge to the specific questions asked in a specific format. Making inferences about a broader area of skills gives you a better idea of your child's strong and weak areas.

A downloadable version of this book.is available for purchase at **http://Homeschool-Books.com**. WIth it you can search for text and and print the pages from your computer.

SECTION I
PHILOSOPHY OF EDUCATION

CHAPTER 1

RENEWING YOUR MIND
PREPARE TO BUILD

As you were growing up and receiving an education, you were taught in certain ways, using systems and procedures that you eventually assumed to be the "correct way" to teach and evaluate students. Public schools teach using the curriculum of the state; that is, subjects that can be evaluated through national achievement testing. As a child, you might have been allowed to pray in school, but Bible or spiritual training was not a part of the state's curriculum. This "measurable academics only" approach is based on Greek philosophy. Today's parents generally believe that achievement testing is the only or the best way to assess a child's development and educational advancement. The purpose of this book is to show you what your child needs to know to be prepared for life, which is different from basic academic skills.

An old story illustrates how easy it is to be conditioned into a wrong thinking pattern. A husband asked his wife why she always cut off the end of the rump roast before roasting it. She replied, "I'm not sure why. I've never thought about it. My mother always cut off the end of the rump roast, so there must be a reason." A few weeks later Mother visited the family. The man asked his wife's mother, "We were wondering, why do you always cut off the end of the rump roast before you roast it?" She replied, "I don't know. I have never thought about it. My mother always cut off the end of the rump roast, so there must be a reason." This made them all curious. They decided to call the wife's mother's mother—the grandmother—to ask her. Grandmother answered the phone. The husband asked her, "Your daughter, granddaughter and I were wondering, why do you always cut off the end of the rump roast before you roast it?" Grandmother replied, "Oh, my roasting pan was too small. I had to cut it off it for it to fit in the pan!"

Many of us have been conditioned to believe that "the state" has all the answers and that the state standards are made by a staff of very educated people. These educated people, chosen by the state, surely know more than parents know concerning what children need to prepare for life.

There are many good home-school books, support groups and workshops available to help re-condition (un-brainwash) parents who realize that the state system does not work. It does not do a good job of educating our children or evaluating our children—there are better ways. It is possible to train and educate our children while maintaining God-honoring perspectives.

Why do I think there are so many misled parents? For many years, I have presented a monthly workshop for parents interested in home education. Each session included a question-and-answer period. Even though the majority of the parents were considering home education for religious reasons, the questions asked made it easy to determine that most parents have been indoctrinated with a "public school mentality." These questions will be answered in Section II. For now, let's look at the motives behind these questions.

The most frequently asked questions pertaining to teaching and evaluating home-schooled students are:

1. How do I find out if my child is required to take the achievement test?

2. How do I know if I am meeting state standards?

3. How do I know if the curriculum I am using includes everything on the Achievement Tests?

4. Shouldn't I use textbooks, such as the schools use?

5. What about college?

6. What about algebra, higher math, and lab sciences?

7. How will Goals 2000, Outcome-Based Education (OBE), or the new national standards affect the achievement tests?

8. How do I know that the material I am using will prepare my child for life?

9. How do I motivate my child to learn?

10. What about grades?

11. How do I really know if I am doing enough?

It seems that the state has conditioned many parents to fear teaching their own children. Even the parents looking into teaching kindergarten or first grade at home fear they are not qualified to teach simple things such as the alphabet and basic addition. Of course, we all want our children to do the best they can do in all areas. But, what is the most important thing you can do to prepare your children for life? Teach him algebra, computer skills, writing skills? In all the workshops I have given I have heard the previous questions over and over.

But never once has anyone asked:

1. How can I find out what God's will is for my child?

2. How do I determine my child's God-given gifts?

3. How will I know if my child is saved?

14

4. What does the Bible say we should teach to our children?

5. How did godly men and women teach their children in Bible times?

Many people tend to view life as quartered: partly religious, partly educational, partly professional, and partly leisure-oriented. Yet, everything we do, regardless of occupation—homemaker, businessman, ditch digger, dentist—we should do unto our King. We should be praising and acknowledging Him in learning, work, recreation, and worship—in all things. In the same way, our children need to see their lives revolving around our King—their writing, reading, daily routine, studies, experiments, and friendships. We need to renew our minds—consider God's ways first!

Before planning the school year, sit down and reflect. The Bible says that no one builds a tower unless they first consider what is necessary (Luke 14:28). The parable on the following few pages is an example of how tragic planning with the wrong focus can be.

BUILDING A HOME: A PARABLE

A man decided he wanted to build a house. It would not be just any house. He dreamed of a big, beautiful, luxury home. He wanted to build the most beautiful house in town.

He carefully thought about the basic building materials, the lumber, the plumbing, roofing, the bricks, and even the nails. He made a list of building materials he would need.

The man found out about a free government program that would help him build his house. He went to the state home builder's office and filled out the proper forms. He was assigned a free set of blueprints, a state government builder, and a lot. The man was thrilled, for by going to the government he was able to save a fortune. He didn't have to pay for the blueprints, the builder, or even the lot!

He met with the state builder and showed him his list of building materials. The builder exclaimed, "What a list! You've listed absolutely everything needed to build a spectacular home! I've never seen someone so well prepared. You have everything from chandeliers to the sewage pump." The builder added, "I have just the right tools to build your home. This will be a fine house."

"Let us look forward to the time when we can take the flag of our country and nail it below the Cross, and there let it wave as it waved in the olden times, and let us gather around it an inscribed for our motto: 'Liberty and Union, one and inseparable, now and forever,' and exclaim, Christ first, our country next!"

—Andrew Johnson

"With the National public school system under humanist control, and our nation's public school under similar control, it is obvious to anyone who can see that, under the guise of secularization, the humanists have created the most powerful and pervasive government-funded establishment of religion that has ever existed in the United States."

—Jay Rogers, Director, Media House International, *A Brief History of Christian Influence in U.S. Colleges*

"...We must ask how we can kill the god of Christianity. We need only to insure that our schools teach only secular knowledge. If we can achieve this, god would be shortly due for a funeral service."

—G. Bozarth, promoting the religion of humanism

Finally, the house was built, and it was truly a magnificent home made with the very best of tools and building materials.

The state building inspector came to check the home. The building inspector was in awe. He said, "You have a fine home. It is beautiful. You have the very best of all the building materials. Your home is in the top ninety-ninth percentile compared to other homes in this area. Your house has passed the state's standards." The man moved into his new beautiful home.

One day the man and his wife were eating dinner. His wife complained that the doors and windows would not shut. Even the beautiful hand-made kitchen cabinet doors would not shut. As they were talking, it started to rain. It wasn't a fierce storm, but it started raining very hard. The man noticed a crack in the wall. He got up to look at the crack and saw another crack in the ceiling. Just then, a few bricks fell out of the fine custom fireplace. The man went into other parts of the house. The bathroom floors started to buckle. The base of the sink was coming out of the floor! The plumbing was backed up. The roof started leaking. The man didn't understand why his beautiful house was falling apart. He called the building inspector. The inspector said he was not responsible for the house. The man called the state home builder's office to get help. The woman who answered told him that they could only help if the man gave them the house. While he was on the phone, the water pipes burst and water poured into every room in the house. The carpets were soaked and the wood floors warped.

The man called his friends to help. A friend brought a truck to help the man save some of his furnishings. While they were moving the furniture into a truck, the electricity went out. The man was close to tears. He had no idea what was wrong with his home. His friend started looking through the house with a flashlight. He soon discovered the problem. He told the man, "This house has shifted. It has a weak foundation. It cannot survive this storm." Before he could finish his sentence, the entire house crashed down around them.

The house was built on sandy ground. All the fine fixtures and furnishings—indeed, the entire house, was worthless. The man was very sad.

This parable parallels the building of a home to the training of a child. The fact that you bought this book indicates you are interested in building a home—training your child. I know you have high goals and expectations for your home (child). The purpose of this book is to take the focus off the tools and materials and keep your focus on the:

- Builder
- Blueprints
- Foundation

The man in the story had a goal to build a fine house (raise a child). His focus was on what would make the house look good to the world (a successful, self-reliant student). The man took the easiest route to have the home built (state). It demanded no time or effort on the part of the man. There was nothing wrong with the basic building materials (knowledge) if the builder used them correctly (curriculum). The man did not know the builder, therefore the builder did not care about the man or the house. The builder used the state's blueprints (curriculum) to provide a foundation of sand (humanism). The man provided sound building materials, but the blueprints called for the builder to bend and distort these materials. The inspector (test examiner) compared the house to the other homes in the area. He focused on the surface results, not the foundation. This book may be able to point you in the right direction to keep your house (child) from destruction. With the right Builder, Foundation, and Blueprints, you can build a strong, fine home.

First you must get to know the right builder. An experienced builder who personally knows and cares for you will help you build a fine home. I know of a wonderful Builder. He is the architect who designed the Blueprints for the world's most stable home. He is known for providing the strongest foundation available, guaranteed to weather any storm. This home will last for eternity. The builder is God through His Holy Spirit leading you through life. The blueprints are the Bible, God's Word, giving instructions for every step of the process. The foundation is Jesus Christ, the Rock of Salvation.

Photos of brand-new, fine house destroyed due to a bad foundation.

God will provide the foundation and build the house as a free gift to you. You and your child only have to ask Him to take over. God expects you to provide the tools and He will show you the best materials for your home (academic training). He will use the materials wisely if, by faith, you allow God to shape the materials according to His will.

Therefore whosoever heareth these sayings of mine, and doeth them, I will liken him unto a wise man, which built his house upon a rock: And the rain descended, and the floods came, and the winds blew, and beat upon that house; and it fell not: for it was founded upon a rock. And every one that heareth these sayings of mine, and doeth them not, shall be likened unto a foolish man, which built his house upon the sand: And the rain descended, and the floods came, and the winds blew, and beat upon that house; and it fell: and great was the fall of it.
(MATTHEW 7:24-27)

	HOUSE ON THE SAND	HOUSE ON A ROCK
BUILDER	State	God
BLUEPRINTS	State Curriculum	Bible
FOUNDATION	Humanism, false gods	Jesus

The academic Check Lists in this book are only a list of basic building materials. You, the child's parent, must decide on the more important foundation and choose whom you want to build the house.

DEFINITION OF "EDUCATION"

A look at the different definitions of "education" from different sources can be quite revealing.

Webster's 1828 Dictionary
This was the original dictionary by Noah Webster, reflecting the thoughts and values of the early American Christian culture.

EDUCATION, n. [L. education.] The bringing up, as of a child, instruction; formation of manners. Education comprehends all that series of instruction and discipline which is intended to enlighten the understanding, correct the temper, and form the manners and habits of youth, and fit them for usefulness in their future stations. To give children a good education in manners, arts and science, is important; to give them a religious education is indispensable; and an immense responsibility rests on parents and guardians who neglect these duties.

ED'UCATE, v.t. [L. educo, educare; e and duco, to lead.] To bring up, as a child; to instruct; to inform and enlighten the understanding; to instill into the mind principles of arts, science, morals, religion and behavior. To educate children well is one of the most important duties of parents and guardians.

To know what is meant by "religious education," one must examine the definition of the word, "religion."

RELIGION: 1. Religion, in its most comprehensive sense, includes a belief in the being and perfections of God, in the revelation of His will to man, in man's obligation to obey His commands, in a state of reward and punishment, and in man's accountableness to God... 2. ...the performance of all known duties to God and our fellow men, in obedience to divine command, or from love to God and His law. [The phrases "divine command" and "His law" are synonymous with what is contained in the Bible.]

God's Word was an essential part of American education in the eighteenth and early nineteenth centuries. Three vital elements contained in the 1828 Webster definition were:

1. The future station (occupation or calling) of the child
2. Religious training
3. Parental responsibility

Compare the 1828 definition to that found in today's Webster's Dictionary (the name "Webster" was kept, but the new dictionaries bear no relation to Noah Webster):

Today's *Webster's New World Dictionary*
EDUCATION: 1. The process of training and developing the knowledge, skill, mind, character, etc., especially by formal schooling 2. knowledge, ability, etc. thus developed 3. formal schooling at an institution of learning 4. systematic study of the methods and theories of teaching and learning.

Today's definition is totally void of the three principles listed in the 1828 Webster definition.

ONE THING IS NEEDFUL

When Martha was too busy preparing her home to learn from Jesus, He said to her, "Martha, Martha, you are worried about so many things, when there is *one* thing that is needful." He was not saying that Martha should never tend to housework, just as we should not ignore the basic skills. But the basic skills are a fraction of a weight on a scale compared to what Jesus said is the *one* needful thing—sitting at His feet learning the paths of God—the *one* thing your child needs to prepare him for life!

Christians are commanded to be anxious for nothing. The achievement test and standards are only tools. Proper use of them will allow us to better evaluate our children—as long as we keep the right perspective.

"I'll take the standards, warnings and solutions God gave to Moses or King David, King Solomon or the Prophets, over anything that Bill Clinton, Ted Kennedy or a pagan Supreme Court could ever offer."

—Terry Randel

All education is indoctrination into a religious worldview, whether it be the true religion of Christianity, or any of the myriad false religions invented by men. All education is undergirded by presuppositions about the origin of the universe, the origin of man, the purpose of man, ethics governing relationships between men, and the continuing existence of the universe in an orderly and predictable manner. It is an inescapable fact that all of these basic assumptions are fundamentally religious. Therefore we must view the schoolroom as the place where children are indoctrinated into the religion of their society. The school is, in effect, a temple. The question which Christians in twentieth century America are late in asking is this: "Into what religion do the government schools educate our children?"

David Sant, The Religious Nature of Education, *Patriarch Magazine*

19

THE PRIMARY PURPOSE OF EDUCATION

The primary purpose of education should be to train the whole person for lifelong, obedient service, just as it was in Bible times (home was the center for education then). God never changes. He still has the same desire for us to know Him.

Our first goal must be to teach our children God's ways and His paths. We home schoolers cannot be so worried about fractions or spelling that we skip the one needful thing: sitting at the feet learning from our Master, through Bible study and prayer. We can prepare our children for whatever direction their gifts and talents lie; however, God may take your child in another direction. A Christian who is striving to find God's Will for his life will be equipped in the important traits, prepared for anything in life.

Knowing the facts and scoring high on achievement tests is not a formula for success. The education required by the state is not true education. Christians' questions should not be, "What score did she get on the achievement test?" or "What job or college is he prepared for?" The questions should be, "Is my child prepared to use the gifts and talents God has given her to carry out His Will in her life? Is this child seriously directed toward holiness, right relationships, and fruitfulness?"

WISDOM ACCORDING TO GOD

God's Word promises that wisdom can be attained by all who seek and follow it. Those who keep God's moral and ethical laws will be rewarded with long life, health, possessions, respect, security, and self-control (Proverbs 3:2-4).

This wisdom begins when man humbles himself before God in reverence and worship and is obedient to His commands. This is quite different from the Greek and American views of wisdom sought through philosophy and man's rationale as a way of explaining the mysteries of existence and the universe.

Christian wisdom appears to be foolishness to the people of the world. But it is wiser than the philosophy of this age, which comes to nothing. The foolishness of God is wiser than men; and the weakness of God is stronger than men. Wisdom is revealed through God and received through His Spirit. Christians have the highest and most complete wisdom in Christ.

For it is written, I will destroy the wisdom of the wise, and will bring to nothing the understanding of the prudent. Where is the wise? where is the scribe? where is the disputer of this world? hath not God made foolish the wisdom of this world?

"The humanism that is being taught in our schools, media, and intellectual circles will ultimately lead people to the Antichrist, because he will be the consummate figure of humanism."
—Pat Robertson, 1989

"Brainwashing is a system of befogging the brain so a person can be seduced into acceptance of what otherwise would be abhorrent to him. He loses touch with reality. Facts and fancy whirl round and change places. However, in order to prevent people from recognizing the inherent evils in brainwashing, the Reds pretend that it is only another name for something already very familiar and of unquestioned respect, such as education or reform."
—Edward Hunter, *Brainwashing*

For after that in the wisdom of God the world by wisdom knew not God, it pleased God by the foolishness of preaching to save them that believe.

For the Jews require a sign, and the Greeks seek after wisdom: But we preach Christ crucified, unto the Jews a stumbling block, and unto the Greeks foolishness; But unto them which are called, both Jews and Greeks, Christ the power of God, and the wisdom of God. Because the foolishness of God is wiser than men; and the weakness of God is stronger than men. For ye see your calling, brethren, how that not many wise men after the flesh, not many mighty, not many noble, are called: But God hath chosen the foolish things of the world to confound the wise; and God hath chosen the weak things of the world to confound the things which are mighty; And base things of the world, and things which are despised, hath God chosen, yea, and things which are not, to bring to nought things that are: That no flesh should glory in his presence. But of him are ye in Christ Jesus, who of God is made unto us wisdom, and righteousness, and sanctification, and redemption: That, according as it is written, He that glorieth, let him glory in the Lord (1 Corinthians 1:19-31).

REQUIREMENTS FOR RECEIVING WISDOM

The requirement for wisdom is a desire to follow and imitate God as He has revealed Himself in Jesus Christ, without self-reliance and especially not in a spirit of pride: *A wise man will hear, and will increase learning; and a man of understanding shall attain unto wise counsels: To understand a proverb, and the interpretation; the words of the wise, and their dark sayings. The fear of the Lord is the beginning of knowledge: but fools despise wisdom and instruction* (Proverbs 1:5-7).

The person who seeks wisdom diligently will receive understanding: *For the Lord giveth wisdom: out of his mouth cometh knowledge and understanding* (Proverbs 2:6). He will benefit in his life by walking with God: *That thou mayest walk in the way of good men, and keep the paths of the righteous* (Proverbs 2:20).

FRUITS OF TRUE WISDOM

The fruits of wisdom are many, and the Book of Proverbs describes the characters of wisdom. In New Testament terms, the fruits of wisdom are the same as the fruits of the Holy Spirit. *But the fruit of the Spirit is love, joy, peace, longsuffering, gentleness, goodness, faith, Meekness, temperance: against such there is no law* (Galatians 5:22-23). *But the wisdom that*

"...Suppose the child, the human being, is an evolutionary product, simply a more complicated animal, without a soul, especially without an immortal soul.... The end of man is doom, pitiless and dark. All the labor of the ages is destined to extinction and must inevitably be buried beneath the debris of a universe in ruins. Suppose on the other hand that God created man in His own image and breathed into him the breath of life, with the result that those redeemed by Christ shall glorify God and enjoy him forever."

—Gordon H. Clark
Christian Philosophy of Education

"A nationwide study using a random sample of 1,516 families from one organization's membership, found home educated students to be scoring, on average, at or above the 80th percentile in all areas on standardized achievement tests. Note: The national average on standardized achievement tests is the 50th percentile. The research findings are consistent that the home educated do equal to or better than conventional school students on achievement tests."

—National Home Education Research Institute

is from above is first pure, then peaceable, gentle, and easy to be entreated, full of mercy and good fruits, without partiality, and without hypocrisy. And the fruit of righteousness is sown in peace of them that make peace (James 3:17-18).

Author David Mulligan said it so appropriately in his book *Far Above Rubies: Wisdom in the Christian Community:*

> We must do more than rail against Godless education. We must identify a distinctly Christian curriculum—one that takes its identity, its motion, from the reality of our redeemed condition—one that begins with authority of the risen Christ speaking through His Word. It is not enough to know what we are against; we must know what we are for. Dismantling the world is one work; building the Kingdom is another. If we fail to make a positive contribution to education, if we keep the same old public school agenda packaged in Christian dress, our children will not prosper as they should. Without fundamental changes, we are only straining out the gnat while swallowing the camel. We cannot let the wolf of antichrist values in because he is wearing sheep's clothing.

Your primary responsibility as a parent is to pass along your faith and corresponding values to your children. Don Stamp's comentary on Colossians 3:20-21 includes a list of thing parents should do to prepare children for life that should preceed academic requirements :

- Dedicate them to God at the beginning of their lives (1 Samuel 1:28; Luke 2:22).
- Teach them to fear the Lord and to turn away from evil, to love righteousness and to hate sin. Instill in them an awareness of God's attitude and judgment toward sin (Hebrews 1:9).
- Instruct them in God's Word, both in conversation and family devotions (Deuteronomy 4:9; 6:5-7; 1 Timothy 4:6; 2 Timothy 3:15).
- Teach them to obey through biblical discipline (Deuteronomy 8:5; Proverbs 3:11-12; 13:20; 23:13-14; 29:15,17; Hebrews 12:7).
- Protect them from ungodly influences by being aware of Satan's attempts to destroy them spiritually through attraction to the world or through immoral comparisons

(Proverbs 13:20; 28:7; 1 John 2:15-17).

- Make them aware that God is always observing and evaluating what they do, think, and say (Psalms 139:1-12).

- Bring them early in life to a personal faith, repentance, and water baptism in Christ (Matthew 19:14).

- Establish them in a spiritual church where God's Word is proclaimed, His righteous standards honored, and the Holy Spirit manifested.

- Teach them the motto, I am a companion to all of them that fear thee…(Psalms 119:63).

- Encourage them to remain separated from the world and to witness and work for God (2 Corinthians 6:14; 7:1; James 4:4).

- Teach them that they are strangers and aliens on this earth (Hebrews 11:13-16), and that their real home and citizenship is in heaven with Christ (Philippians 3:20; Colossians 3:1-3).

- Through example and exhortation, encourage them to live lives devoted to prayer (Acts 6:4; Romans 12:12; Ephesians 6:18; James 5:16).

SUMMARY

In our achievement-oriented society, significance or importance is equated with intellectualism. Even Christians tend to evaluate worth on the basis of achievement scores instead of who we are in Christ. Is it right to put our children on a performance scale to measure their worth and significance?

We've got to give up cookie cutter academic achievement goals and seek God's standards. We must view each child as a unique individual (with different gifts and talents). God gave us these precious blessings with an instruction Manual —the Bible. The more familiar we are with the Manual, the more effective we will become in our teaching. God promises to show us the way when we obey Him. F. B. Meyer writes about Abraham's obedience, "There is nothing that God will not do for a man who dares to step out upon what seems to be the mist; who then finds rock beneath him as he puts his foot down."

"The gains of education are never really lost. Books may be burned and cities sacked, but truth, like the yearning for freedom, lives in the hearts of humble men."
—Franklin D. Roosevelt, *speech, Democratic National Convention*, June 27, 1936.

"Every child in America entering school at the age of five is mentally ill, because he comes to school with certain allegiances toward our founding fathers, toward elected officials, toward his parents, toward a belief in a supernatural being. It's up to you teachers to make all of these sick children well by creating the international children of the future."
—A Harvard Professor of Education and Psychiatry at a childhood-education seminar for public schools

"Many in the secular world are often adrift and anchorless. Only an education which educates for eternity has the wholeness which humans need. When we separate learning from divine moral truth, it quickly deteriorates into a restless, roving search for meaning and often drifts into sensual selfishness."
—President Spencer W Kimball, *The Teachings of Spencer W. Kimball*, p. 387

CHAPTER 2

WORLD VIEWS
Choosing a Carpenter

The importance of world view cannot be overstated. To provide a Christian education you must have a Christian philosophy. Philosophy is the way of looking at our experience in the world—a world view. Major world religions are based on world views. God expects His people to seek earnestly for the truth. As the Apostle Paul faced the humanists of his day, so the faithful and aware Christian must, if he is truly to follow Christ, face the humanist of our day. Our children will eventually be in company with those taught totally humanistic values in the public school system. If our young people have no concept of worldview (and this is the case with the vast majority), they will be totally unprepared to defend their beliefs. It is of extreme importance for our children to study and understand the different worldviews being taught.

What *your child* needs to know depends upon your world view. Let me repeat, it's *your* world view (not the state's world view, not your mother-in-law's view, not the neighbor's view, and not Susie's view from your support group). Worldviews in education are unavoidable. Neutrality is impossible. Jesus said, *He who is not with Me is against Me, and he who does not gather with Me scatters abroad* (Matt. 12:30). Everyone has a world view. You may not have written it down, but you have one. Your world view determines your values. It separates what is important to you from what is not. Walsh and Middleton in *Transforming a Vision* suggest that there are four questions that identify a person's world view:

1. Who am I?

2. Where am I?

3. What is wrong? Why am I often frustrated, disappointed, and defeated?

4. How can it be fixed? How can I solve my problems and satisfy my desires?

Before you turn the page, take this opportunity to spend a few minutes answering each of these questions on paper. Save your answers and compare them with the answers of the two world views which follow. The majority of Americans tend to answer the questions in one of two ways—from a secular view (without God) or from a Christian world view.

SECULAR WORLD VIEW

The World View Taught in America's State Schools:

1. Who am I?

I am a human being, an accident. My species evolved from a monkey.

2. Where am I?

I am on Earth, a planet that just happened by accident. The accident is called "The Big Bang."

3. What is wrong?

There is a lack of education and a lack of money; therefore, people are frustrated, disappointed, and defeated.

4. How can it be fixed?

By providing money and education. The more money and education one has, the happier and more fulfilling his life will be.

Those who do not believe in God have to find a way to explain the universe. They have twisted and tortured the limits of both nature and psychology in an effort to escape God's natural law. (Mulligan p. 58)

Humanism, for example, is a world view which states that the universe is centered on man and his achievements. Marxism is a world view which asserts the inevitability of class struggle based on economic factors.

A secular world view does not always value human life. If the only thing a child has ever been taught is that we are all accidents—is it really so unusual that there are so many abortions, murders, and suicides? Let's look at the answers from a Christian world view. What value does a Christian place on life? On education? On material gain?

CHRISTIAN WORLD VIEW

Look again at these four questions, from a biblical view:

1. Who am I?

I am a human being created by an awesome, wonderful, loving God. He especially put me here for a specific reason.

WHAT YOUR CHILD NEEDS TO KNOW WHEN

2. Where am I?

I am on the Earth created by God. This Earth is so marvelously created that if it were hung differently in the universe, one degree more or less, it would not be in existence.

3. What is wrong?

Sin. Our disobedience to God. When sin entered the world it severed our relationship with God, our Creator. We need our relationship with God to be restored.

4. How can it be fixed?

Jesus Christ, God's only begotten Son, came into the world in human form and gave His life as a sacrifice for our sins. Accepting His sacrifice and making Him Lord of our lives is our only hope.

The public school system teaches a secular world view. Children are taught that the answers to all of life's problems are money and education. Much of this philosophy has crept into the church; so much so, that many Christians value education to the extent that they will choose a "good education" over God's command to "be not unequally yoked." Or they will choose curriculum because it is equivalent to the academic requirements of a traditional education.

Developing a Christian world view is of extreme importance in order to advance Christ's kingdom. False systems will collapse under their own corrupted weight. One reason for the decline of Christianity in Western culture is the lack of a Bible-based world view. Instead, the cultural world view of materialism, selfishness, and greed has become the predominant vision.

In education, a Christian world view seeks knowledge, wisdom, and understanding as outlined by God's Word. A secular world view focuses on SAT testing and rote memorization with no thought to character, morals, and values.

Thus, if we were to properly understand the role of the world view, we would understand it as a set of rules that reside at the very core of our beings. If our set of values is earthly, carnal, and debased, then our actions will reflect such rot; however, a change in this set of values will bring a change in our actions. If we are taught a Bible-based world view, radical change will take place. Believers the world over will experience revival, and evangelism will become more effective than ever.

All of life is lived out before God, not just certain parts (i.e. gospel proclamation, church, etc.) All science, art, literature, philosophy, theology, business, and culture must be conformed to Scripture. Salvation of individuals is not the primary theme of Scripture,

"[Jesus] is the image of the invisible God, the firstborn over all creation. For by him all things were created: things in heaven and on earth, visible and invisible, whether thrones or powers or rulers or authorities; all things were created by him and for him. He is before all things, and in him all things hold together. And he is the head of the body, the church; he is the beginning and the firstborn from among the dead, so that in everything he might have the supremacy. For God was pleased to have all his fullness dwell in him, and through him to reconcile to himself all things, whether things on earth or things in heaven, by making peace through his blood, shed on the cross. In Christ are hidden all the treasures of wisdom and knowledge. I tell you this so that no one may deceive you by fine-sounding arguments."
(COLOSSIANS 1:15-20; 2:3-4).
—Francis A. Schaeffer

"We demolish arguments and every pretension that sets itself up against the knowledge of God, and we take captive every thought to make it obedient to Christ."
(2 Corinthians 10:5)

"The Christian belief system, which the Christian knows to be grounded in divine revelation, is relevant to all of life."
—Carl F. H. Henry,
Toward a Recovery of Christian Belief

"And just knowing that our children really love the Lord is a faithful parent's passion and reward."
—Jon Mohr

"Because God is considered irrelevant in the classroom, there is no longer any basis from which to form opinions on morality, ethics and religion. Our society's motto has become, 'Hey, it doesn't make any difference what you believe, as long as you believe it.' Our society has become a little schizophrenic, thinking that right answers exist for any area of life except religion and morality. Again, if God exists and spoke, then absolutes exist and we have a basis for deciding right from wrong. Yet, people reject Christianity, not because they researched the historical evidence and found it lacking, but because they simply don't like what it says. That's a classic bias.

We are to respect authority because God, the ultimate authority over all He has created, has called us to do so. A teacher has legitimate authority over his students because the parents have delegated authority to him by enrolling their child in the school. A student who does not respect the authority of his teacher will be hindered in what he can learn from his teacher due to this lack of submission. A submissive spirit is a teachable spirit, but contentiousness blockades the path to true knowledge and wisdom.

The basic problem of the Christians in this country in the last eighty years or so, in regard to society and in regard to government, is that they have seen things in bits and pieces instead of totals."
—Brent Knox, The Christian Cause,1988

and to interpret it as such is to squeeze Scripture into the hyper-individualism of this age. There is a reason why people interpret the Bible strictly from the Gospel, but it is not a noble, well-contemplated Biblical reason. (Noebel)

The principles listed below are a small portion of *Seven Principles of Effective Biblical Worldview* by Kevin J. Price, President of Worldview Ministries.

These principles are discussed in detail in the Worldview Ministries book, *Understanding God's Worldview*, and summarized in the booklet *Seven Principles of Effective Biblical Worldview* (ordering information is at the end of this chapter). They are not the only principles that are important; in fact, they may not be the most important, but they are useful in understanding how the Christian is to relate to the world.

1. Worship is a twenty-four-hour-a-day activity.

In John 4:20-24, Jesus said that people should worship God in spirit and in truth. In essence, Jesus was saying that worship should not be isolated to a time or place, but that our whole lives were to be acts of worship. This differs from the modern view of "going to worship." In God's view, we become worship ourselves (Romans 12:1,2). On a practical level, this means that Christians are called by God to be an influence in everything we do and that we should not limit ourselves to areas which are religious.

2. Biblical world view is crucial in maintaining a stable, healthy society.

In Colossians 1:16-17, Paul noted that Jesus Christ holds all things together. The reason why much in our society is chaotic and confused is that there is a lack of a Christian influence.

3. There are two forces: life and death.

This isn't some New Age concept; it is scriptural. In John 10:10 we are informed that Satan comes to kill, steal, and destroy, whereas Jesus came to give life. This view transcends virtually everything. For example, in the realm of economics, Satan's pro-death views have led to population control, abortion, wealth redistribution, and other policies which have harmed the economy and the very people these policies were supposed to help.

4. Exercising biblical world view requires recognizing God's authority.

Everything, including the government, is subject to God's authority (Romans 13:1-4; Acts 4:16-20; Acts 5:27-29). When you live in a country where Christians are allowed to be involved, it is imperative that you work to keep your nation in submission to God.

5. History supports Christianity rather than humanism.

In government schools throughout America there has been a divorce of Christianity from history, although all of the founders of this nation argued that America's success was contingent on its relationship with God. They knew that America would eventually collapse without sound policies based on God's law.

6. Be bold in the fact that Christianity is intellectually, as well as spiritually, superior to humanism.

The prophets of humanism—Marx, Rousseau, Darwin, and others—often lived immoral lives, and their philosophies contributed to genocide, racism, and slavery. God's world view is superior to any of the immoral ideas of the philosophers.

7. Think and behave with a biblical world view.

Christians must learn to test all things, study God's Word, focus on the cause and not the symptoms of problems, and strive for consistency in their thinking (1 John 4:17; Psalms 40:8; Ephesians 4:14-15). Furthermore, Christians need to strive to solve problems rather than pass them on to the government and others.

The Church is a social institution with a mandate from God to care for the widows, the poor, and the fatherless (orphans). If people would follow God's plan, there would be no need for governmental agencies that work to alleviate poverty and abuse.

GREEK VS. HEBREW WORLDVIEWS

Now that we've explored the differences between a secular and Christian world view, we need to examine the effects of the ancient Greeks and Romans on a Christian world view to see the effect upon education. We must understand the myriad differences between Hebrew and Greek thought. Intellectually, we (Westerners) are Greeks, not Hebrews. Aristotelian and Socratic thought patterns are apparent in most Western educational approaches. The ancient Greek world's view of teaching was that it primarily involved the transference of knowledge in the intellectual and technical areas, such as music, art, reading, or athletics. The primary purpose of education in

Do not conform any longer to the pattern of this world, but be transformed by the renewing of your mind. Then you will be able to test and approve what God's will is—his good, pleasing and perfect will.

(ROMANS 12:2)

"Once a Christian discovers that there is a total divorce between mind and spirit in the schools and universities, between the perfection of thought and the perfection of soul and character, between intellectual sophistication and the spiritual worth of the individual human person, between reason and faith, between the pride of knowledge and the contrition of heart consequent upon being a mere creature, and once he realizes that Jesus Christ will find Himself less at home on the campuses of the great universities, in Europe and America, than almost anywhere else, he will be profoundly disturbed, and he will inquire what can be done to recapture the great universities for Jesus Christ, the universities which would not have come into being in the first place without Him."

—Charles Malik, *at the dedication of the Billy Graham Center in Wheaton, Illinois*

"We believe that 'the propitious smiles of heaven can never be expected on a nation which disregards the eternal rules of order and right which heaven itself has ordained.'"

—George Washington

For other foundation can no man lay than that is laid, which is Jesus Christ.

(1 CORINTHIANS 3:11)

Bible times was to train the whole person for lifelong, obedient service in the knowledge of God (Prov. 1:7; Eccl. 12:13). The ancient Greeks believed that education was for the wealthy and leisure classes. The Hebrews believed education was for all people. Teaching had to do primarily with the communication of the God's laws and was done by God himself, by the father of the family, or by a religious leader within the community.

We need to understand the Hebrew culture, not only to understand the Bible but to learn how God wants us to educate our children. Marvin Wilson explains in *Our Father Abraham*,

> Christianity does not derive from pagan, Hellenistic sources or from speculative worldviews. Neither is it a syncretistic religion deeply rooted in mystery cults, Gnostic sects, naturalistic philosophies, or polytheistic thought. Rather, the Christian faith is divinely revealed and is securely anchored in the Hebrew Bible–the Law, Prophets, and Writings. God breathed his word into the minds of the biblical authors within a Jewish cultural environment. Consequently, for us, in the most succinct terms, 'to ignore Hebraic ways of thinking is to subvert Christian understanding.' We must, therefore, focus on the language and thought-patterns found in the Scriptures so that we are able to penetrate the mind of the Hebrew people. When we enter their civilization and view it through their eyes, we find that the contour of their thought is vibrant, rich, and colorful. It has its own nuances and features. Indeed, the Hebraic background to Christian thought is at the heart of the rich spiritual legacy that the Jews have shared with Christians.

William Barrett explains that one of the most fundamental differences between the Western, Hellenistic mind and the Hebrew mind is found in the area of knowing vs. doing. Says Barrett, "The distinction...arises from the difference between doing and knowing. The Hebrew is concerned with practice, the Greek with knowledge. Right conduct is the ultimate concern of the Hebrew, right thinking that of the Greek. Duty and strictness of conscience are the paramount things in life for the Hebrew; for the Greek, the spontaneous and luminous play of the intelligence. The Hebrew thus extols the moral virtues as the substance and meaning of life; the Greek subordinates them to the intellectual virtues...the contrast is between practice and theory, between the moral man and the theoretical or intellectual man."

WORLD VIEW RESOURCES

Assumptions That Affect Our Lives by Christian Overman. The visible actions of people are first shaped by invisible thoughts, deep in the unseen world of the human mind and heart. What factors influence those invisible ideas? For people who live in the Western world, the answers can be found by examining the two major roots of Western thought— the ancient Greeks and the ancient Hebrews. *Assumptions That Affect Our Lives* takes the reader back to the roots of the modern conflict between Christianity and secular humanism through a comparison of ancient Greek and Hebrew culture. What the reader will discover is, the current tension between evangelical Christians and the non-biblical ideas with which they are surrounded is an age-old conflict. By viewing the current situation in the context of the ancient Greeks and Hebrews, contemporary Christians can be better equipped to deal with the challenges of living in a predominately Greek-based culture today. Paperback - 273 pages 1 edition (November 27, 1996) Micah 6:8; ISBN: 1883035503.

Understanding the Times: The Religious Worldviews of Our Day and the Search for Truth by David A. Noebel. From Summit Ministries. This study was designed especially for Christian high school and college students. It emphasizes the importance of understanding the Christian worldview's relevance in an academic environment. When students complete the study, they will have a comprehensive grasp of the major ideas, issues, and personalities that shaped the twentieth century and which will shape the twenty-first. They will be able to recognize how these humanistic ideas are growing in acceptance and how these ideas affect our lives. *Understanding the Times* is very easy to read, easy to use and well laid out. It looks at ten categories: theology, philosophy, ethics, biology, psychology, sociology, law, politics, economics, and history. Each category goes into fascinating and interesting details of three worldviews: Secular Humanism, Marxism/Leninism (a branch of secular humanism) and Biblical Christianity. Harvest House Publishers, Inc.; ISBN: 1565072685.

Seven Principles of Effective Biblical Worldview by Kevin J. Price. An easy-to-read booklet with concise information on worldviews. ($1.50 plus postage and handling) or ***Understanding God's Worldview*** ($10.00 plus p+h) at Worldview Ministries; 6338 Limestone Houston TX 77092. E-mail K_J_P@email.com.

A Christian View of Men and Things by Gordon H. Clark. The presentation of Christianity as it applies to history, politics, ethics,

"The categories within which philosophical reflection about religion has been operating are derived from Athens rather than from Jerusalem.'"
—Abraham Heschel, *God in Search of Man*

"The Greeks learned in order to comprehend. The Hebrews learned in order to revere. The modern man learns in order to use."
—ibid

The goals of Jewish education may be broadly summed up:

1. To transmit knowledge and skills from generation to generation;

2. to increase knowledge and skills; and

3. to concretize cultural values into accepted behavior. The three main orders of study in ancient Israel consisted of religious education, occupational skills, and military training, with the essence of all knowledge being the fear of the Lord (Psalms 111:10; Proverbs 1:7).
—Ron Mosley, "Jewish Education in Ancient Times," *Restore Magazine*

...there is a long tradition in this country of resistance to the wisdom of the Greeks: Thomas Paine, Benjamin Franklin, and Noah Webster all judged the classics to be of scant use, and advocated that Americans receive, instead, a properly American education.
—Algis Valiunas, *Learning from the Greeks, Commentary Magazine, August, 1998*

"From these Greek thinkers came much that is good, including mathematics, the scientific method, the beautiful language of the New Testament... But our inheritance from the Greeks also came with some serious baggage. The Greek thinkers, shunning the God of the Hebrews, came up with man-centered and mystical notions to define the world around them.

Some have been largely discarded, like Homer's gods of fire and thunder, living on mountain peaks. Four hundred years after Homer, and four hundred years before Christ, Aristotle departed from mythology to describe "God" as an infinite but impersonal 'energizing form,' a self-developing energy source—the very root of modern New Age philosophy.

Without the God of the Bible, human beings are left with only themselves. Protagoras, in the fifth century B.C., put it crisply when he offered his famous maxim, 'Man is the measure of all things.'"
—John D. Beckett,
Loving Monday

science, religion, and epistemology. Clark's command of both worldly philosophy and Scripture is evident on every page, and the result is a breathtaking and invigorating challenge to the wisdom of this world. (September 1998) Trinity Foundation; ISBN: 1891777017.

Seven Men Who Rule the World from the Grave by Dave Breese. David Breese identifies seven men who, even though they rest in their graves, influence the world in negative ways through their ideas: Darwin, Marx, Wellhausen, Dewey, Freud, Keynes, and Kierkegaard.

Thinking Christianly by Dr. Albert Green. This Bible study explains why we ought to think in a distinctively Christian way. To learn what it means to have Jesus be the Lord of our thought life is a freeing, delightful experience. It is not easy, for we have all accumulated a history of secularized thinking which is not readily disposed of. This study will lead you into a joyful new way of approaching life because you will learn to think more Christianly about it. The author writes: "On the surface, it seems as if Christians and non-Christians think in the same way . . . but thoughts have their roots in our hearts. When God changed your heart, he laid the basis for a radical change in the way you think. This study booklet is intended to help you see how deep that change is meant to be . . ." This study guide is suitable for individual or group settings. Alta Vista 1719 NE 50th Street Seattle, Washington 98105. Phone: (206) 524-2262.

See our web site at Homeschool-Books.com for more resources and links to articles.

CHAPTER 3

HISTORY OF STATE EDUCATION
Foundation of Sand

HOW DID WE GET HERE?

The roots of modern American culture can be traced to two historic influences: the recorded experiences of the Greco-Roman civilization and philosophies on one side, and the Hebrew-Christian ideals set forth in the Bible on the other. The last 2,500 years of Western history record the intense struggle between people influenced by these two basic cultural forces. (Tom Eldredge, *Safely Home*).

In this chapter we will trace the history of education and identify the problems with Greco-Roman ways. We will see that biblical wisdom does not depend on Greek intellectual knowledge or nationality. Wisdom ultimately rests in our relationship with Jesus Christ, having the mind of Christ (1 Cor. 1 and 2). Biblical wisdom embodies a love for the author of wisdom and for what He enables us to know, and therefore applies knowledge with compassion and justice.

The American educational system is based on Greek philosophy. The word philosophy is from the Greek word *philosophia,* which means "love of wisdom" (from *phileo,* "to love," and *sophia,* "wisdom"). As used originally by the ancient Greeks, the term philosophy meant "the pursuit of knowledge for its own sake." Every Christian should know the differences between the pagan Greek philosophies and the education of the Bible. The Greek philosophies are not only prevalent in the public school system but are also creeping into our churches.

ANCIENT GREECE: THE ROOTS OF MODERN EDUCATION

The roots of modern America's educational system and traditions come from the ancient Greeks. They were the first to separate education from religious control.

Two contrasting types of education appeared early in ancient Greece: that of Sparta, wholly controlled by the state, and that of Athens, left almost entirely to the home or to private schools. Up to the age of seven, the education of both boys and girls was left to the home; at the age of seven, boys were gathered in barracks, where emphasis was placed upon physical development through games, exercises, and the pentathlon (running, jumping, throwing the discus, casting the javelin, and wrestling), and upon memorizing both the laws of Lycurgus (the Spartan lawgiver) and selections from Homer. The whole process was designed to develop endurance, resourcefulness, and discipline. At eighteen, definite training in the use of arms and warfare began; from twenty to thirty, service in the army and guarding the borders of the state were required, and even after thirty, men were required to live in barracks and assist in the training of the boys. Physical training was also emphasized in the education of girls and women, so that they might bear sturdy children. The whole purpose of education was to subordinate the individual to the needs of the state. (Kandel 1996)

The ancient Greeks' interest in learning was evident in their art, politics, and philosophy. Teachers lived in their households; these teachers were often slaves from conquered states. Later, when the Roman Empire was at its height, its citizens also followed the practice of having teacher-slaves, usually Greeks, in their households. Several Greek writers served as the models for the educational systems of ancient Greece, which stressed gymnastics as well as mathematics and music.

Have you ever wondered about the origins of the subject divisions used in modern education: literature, history, language? The Greeks divided God's creation into topics. When you divide life into topics, you can separate the topic from the Creator.

The basic divisions of knowledge were grammar, rhetoric, and dialectic. These were meant to help students communicate effectively, and included a study of literature and language, arithmetic, music, geometry, and astronomy. These subjects later became known as the liberal arts. They survive in one form or another in many universities today. Anatomy, biology, and botany were also regarded as valid fields of study.

Education, in general, was considered a leisure pursuit only available to the privileged few. The majority of the population that were Greek or Roman received no education. The pursuit of literature was considered the ultimate goal—an idle life of leisure void of manual labor. This pagan goal of the idle rich is pervasive in America today.

The Greeks were history's first humanists, believing that man was the measure of all things. The Greek aim was to prepare intellectually well-rounded young people to take leading roles in the activities of the state and society. Greek concepts served as the basis for the liberal arts, the teaching of the various branches of philosophy, the cultivation of the aesthetic ideal, and the promotion of gymnastic training. There is a problem with the educational system based on the philosophies of these non-believers!

According to *Microsoft Encarta Encyclopedia,* the intuitive hypotheses of the ancient Greeks foreshadowed many theories of modern science, and many of the moral ideas of pagan

Greek philosophers have been incorporated into Christian moral doctrine...With their emphasis on the importance of human perception, Greek philosophers doubted that humanity would ever be able to reach objective truth through reason, and taught that material success rather than truth should be the purpose of life.

GREEK PHILOSOPHERS

The ideas of the Greeks have had a profound effect on the modern educational system. The way the Greeks interpreted life is how life is studied in the modern educational system. We must understand this thought and compare it to what the Bible says about understanding, knowledge, and wisdom. To the Greek, knowledge was the primary way to goodness.

Greek philosophy formed the basis of all later philosophical speculation in the Western world. Greek philosophy is divided among those philosophers who sought an explanation of the world in physical terms and those who stressed the importance of non-material forms or ideas. Aristotle, Plato, and Socrates have the prestige of being the most famous of ancient philosophers.

The Ionian School

The first important school of Greek philosophy, the Ionian or Milesian, was largely materialistic. Thales of Miletus in the sixth century B.C. was considered one of the Seven Wise Men of Greece. Thales became renowned for his knowledge of astronomy after predicting the eclipse of the sun that occurred on May 28, 585 B.C. He is also said to have introduced geometry in Greece. Thales believed that water was the basic substance out of which all matter was created.

Pythagoras

The doctrines held by Pythagoras (sixth century B.C.) strongly influenced Plato. The Pythagoreans adhered to several mysteries. They prescribed obedience and silence, frequent fasting, simplicity in dress, limited possessions, and the habit of frequent self-examination. They believed in immortality and in the transmigration of souls—reincarnation.

Socrates

Socrates (470?-399? B.C.) profoundly affected Western philosophy through his influence on Plato. Socrates believed in the superiority of argument over writing and, therefore, spent the greater part of his mature life in the

"Philosophers preach 'The Age of Reason' and say we no longer need God. Western universities worship at the feet of Godless teachers such as Plato and Socrates. They have purchased these doctrines of men with all their wealth. Yet, their graduates are as bankrupt as their philosophies. They cannot answer the true needs of mankind. Western universities and seminaries dispense knowledge without establishing either its need or revealing its source. What has it gotten us? It has resulted in lawlessness, immorality, alternative lifestyles and disease. Have they forgotten that society is held together by Godly families? It appears so as they oppose "traditional family values" by more openly teaching "sexual freedom." "To your own self be true" is their creed. Their Bible is situational ethics, and psychologists are their "accredited" pastors. "Enough," I say. Let us return at once to God's learning procedure of wisdom !

—Karl D. Coke, Ph.D., *Restore!* Magazine

public places of Athens, engaging in dialogue and argument with anyone who would listen. He believed in a purely objective understanding of such concepts as justice, love, virtue, and self-knowledge as the basis of his teachings. He believed that all wickedness is the result of ignorance, and that no person was willingly bad; accordingly, virtue is knowledge, and those who know what is right will act correctly.

Plato

Plato (428?-347 B.C.) is considered one of the most creative and influential thinkers in Western philosophy. His view of knowledge, his psychology, his concept of the state, and his perspective of art must be understood in terms of his theories. Influenced by Socrates, Plato was convinced that knowledge was attainable. He insisted that knowledge must be certain and infallible. He regarded the objects of the real world as mere shadows of eternal forms or ideas. Only these changeless, eternal forms could be the objects of true knowledge; all observations made with our senses are changeable and, therefore, not necessarily valid. He believed that reason, properly used, resulted in intellectual insights that were certain.

Aristotle

Aristotle (384-322 B.C.) was a philosopher and scientist. Aristotle believed that the world was made up of individuals (substances) occurring in fixed natural kinds (species). Each individual had its built-in, specific pattern of development and grew toward proper self-realization as a specimen of its type; thus, growth, purpose, and direction were built into nature.

Aristotle insisted that something could be better understood when its causes were stated in specific terms rather than in general terms. Thus, it would be more informative to know that a sculptor made the statue than to know that an artist made it; and even more informative to know that Polycleitus chiseled it rather than that a sculptor had done so (Encarta 1997).

The influence of Aristotle's philosophy has been pervasive; it has even helped to shape modern language and rational thought. His doctrine of the Prime Mover as final cause played an important role in theology. Until the twentieth century, "logic" meant Aristotle's logic. Until the Renaissance, and even later, astronomers and poets alike admired his concept of the universe. Zoology is based on Aristotle's work.

WHAT YOUR CHILD NEEDS TO KNOW WHEN

GREEK PHILOSOPHY IN A NUTSHELL

The Greeks sought answers in two different realms, first of all in the areas of *polis* [meaning "city," but referring to the whole society]. The Greeks found that society as society could not give ample meaning [to life]. ...Second, they tried to place particulars in relation to their gods. The difficulty with the Greek gods is they were never big enough to be an infinite reference point...Thus neither society or the gods gave the Greeks a sufficient universal understanding. (Schaffer)

THE BIBLE SPEAKS TO THE DANGERS OF GREEK EDUCATIONAL PHILOSOPHIES

True knowledge cannot be gained by unaided human reason. *Canst thou by searching find out God? canst thou find out the Almighty unto perfection?* (Job 11:7). *O the depth of the riches both of the wisdom and knowledge of God! how unsearchable are his judgments, and his ways past finding out!* (Romans 11:33).

Teachers of philosophy give their lives to examining convictions by which people can live in order to develop a consistent world view and way of life based on reliable evidence. The Bible warns against philosophies whose highest realities and concerns are atoms, energy, cosmic laws, or humanity—those founded on the basic principles of the world, and not according to Christ.

Beware lest any man spoil you through philosophy and vain deceit, after the tradition of men, after the rudiments of the world, and not after Christ (Colossians 2:8).

Christians ought to beware that their minds not be taken captive by such philosophies as secular humanism, communism, and capitalistic materialism. These philosophies are best fought with spiritual weapons.

> *(For the weapons of our warfare are not carnal, but mighty through God to the pulling down of strong holds;) Casting down imaginations, and every high thing that exalteth itself against the knowledge of God, and bringing into captivity every thought to the obedience of Christ* (2 Corinthians 10:4-5).

> *For ye see your calling, brethren, how that not many wise men after the flesh, not many mighty, not many noble, are called: But God hath chosen the foolish things of the world to confound the wise; and God hath chosen the weak things of the world to confound the things which are mighty; And*

."..some proponents of "classical Christian education" seek to revive the writings of ancient pagans, Roman, Greek or otherwise, and present them to our children as possible sources of wisdom and true knowledge, we must strongly object. In the case of the Greeks, many of the "great teachers" were not only idolaters, but sodomites and pedophiles with minds which were deeply affected by their perversions. This is precisely the type of reasoning and thinking from which God has redeemed us. We are to build our worldview exclusively on Holy Scripture, taking every thought captive to the obedience of Jesus Christ. To the extent that our mature children should study classical culture and writings, it is to identify the many false philosophies and intellectual strongholds which have infected Western civilization, and against which the Christian soldier is to wage war. "
—Doug Phillips,
The Vision Forum, Inc., 2000

..."for the wisdom of their wise men shall perish, and the understanding of their prudent men shall be hid (Isaiah 29:14). All the valued learning of this world was confounded, baffled, and eclipsed by the Christian revelations and the glorious triumphs of the Cross. The heathen politicians and philosophers, the Jewish rabbis and doctors, the curious searchers into the secrets of nature, were all posed and put to a nonplus. This scheme lay out of the reach of the deepest statesmen and philosophers, and the greatest pretenders to learning both among the Jews and Greeks."
—Matthew Henry's Commentary

base things of the world, and things which are despised, hath God chosen, yea, and things which are not, to bring to nought things that are (1 Corinthians 1:26-28).

PAUL SPEAKS TO THE STUDENTS OF PHILOSOPHY

The chief biblical example of how to help students of philosophy who do not accept biblical authority is found in Paul's ministry to the Epicureans and philosophers at Athens. Paul commended their zeal, quoted them favorably on a point of agreement, declared the truth about the living Lord of all, announced their accountability to Christ (not to Socrates, Plato, Aristotle, Epicurus, or Zeno), and called on them to repent and trust Jesus Christ.

Now while Paul waited for them at Athens, his spirit was stirred in him, when he saw the city wholly given to idolatry. Therefore disputed he in the synagogue with the Jews, and with the devout persons, and in the market daily with them that met with him. Then certain philosophers of the Epicureans, and of the Stoicks, encountered him. And some said, What will this babbler say? other some, He seemeth to be a setter forth of strange gods: because he preached unto them Jesus, and the resurrection. And they took him, and brought him unto Areopagus, saying, May we know what this new doctrine, whereof thou speakest, is? For thou bringest certain strange things to our ears: we would know therefore what these things mean. (For all the Athenians and strangers which were there spent their time in nothing else, but either to tell, or to hear some new thing.)

Then Paul stood in the midst of Mars' hill, and said, Ye men of Athens, I perceive that in all things ye are too superstitious. For as I passed by, and beheld your devotions, I found an altar with this inscription, TO THE UNKNOWN GOD. Whom therefore ye ignorantly worship, him declare I unto you. God that made the world and all things therein, seeing that he is Lord of heaven and earth, dwelleth not in temples made with hands; Neither is worshiped with men's hands, as though he needed any thing, seeing he giveth to all life, and breath, and all things; And hath made of one blood all nations of men for to dwell on all the face of the earth, and hath determined the times before appointed, and the bounds of their habitation; That they should seek the Lord, if haply they might feel after him, and find him, though he be not far from every one of us: For in him we live, and move, and have our being; as certain also of your own poets have said, For we are also his offspring.

	Ancient Greek Education	Ancient Hebrew Education
Goal	Prepare individuals to serve the state.	Prepare individuals to serve God.
	(1) Memorize the laws of Lycurgus, the Spartan lawgiver. (2) Memorize selections from Homer. (3) Develop physical excellence through games, exercises, and the pentathlon (running, jumping, casting javelin, wrestling).	(1) Transmit knowledge and skills from generation to generation. (2) Increase knowledge and skills. (3) Concretize cultural values into accepted behavior.
	Teach students to trust the state.	Teach children to trust God in everything.
	Prepare for the state.	Prepare for eternity.
	Examine the world by classifying whole things into parts-removing them from the Creator. Redefine knowledge: Final reality is impersonal matter or energy shaped into its present form by impersonal chance.	Look at God's world as a whole–interconnecting–revealing God in every area. *The heavens declare the glory of God; and the firmaments sheweth his handywork* (Psalms 19:1).
	Immerse students in literature written by Greek philosophers.	Teach children to love learning so they will become self-motivated, lifelong learners.
	Focus on self-esteem, emotional adjustment, and external training of the body. Develop endurance, resourcefulness, and physical prowess.	Discover a child's God-given gifts and talents, and develop them to their fullest potential. Focus on spiritual training.
Result	Self-centered. My will be done. Violence, pornography, racial tensions, promiscuity, abortion, infanticide, etc.	God-centered. "Thy will be done." Authority with responsibility. Literacy, strong family ties, love of learning, security, independent thinking, high morals and values.
Curriculum Subjects	Humanism Evolution Social Studies	Bible Creation Science His Story (true history) Character Self-Government (internal obedience to God).
Curriculum Content	Trivium, the three stages: Grammar Logic (Dialectic) Rhetoric	The three main orders of study in ancient Israel consisted of: Religious education, Occupational skills, Military training with the basis of all knowledge being the fear of the Lord (Psalms 111:10; Proverbs 1:7). The three learning stages are knowledge, understanding and wisdom.
Curriculum Text	Books by Homer, Aristotle, Virgil, Pliny, Cicero.	God's Word. Orthodox schools did not study subjects derived from Classical tradition.
Heroes	Homer, Plato, Socrates, Aristotle, Epicurus, etc	Abraham, Isaac, Jacob, Joshua, and David.
	Lawlessness: To each his own. Look out for #1. There are no absolutes.	Lawfulness: Love one another. The last shall be first. Deny thyself. Obey the Commandments.
	That this is a rebellious people, lying children, children that will not hear the law of the Lord (Isaiah 30:9).	*Submit yourselves to every ordinance of man for the Lord's sake: whether it be to the king, as supreme; or unto governors, as unto them that are sent by him for the punishment of evildoers, and for the praise of them that do well* (1 Peter 2:13-14).

The Greek classical education model focuses on literature and logic. The Hebraic education model focuses on God's Word and faith.

But were mingled among the heathen, and learned their works.

(PSALMS 106:35)

"It may sound appealing to join great men in history in learning the Greek and Roman cultures, cultures which have influenced history but have not proven to be true! We ask ourselves and our readers the questions: "Will God be displeased if a generation grows up who do not know the names of the idols of Greece and Rome? Will God be displeased if a generation grows up knowing the Bible while ignorant of pagan thinkers?" If these cultures of antiquity were destroyed in their idolatry, why do we want to mimic their unbelieving practices? The Roman Coliseum stands as a gruesome testimony to the battle of Christ for men's souls —dash; a sporting event that enthusiastically killed Christians!"
—Earl & Diane Rodd, "Questioning Secular Classical Education," *Homeschool Digest*, 1998

Forasmuch then as we are the offspring of God, we ought not to think that the Godhead is like unto gold, or silver, or stone, graven by art and man's device. And the times of this ignorance God winked at; but now commandeth all men every where to repent: Because he hath appointed a day, in the which he will judge the world in righteousness by that man whom he hath ordained; whereof he hath given assurance unto all men, in that he hath raised him from the dead. And when they heard of the resurrection of the dead, some mocked: and others said, We will hear thee again of this matter (Acts 17:16-32).

Most of us experienced this Greco-Roman education. Modern education tried to change the liberal arts in order to fill the gaps, but ended up destroying the true principles discovered by the Greeks. There were several philosophies in the classical world directed at gaining knowledge about our world. The Greeks wanted to conform to the good and natural things of the world, but without God. This is not possible.

ANCIENT ROME

Rome absorbed the Greek culture in the second century and attempted to establish pagan schools throughout the Empire by way of taxes. The public school during this period was primarily literal in curriculum and rhetorical in content.

Remember, during this time the Hebrews continued educating their children with the foundation of the Torah (first five books of the Bible). The majority of the first church was Hebrew. They taught their children as commanded in Deuteronomy 6—teaching them the commands and statutes of God first and foremost.

During the first three centuries of the Christian church, there was little contact between the believers (later called Christians) and the pagan educational system. The denial of original sin always leads to disaster. The classical schools, with their intention to produce perfect citizens through education, produced only an artificial and cruel society. Men still look back on the "golden Days" of Greece for personal and cultural inspiration, but they fail to realize that the true nobility that they aspired to was never obtainable on any humanistic premise. True nobility, which the Greek and Roman ideal correctly identified, to some extent, is only available through the obedience to the Gospel of Christ, with its insistence on our recognition and confession of sin and its promise of containing sanctification. This is never attainable though education, but only through the free mercies of Christ our Saviour. (Mulligan)

MIDDLE AGES

The medieval Christian curriculum focus was on study. The medieval scholars used classical learning for Christian purposes. Judaism rejected the world's standards of the pagan culture and education. By this time, the church had gone from mostly Hebrew to mostly Gentile. Christianity embraced the world views with open arms.

David Mulligan's book *Far Above Rubies: Wisdom in the Christian Community* illustrates how the medieval approach to education used many non-biblical sources—even to the point of neglecting Scripture.

> Two traditions of classical literature and philosophy separated the classical world, but were brought together for the first time in fruitful union by the church and rearranged into an educational method that would be the standard of learning for the next one thousand years.
>
> The joining of the literary and scientific world views in Christ was the unique contribution of Medieval Christianity. The sciences of grammar and rhetoric were brought into conjunction with the science of dialectic (logic). They were arranged progressively, so that the student could use them to achieve his true goal, which in many cases was the science of theology. This system, known as the Trivium, was the foundation of the seven liberal arts programs that became universal throughout the Middle Ages.
>
> This methodology was kept alive in the West. It used textbooks and examples from the ancient world [Greek and Roman] and never saw a need for writing new ones. That was not because it accepted paganism, but because it believed that in many cases the basic curricula of certain structures had been worked out in the ancient world and did not need to be written again. This explains, for instance, the medieval emphasis on philosophy.
>
> Natural knowledge became prevalent at the end of the Middle Ages. Philosophy was discredited, the link between theology and the sciences broken; and man began to work out an approach to life that was independent of religion, independent of God. Secularism was born.

And delivered just Lot, vexed with the filthy conversation of the wicked: (For that righteous man dwelling among them, in seeing and hearing, vexed his righteous soul from day to day with their unlawful deeds;).
(2 Peter 2:7-8)

Christian education must therefore present all subjects as parts of an integrated whole with the Scriptures at the center. Without this integration, the curriculum will be nothing more than a dumping ground for unrelated facts. When God is acknowledged, all knowledge coheres.
—Doug Wilson
The Biblical Antithesis in Education, *Family Matters,* issue 2, 1995

During this period the Hebrew people continued to teach their children the ways of God, rejecting pagan culture. Anti-Semitism continued to flourish. Christians believed horrendous lies about the Jews and therefore continued to separate from anything Jewish.

Michael Brown explains the attitude toward the Jews during the later Middle Ages in his book *Our Hands are Stained With Blood*:

> The Black Death that ravaged Europe, wiping out about one-third of Europe's entire population, was blamed on the Jews. Christians believed the lies that the Jews secretly contaminated the wells with a poison mixture made of spiders, lizards, and the hearts of Christians. As a result, thousands of Jews were butchered by angry mobs and Jewish children under the age of seven were baptized and reared as Christians after their families were murdered.

Mulligan continues to explain in *Far Above Rubies: Wisdom in the Christian Community*

> After the peace of the church, in the reign of Constantine, Christianity began to make converts amid the educated classes. More than ever before, the church was brought into direct confrontation with the dilemma offered by pagan ideals of education and the perfect man. To a large extent the confrontation took place over classical literature. A majority of citizens were of the literary/rhetorical tradition. The issue was over the classical world view. Was the church to discard all pagan culture, or was it to attempt a synthesis between Christian and classical thought? Within the circle of orthodoxy many answers were given. After long trial and debate, what was finally settled upon has affected our intellectual culture to this day.

> By the time the church confronted the issue of education on an institutional level, several important events had already occurred:

> 1. The Church had transferred from Jewish to Gentile soil.

> 2. The standard of orthodoxy was moving in a more theological direction.

> 3. The Judaic roots of Christianity were radically de-emphasized as the Gospel message was universalized.

4. The biblical wisdom tradition was discarded in exchange for Greek education.

5. Wisdom was redefined in classical terms.

6. As the Church became more and more Gentile, less and less Judaic, an education system arose. The Bible standards that would have caused friction with the classical paideia [education] had retreated into the distance. The Church had undergone a strange transformation.

THE PURITANS

Let us move rapidly, a few hundred years, to the time of the Puritans. We see the Puritans throwing off the lies from the churches and returning to the early church's Hebrew heritage. Marvin Wilson's book, *Our Father Abraham*, explains (pp. 127-128):

> During the period of the Protestant Reformation (16th century), some signs of the re-Judaization of the Christian faith began to surface, as certain Hebrew categories were rediscovered. The Reformers put great stress on *sola scriptura* (Scripture as the sole and final authority of the Christian). The consequent de-emphasis on tradition brought with it a return to the biblical roots. Accordingly, during the two centuries following the Reformation, several groups recognized the importance of once again emphasizing the Hebraic heritage of the Church. Among these people were the Puritans who founded Pilgrim America, and the leaders who pioneered American education. We shall comment briefly on the first of these groups before concentrating on the second.

The Puritans came to America deeply rooted in the Hebraic tradition. Most bore Hebrew names. The Pilgrim fathers considered themselves as the children of Israel fleeing "Egypt" (England), crossing the "Red Sea" (the Atlantic Ocean), and emerging from this "Exodus" to their own "promised land" (New England). The Pilgrims thought of themselves as "all the children of Abraham" and, thus, under the covenant of Abraham (Feingold p. 46). The President of Yale College used these words before the Governor and General Assembly of the state of Connecticut in 1783: "Their influence on American society was not soon forgotten: more than a century and a half

Thus saith the LORD, Learn not the way of the heathen,...
(JEREMIAH 10:2)

"The philosophy of humanism began with Satan and is an expression of Satan's lie that humans can be like God. (ROMANS 1:25). Scripture identifies humanists as those who have "exchanged the truth of God for a lie, and worshipped and served created things rather than the Creator..."

Many who propose a classical education seek to be educated like the American founders were educated. It is true that most American founders received a classical education, being trained in Greek and Latin and studying Greek and Roman writers and philosophers as well as a variety of other writers and philosophers, Christian and non-Christian.

We believe that the classical education of the founders was their weakness, not their strength. While many were men of strong Christian character and practice, their classical education caused them to use a mixture of the philosophies of men and the Bible as their starting point in designing our system of government. When institutional education finally replaced parental discipleship in the 1800s, the dominant education was classical, not Biblical. The institutions continued teaching the classical while the Biblical, which previously had roots in some homes, fell by the wayside. As a result, the nation lost the essential ingredient necessary for our form of government: people with Godly wisdom, knowledge, and integrity and the power of the Holy Spirit to govern themselves.
—Earl & Diane Rodd, Questioning Secular Classical Education, *Homeschool Digest*, 1998

after the first Puritan settlers reached New England, the American people were referred to in a State Assembly as 'God's American Israel.'" (Feldman p. 5)

A.D. 1600 TO 1800

The International Institute for Christian Studies reports:

> Just as in Europe with the birth of the earliest universities, "the Christian worldview, more than any other system of thought, dominated American intellectual development during the colonial period.... Regardless of the vocation for which a student was preparing, the colonial college sought to provide for him an education that was distinctly Christian." ..."If colonial higher education operated from a Christian foundation, it did so primarily because such an intellectual framework also characterized the European institutions that served as models for the colonial college founders." ..."Thirty-five of the university men in early New England, including a large majority of the Harvard founders, had attended Emmanuel College of Cambridge University."
> The key [Bible] verse of the Puritan educators was, "The fear of the Lord is the beginning of wisdom." ...Education, for them, had to have at its heart the purpose of creating character and producing leaders. The very word *education* comes from a Latin word meaning "to lead out." This meant that what God worked inside a person, got processed out into his daily life and thinking. The professor's role was to draw out that which God was putting into the student. (Millar ed.)

During the 1700s Harvard began moving away from its Puritan roots to become thoroughly Unitarian by the early 1800s.

A Brief History of Christian Influence in U.S. Colleges by Jay Rogers explains:

> Harvard was founded in 1636 by Puritan Calvinists who recognized the necessity for training up a clergy if the new Bible commonwealth was to flourish in the wilderness.

> The kind of teaching that Harvard College was to provide was spelled out in its "Rules and Precepts" as follows: "Let every Student be plainly instructed, and earnestly pressed to consider well, the main end of his life and studies is, to know God and Jesus Christ which is eternal life, John 17:3, and therefore to lay Christ in the bottom, as the only foundation of all found knowledge and Learning...."

Secularization of the American university began with the takeover of Harvard by the Unitarians in 1805. Actually, the Unitarian takeover was preceded by a protracted struggle between orthodoxy and liberalism, which began in 1701 when Increase Mather stepped down from the presidency. The liberals, who had obtained a definite majority in the governing Corporation, elected John Leverett as president of Harvard College. Leverett, a religious liberal and a layman, set the college on its course away from Calvinist orthodoxy.

The rebellion against Calvinism was a rebellion against the Biblical view of man and God. For Unitarians, the worship of God depended on His being what they thought He should be, not what He actually was.

The Unitarians also rejected the Calvinist view of man as being innately depraved. Man, they were convinced, was not only basically good, but perfectible. For this reason, social action became the principal mode in which Unitarians practiced their religion. They were convinced that evil was caused not by man's sinful nature, but by ignorance, poverty, and social injustice. Thus, by eliminating ignorance (through universal public education), they would eliminate poverty and thereby eliminate social injustice. Once this was done and the happy results observed by all, the Unitarians would have proven that they were right and the Calvinists were wrong (*A Basic History of the United States*).

While the early Harvard Unitarians believed that their rational form of Christianity was quite scriptural, the newer generation, influenced by the enlightenment and the intoxicating elixir of Hegelian pantheism, saw no reason why they should subject their emotional, spiritual, and intellectual aspirations to the stultifying restrictions of the Bible.

The seeds of religious liberty for the American Church did not come from New England leaders such as Roger Williams and Anne Hutchinson—as noble as they and others were. Rather, they[the seeds] came from the Hebrews themselves, whose sacred writings inspired the Puritans. Accordingly, many of the Puritans in seventeenth-century England were learned Hebraists. William Bradford (1590-1657), prominent early American and Governor of Plymouth Colony for more than three decades, maintained an intense interest in Hebrew. Bradford stated that he studied Hebrew so that when he died he might be able to speak in the "most ancient language, the

"The United States is attempting to implement major educational changes. There is substantial agreement that other industrialized democracies are doing a better job of educating their students than we are. This holds true not only for their highest achievers but for their middle and lowest tracks as well. Many of these countries differ as much from each other as they do from us. Also, with few exceptions, they are now quite diverse in their student populations."
—*Education Reform: What's Not Being Said*
Albert Shanker,
President, American
Federation of Teachers,
Washington, D.C.

"The Greeks study in order to understand while the Hebrews study in order to revere."
—Abraham Joshua Heschel

"The Jewish Talmud tells a story of an elderly rabbi's counsel to his young nephew. The boy already knew the Torah, the Old Testament Law. Now he wanted to study the wisdom of the Greeks.

The rabbi recalled God's words to Joshua: 'You shall meditate on it [biblical law] day and night.'

'Go, then,' said the rabbi. 'Find a time that is neither day nor night, and learn then Greek wisdom.'

Like that rabbi, who put little stock in the value of studying Greek philosophy, Tertullian, an early Christian theologian, wrestled with the conflict in his day between Greek and Hebrew thought. He asked: 'What has Athens to do with Jerusalem?'"
—Christian Overman,

Holy Tongue in which God and, the angels, spake." Cotton Mather (1663-1728), a well-known Puritan minister and scholar from Massachusetts, had a similar deep respect for the Hebrew language. Concerning its importance, Mather once observed, "I promise that those who spend as much time morning and evening in Hebrew studies as they do in smoking tobacco, would quickly make excellent progress in the language" (Rosovsky).

AMERICA'S GODLY HERITAGE

Early American educators are another influential segment that placed a strong emphasis upon Old Testament and Hebrew studies. These people were closely connected to the "olive root" and insisted, in keeping with their Puritan heritage, that Hebrew be central in the realm of higher education. A study of the beginnings and curricula of many of the Ivy League colleges in the East is a case in point. Hebrew inscriptions, for example, are found on the insignias or seals of such schools as Columbia and Dartmouth. Of particular interest for our purposes are the early years of Harvard, Yale, and Dartmouth.

The last three generations of Americans simply have not been told the truth about American history. Active humanists and the liberal media have for years undertaken a concentrated effort to misinform the American public by attacking the "Religious Right" and rewriting America's Judeo-Christian history in a humanistic tone. The motto at the heart of the American expression "In God we trust" has been exchanged for "In man we trust."

Examine the quotes below. Have you heard them before? If so, you did not hear them in an American public history class:

- 1490-1492 - Columbus's commission was given to set out to find a new world. According to Columbus's personal log, his purpose in seeking undiscovered worlds was to "bring the Gospel of Jesus Christ to the heathens. …It was the Lord who put into my mind…that it would be possible to sail from here to the Indies…I am the most unworthy sinner, but I have cried out to the Lord for grace and mercy, and they have covered me completely … No one should fear to undertake any task in the name of our Saviour, if it is just and if the intention is purely for His holy service" (*Columbus's Book of Prophecies*).

- 1606 - The Charter for the Virginia Colony read in part:

"To the glory of His divine Majesty, in propagating of the Christian religion to such people as yet live in ignorance of the true knowledge and worship of God."

• 1620 - King James I granted the Charter of the Plymouth council. "In the hope thereby to advance the enlargement of the Christian religion, to the glory of God Almighty."

• 1620 - The Pilgrims sign the Mayflower Compact aboard the Mayflower, in Plymouth Harbor. "For the glory of God and advancement of ye Christian faith… doe by these presents solemnly & mutually in ye presence of God and one of another, covenant & combine our selves together into a civil body politick."[sic]

• 1623 - "But God gave them health and strength in a good measure; and showed them by experience the truth of the word, Deuteronomy 8:3: 'Man does not live on bread alone but on every word that comes from the mouth of the Lord'" (William Bradford, in BHOPP, p. 175).

• 1629 - The first Charter of Massachusetts read in part: "For the directing, ruling, and disposing of all other Matters and Thinges, whereby our said People may be soe religiously, peaceablie, and civilly governed, as their good life and orderlie Conversacon, maie wynn and incite the Natives of the Country to the Knowledg and Obedience of the onlie true God and Savior of Mankinde, and the Christian Fayth, which in our Royall Intencon, and The Adventurers free profession, is the principall Ende of the Plantacion…."

• 1638 - The towns of Hartford, Weathersfield, and Windsor adopt the Fundamental Orders of Connecticut. "To mayntayne and presearve the liberty and purity of the Gospell of our Lord Jesus, which we now professe…."

• 1639 - The governing body of New Hampshire is established. "Considering with ourselves the holy will of God and our own necessity, that we should not live without wholesome laws and civil government among us, of which we are altogether destitute, do, in the name of Christ and in the sight of God, combine ourselves together to erect and set up among us such government as shall be, to our best discerning, agreeable

Obey them that have the rule over you, and submit yourselves: for they watch for your souls, as they that must give account, that they may do it with joy, and not with grief: for that is unprofitable for you.
(HEBREWS 13:17)

But the natural man receiveth not the things of the Spirit of God: for they are foolishness unto him: neither can he know them, because they are spiritually discerned.
(1 CORINTHIANS 2:14)

"Sort children by judgments of learning capacity; separate the bright from the dull. This is the fundamental operating principle of our education program, the imperative that drives norm-referenced testing, tracking, ability grouping, gifted and talented programs and all the rest. Practices explicitly designed to exclude millions from rigorous education seem entirely reasonable if you believe the requisite abilities to be unequally distributed. By now five generations have received this treatment; we have come to accept it as a fundamental aspect of 'the way things are.'"
—Jeff Howard,
President, The Efficacy Institute

Any moral system that does not put Jesus Christ at its center, denies Christ: "No one can serve two masters; for either he will hate the one and love the other, or he will hold to one and despise the other…" (Matthew 6:24); and, "He who is not with Me is against Me; and he who does not gather with Me scatters" (12:30).

to the will of God...."

- 1775 - In Patrick Henry's speech: "We shall not fight alone. God presides over the destinies of nations, and will raise up friends for us. The battle is not to the strong alone; it is to the vigilant, the active, the brave... Is life so dear, or peace so sweet as to be purchased at the price of chains and slavery? Forbid it Almighty God! I know not what course others may take, but as for me, give me liberty or give me death!"

- 1787 - Article III of the Northwest Ordinance of 1787: "Religion, morality, and knowledge, being necessary to good government and the happiness of mankind, schools and the means of education shall forever be encouraged."

- 1789 - George Washington said "Let us with caution indulge the supposition, that morality can be maintained without religion" (Schroeder ed. p. 106).

- 1794 - John Jay, first Chief Justice of the U.S. Supreme Court, in a letter to his wife, stated "God's will be done; to him I resign—in him I confide. Do the like. Any other philosophy applicable to this occasion is delusive. Away with it" (Johnston ed. vol. 4, p. 7).

America, founded as a Christian nation, originally taught children in their own homes. Parents had sole responsibility for their children's education. The focus, from the Puritan Calvinists, was on studying God's Word. (See chart on page 43.)

Charles Spurgeon (1834-1892), speaking of education said, "It seemed to me that the preachers of the grand old truths of the gospel, were likely to be found in an institution where preaching and divinity would be the main objects, and not degrees and other insignia of human learning."

A portion of the prospectus for Spurgeon's Pastor's College:

> The College aims at training preachers rather than scholars. To develop faculties of ready speech, to help them to understand the Word of God, and to foster a spirit of consecration, courage, and confidence in God, are objects so important that we put all other matters into a secondary position. If a student should learn a thousand things and yet fail to preach the gospel acceptably, his college course will have missed its

true design. Should the pursuit of literary prizes and the ambition of classical honors so occupy the mind as to divert the attention from his life work, they are perilous rather than beneficial. To be wise, to win souls is the wisdom ministers must possess.

With a few adjustments, this portion of the prospectus for Spurgeon's School for Pastors is an excellent outline for a home school family's education statement. For example:

> *Our home school* aims at training godly men and women rather than scholars. To help them to understand the Word of God, and to foster a spirit of consecration, courage, and confidence in God, are objects so important that we put all other matters into a secondary position. If our students learn a thousand academic things and yet fail to find God's paths, this home school will have missed its true design. Should the pursuit of literary prizes and the ambition of classical honors so occupy the mind as to divert the attention from our children's life work, they are perilous rather than beneficial. To be wise, to follow God's ways is the wisdom that Christians must possess.

The reason we have lost so many of our religious freedoms is that the liberal educational establishment has worked hard to eliminate our knowledge of the godly heritage of America. The facts, nonetheless, reveal the true convictions of our founders. Without question, they believed that, although no single Christian denomination should dominate the nation, the principles of the Bible and Christianity should underlie our government and the American educational system as well.

The Puritans knew that the pagan Greek classical educational system could ruin America. Look at these excerpts written by John Wesley in *The Education Of Children*:

- "And education under Pythagoras or Socrates had no other end, but to teach children to think and act as Pythagoras and Socrates did. And is it not reasonable to suppose that a Christian education should have no other end but to teach them how to think, and judge, and act according to the strictest rules of Christianity?"

- "At least one would suppose, that in all Christian schools, the teaching them to begin their lives in the

But shun profane and vain babblings: for they will increase unto more ungodliness.

(2 Timothy 2:16)

"Congress shall make no law respecting an establishment of religion, or prohibiting the free exercise thereof" had always meant that Congress was prohibited from establishing a national religious denomination, that Congress could not require that all Americans become Catholics, Anglicans, or members of any other denomination.
This understanding of "separation of church and state" was applied not only during the time of the Founders, but for 170 years afterwards. James Madison (1751-1836) clearly articulated this concept of separation when explaining the First Amendment's protection of religious liberty. He said that the First Amendment to the Constitution was prompted because "The people feared one sect might obtain a preeminence, or two combine together, and establish a religion to which they would compel others to conform."
-The Separation of Church and State, Jeremiah Project

spirit of Christianity,—in such abstinence, humility, sobriety, and devotion as Christianity requires,—should not only be more, but a hundred times more, regarded that nay or all things else."

- "Let it be carefully remembered all this time, that God, not man, is the physician of souls; that it is He, and none else, who giveth medicine to heal our natural sickness; that all 'the help which is done upon earth, he doeth it himself'; that none of all the children of men is able to 'bring a clean thing out of an unclean'; and, in a word, that 'it is God who worketh in us, both to will and to do of his good pleasure.' But is generally his pleasure to work by his creatures; to help man by man. He honours men to be, in a sense, 'workers together with him.' By this means the reward is ours, while the glory redounds to him."

- "Ye that are truly kind parents, in the morning, in the evening, and all the day beside, press upon all your children, 'to walk in love, as Christ also loved us, and gave himself for us'; to mind that one point, 'God is love; and he that dwelleth in love, dwelleth in God, and God in him.'"
(Millar ed.)

John Wesley often quoted William Law. Review the excerpt below from Law's writing, *A Serious Call to a Devout and Holy Life*, first published in 1728. In all of the Puritan writings, God—not academics—is the primary source of wisdom.

Devotion is neither private nor public prayer; but prayers, whether private or public, are particular parts or instances of devotion. Devotion signifies a life given, or devoted, to God.

He, therefore, is the devout man, who lives no longer to his own will, or the way and spirit of the world, but to the sole will of God, who considers God in everything, who serves God in everything, who makes all the parts of his common life parts of piety, by doing everything in the Name of God, and under such rules as are conformable to His glory.

We readily acknowledge, that God alone is to be the rule and measure of our prayers; that in them we are to look wholly unto Him, and act wholly for Him; that we are only to pray in such a manner, for such things, and such ends, as are suitable to His glory.

WHAT HAPPENED TO AMERICA'S

GODLY EDUCATIONAL SYSTEM?

America: The First 350 Years by J. Steven Wilkins is an extraordinary study of the true history of America (the facts left out of the public school system for the last one hundred years). This "must have" for all educators is available on sixteen cassette tapes, with a cassette container and a study guide. Wilkins explains in *The Beginning of Public School Movement* (Lecture #29 audio cassette):

One of the most successful reform movements of the 1830s and '40s was the push for a nationwide, state-supported (and state-controlled) school system. The educational level of our nation was far better than Europe and much higher than the literacy rate today. The male literacy rate at that time ran from 70 to 100 percent (Blumefield, p. 20). There were numerous private schools and even charity schools for the poor—all without government assistance. Outside of New England, the country had almost complete educational liberty. This being the case, why a desire for state controlled schools? They were motivated by two things:

1. The desire to destroy the Christian foundations of the nation; and

2. The humanistic belief of salvation through education

The public school movement was always more than simply an effort to have schools at taxpayers' expense. Nor was it simply an effort to have educated electorate as the franchise was extended to more people, as sometimes alleged. The most zealous of reformers were determined to use the power of the state by the way of the schools to break hold of religious traditions and the inherited culture and to change society through the child's training. (*A Basic History of the United States*, vol. 3, pp. 90-91)

Charles Darwin and his colleagues were probably the most influential persons, in terms of changing an established way of thinking, since Nicolaus Copernicus. Darwin claimed that "natural selection" is what determines life and how it will proceed throughout history. His book, Origin Of Species, changed the way scientists, educators, and even the Church, viewed the origin and development of life. Just recently the Catholic Pope announced that Darwin's evolution theory was probably true.

SOME OF THE LEADERS OF THE "PUBLIC SCHOOL" MOVE-

Because that, when they knew God, they glorified him not as God, neither were thankful; but became vain in their imaginations, and their foolish heart was darkened. Professing themselves to be wise, they became fools,

(ROMANS 1:21-22)

"Active humanists and the liberal media have for years undertaken a concentrated effort to misinform the American public by attacking the "Religious Right" and rewriting America's Judeo-Christian history in a humanistic tone. The motto at the heart of the American experiment "in God we trust" has been exchanged for "in Man we trust."

—David Barton , *America's Godly Heritage*

"The First Amendment has a dual aspect. It not only "forestalls compulsion by law of the acceptance of any creed or the practice of any form of worship" but also "safeguards the free exercise of the chosen form of religion." The First Amendment was a safe-guard so that the State can have no jurisdiction over the Church. Its purpose was to protect the Church, not to disestablish it."

—Justice Douglas, Supreme Court in the United States vs. Ballard, 1944

MENT

America: The First 350 Years Study Guide, (pp 131-132) gives brief biographical sketches of some of the leaders of the modern school system:

Robert Owen
The father of modern socialism, Owen denounced all religion as the chief cause of human misery. In 1830 he wrote, "Now, when the effects of religion, as it has been hereto taught, and impressed by the human race, shall be followed throughout all their ramifications, it will be discovered that the religion of the world is the sole cause of all disunion, hatred, uncharitableness, and crime which pervade the population of the earth" (Samual Blumfield, *Is Public Education Necessary?* p 204).

The "salvation" of the world (which in Owen's mind represented embracing of socialism) depended upon the eradication of biblical education. The populace had to be re-educated. Blumfield observes: "To the Owenites in 1828 it was clear that national public education was the essential first step on the road to socialism and that this would require a sustained effort of propaganda and political activism over a long period of time." Owen was willing to give up on his own generation for socialism. He knew he needed a national school system that could change the nation—that was their vision in 1828. The Owenites knew that public education was the first step on the road to socialism and it would require many years, over a hundred. They had a vision for long-term victory. Owen was so outspoken against Christianity that Christians despised him, so he could not be the "up-front" person or the leading man. (He dropped into the background but was still very active. All orders were from him.) Abram Combe replaced him.

Abram Combe
A disciple of Owen, Combe shared, along with the others, a revulsion of Biblical faith. Combe was converted from Calvinism to a philosophy of human nature called Phrenology, which was developed by a German physician, Franz Joseph Gall. He realized his conversion would have to be repeated several times in the lives of other men before a secular, national educational system dedicated to the improvement (salvation) of men could be a reality.

Horace Mann
Like his cohorts, Mann was a Calvinist but rejected it

"A declared atheist who sometimes used religious terminology, Dewey was a Hegelian, holding that truth is in process; it never is eternally fixed. Morals change, he believed, as society changed. Students should, therefore, be taught to adjust socially and ethically to change as it occurs."
— Mel and Norma Gabler, textbook analysts

"To destroy a people you must first sever their roots."
—Alexander Solzhenitsyn, Russian writer

Finally, brothers, whatever is true, whatever is noble, whatever is right, whatever is pure, whatever is lovely, whatever is admirable - if anything is excellent or praiseworthy - think about such things. Whatever you have learned or received or heard from me, or seen in me - put it into practice. And the God of peace will be with you.
(Phil. 4:8-9)

"Over 70% of parents and the general public characterized today's children & teens as rude, irresponsible, and wild."
—Public Agenda
Kids These Days '99: What Americans Really Think About the Next Generation

when he was twelve years old. To Mann, inequality was man's great enemy. If man was ever to be equal, there must be equality of education and character. This made public schools with common curriculum necessary. Horace Mann believed the STATE to be the true parent of the child!

Robert Dale Owen

Son of Robert Owen, Robert Dale Owen followed his father's judgment. He wanted to replace Christian education with a "religiously neutral" education. He and his father felt that religion was superstition.

THE MEN THAT BEGAN THE STATE SCHOOL MOVEMENT REJECTED CHRISTIANITY

These men wanted public education to be the "redeemer" or "regenerator" of this present age. The Owenites later formed a secret society to work toward attaining their goals. They infiltrated other movements, educational groups, political groups, and other areas by volunteering or being elected. They then spread their ideas among those groups. Orestes Brownson (later a leader in their society) wrote:

> The great object was to get rid of Christianity, and not to convert our churches into halls of science. The plan was not to make open attacks on religion, although we might belabor the clergy and bring them into contempt where we could; but to establish a system of state—we said— national schools, from which all religion was to be excluded and to which all parents were to be compelled by law to send their children. (ibid 95, 96)

The Owenites didn't openly attack religion, but undermined it in any way possible, and kept promoting the public school system. Surprisingly, the majority of Christians supported their movement. The reasons were threefold:

1. There was a decline in Calvinism among evangelicals in general. The majority of Christians were in basic agreement with the Unitarians and Owenites in their opposition to Calvinism.

2. There was a great influx of immigrants from Europe, many of whom were Roman Catholic, who had been greatly influenced by rationalism. These people posed a threat to the historic Protestantism consensus, and believed that government schools would ward off their

The fear of the Lord is the beginning of knowledge; fools despise wisdom and instruction.

(Proverbs 1:7)

This know also, that in the last days perilous times shall come. For men shall be lovers of their own selves, covetous, boasters, proud, blasphemers, disobedient to parents, unthankful, unholy, Without natural affection, trucebreakers, false accusers, incontinent, fierce, despisers of those that are good, Traitors, heady, highminded, lovers of pleasures more than lovers of God; Having a form of godliness, but denying the power thereof: from such turn away. For of this sort are they which creep into houses, and lead captive silly women laden with sins, led away with divers lusts, Ever learning, and never able to come to the knowledge of the truth.

(2 Timothy 3:1-7)

Cease, my son, to hear the instruction that causeth to err from the words of knowledge.

(Proverbs 19:27)

Stand fast, and hold the traditions which ye have been taught, whether by word, or our epistle.

(II Thes. 2:15)

"I am much afraid that schools will prove to be the gates of hell, unless they [schools] diligently labor in explaining the Holy Scriptures, engraving them in the hearts of youth. Every institution in which men are not unceasingly occupied with the Word of God must become corrupt."
—Martin Luther

In a nationwide web-based survey of nearly 70,000 students in grades 6-12, students voiced their perceptions on school climate. Survey data reveals that nearly 59 percent of the respondents report feeling safe at school and 44 percent believe that school rules are enforced fairly.

37 percent of those surveyed said students show respect for one another.

One-third agreed with the statement "students say things to hurt or insult me."

While 80 percent of the girls surveyed said it bothered them "when others are insulted or hurt verbally," only 57 percent of the boys expressed a similar attitude.

Fewer than half considered themselves positive role models for other students.

Just over one-third said that students show respect toward teachers.
—National Center for Student Aspirations, 2001

influence.

3. It was the belief of many citizens that public schools would be turned over to the control of Christians once they were established.

These things resulted in the strange coalition of Socialists, Unitarians, and evangelical Christians, all supporting a governmental system for their own reasons. This, coupled with those who wanted to make money from the system (textbook publishers, professional educators, and others), brought tremendous pressure in favor of government-financed schools. The pro-school propaganda became increasingly vicious and outrageous. Opponents of the school were labeled the "enemies of light and knowledge" and "of the betterment of mankind."

By the year 1850 it was a foregone conclusion that this country would have a system of government-supported schools. They were not to be schools of learning, but engines of change and "reform." Schools were no longer extensions of parental authority but, instead, powerful instruments for state control over the population. The reformers sought to deny parents' authority over the education of their children. Children increasingly became "wards of the state." The public schools would become the chief instrument in implementing the revolution which the enemies of Christianity desired.

The schools became the new temples of the new religion of man, and teachers became the new priests. Man, or more precisely "humanity," as incorporated in the state, became the new god and has remained so to this day.

Today, denouncing the public school system in this country offends more people than denouncing God. Why? Because people believe education is salvation. Survival from poverty comes from education. If you don't have formal education, you are a second-class citizen. (God's Word tells us that this is the world's view, not God's. The Bible clearly states that wisdom and knowledge come from God.) Christians believe in education, and we will educate our children as God commands, but education is not considered salvation. Education is still to the world—and to Christians who have believed the lie—the great thing that will save the state.

WHEN PRAYER WAS TAKEN OUT OF SCHOOL

David Breese, author of *Seven Men Who Rule the World From*

the Grave, explains that through the teachings of John Dewey's humanism, his atheism, his autonomous man, amorality, evolution, and one-world socialism permeated our educational system and excluded from our textbooks the moral and biblical teachings which were the bedrock of our American culture. Thus, our American youth have been disenfranchised from our Christian heritage. Now two generations of graduates have been subjected to these godless philosophies through our schools. What are the results?

The results are a spiritually apathetic society that hardly murmured when, in 1962, citing no precedents, a liberal Supreme Court abolished prayer from the public schools and the next year abolished Bible reading from the schools. ... *Because iniquity shall abound, the love of many shall run cold* (Matthew 24:12).

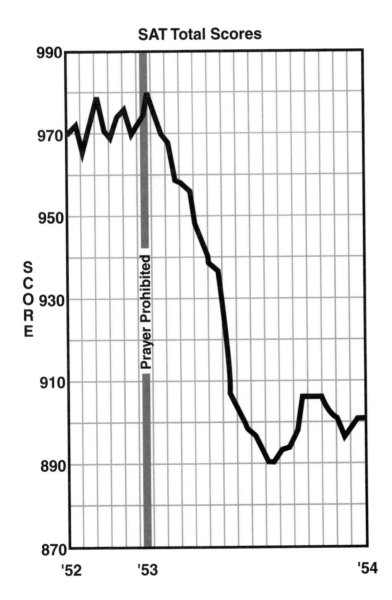

Nearly one third of U.S. students report they experience bullying, either as a target or as a perpetrator, according to survey of 15,686 public and private school students; this survey is among the first to document the prevalence of bullying in the U.S.

Overall, nearly 30 percent of the children reported that they had been involved in bullying. More than 16 percent said they'd been bullied at least occasionally during the current school term, and 8 percent reported bullying or being bullied at least once weekly. Other significant findings include:

Of the 30 percent who reported being involved in bullying, 13 percent reported that they had bullied other children while just over 10 percent said that they had been bullied. Approximately 6 percent of the children reported that they had, at different times, been bully and victim.

The frequency of bullying was higher among 6th- through 8th-grade students than among 9th- and 10th-grade students.

Children who said they were bullied reported more loneliness and difficulty making friends, while those who did the bullying were more likely to have poor grades and to smoke and drink alcohol, the survey found.
—National School Safety Center Report, 2001

STANDARD EIGHTH GRADE ACHIEVEMENT TEST IN 1907

An excerpt from "Small World Gone: A Family Record of an Era" published by the *Wall Street Journal*. The author talks of the evening she received her eighth grade diploma from a small-town school.

Science

The 'orthography' quiz asked us to spell twenty words, including "abbreviated," "obscene," "elucidation," "assassination" and "animosity." We were also required to make a table showing the different sounds of all the vowels. Among the other eight questions (each subject had ten questions) was one which asked us to divide words into syllables and mark diacritical, defiance, priority, remittance and propagate.

Math

Two of Arithmetic's ten questions asked us to find the interest on an 8 percent note for $900 running two years, two months, six days; and also to reduce three pecks, five quarts, and one pint into bushels.

Reading

In reading we were required to tell what we knew of the writings of Thomas Jefferson and, for another of the ten questions, to indicate the pronunciation and give meanings to the following words: zenith, deviated, coliseum, misconception, panegyric, Spartan, talisman, eyre, triton, crypt and others.

Geography

Among Geography's ten questions were these two: "Name two countries producing large quantities of wheat, two of cotton, two of coal, two of tea." and "Name the three important rivers of the U.S., three of Europe, three of Asia, three of South America, and three of Africa."

Physiology

As one of Physiology's ten we were asked to write 200 words on the evil effects of alcoholic beverages. Another directed us to define boards of health and what their duties were.

Grammar

In Grammar's ten were two directing us to analyze and diagram: "There is a tide in the affairs of men, which, taken at the flood, leads on to a fortune," and then to parse tide, which, taken, leads.

History

In History we were to "give a brief account of the colleges, printing and religion in the colonies prior to the American Revolution," to "name the principal campaigns and military leaders of the Civil War," and to "name the principal political questions which have been advocated since the Civil War and the party which advocated each."

Aavis Carlson took and passed that standard eighth grade test when she was eleven years and eight months old. So much for a one-room school in Kansas, 1907.

PUBLIC SCHOOL TODAY

Let us move from the primitive one-room schoolhouse to the bright and better future of 1986, where our tax dollars were hard at work educating tomorrow's leaders.

Reading

In 1990, Secretary of education Cavazos released the results of two nationwide tests. Fifty-eight percent of seventeen-year-olds cannot understand a twelfth grade textbook or articles in the *Wall Street Journal, Time* or *Newsweek*. Ninety-five percent do not have the reading skills to understand a college textbook. Forty two percent of thirteen-year-olds and fourteen percent of seventeen-year-olds cannot read at an eighth grade level.

History and Literature

In 1986, 7,812 eleventh graders took a national test of their knowledge of history and literature. This was a multiple choice affair, in which there was no penalty for skipping a question altogether. Even so, of all the answers given to the 141 questions on history, only 54.5 percent were correct. The results in literature were even more depressing. As a group, these seventeen-year-olds demonstrated no sense of chronological history. Almost 25 percent thought the Civil War was before 1800. One third thought Columbus discovered the new world after 1750. Three out of four could not place Lincoln within twenty years. Forty-three percent guessed wrong on wnich half century included World War I. Not even half could identify Patrick Henry.

Math

In 1987 the *News / Sun Journal* in Fort Lauderdale stated, "New evidence ranks the mathematical ability of American primary and high school students among the lowest of any country."

Geography

The Monitor, McAllen, Texas, ran an article titled, "Study: One fifth of students can't find the U.S.A. on a map." A report from the National Council for Geographical Education found that in a 1983 test on geography, American twelve-year-olds often confused Brazil on the map for the United States. American youngsters placed fourth among an international field of eight. Their median scores were 42.9 of a possible 101.

Composition

A study by Educational Writers in Sioux Falls, South Dakota in 1986 stated: "76 percent of seventeen-year-olds could not write an adequate piece of creative writing, 62 percent could not write a satisfactory piece of prose, and 80 percent could not write a persuasive letter."

Our future leaders?

From that time on, there was a startling rise in teenage pregnancies, up 556 percent; venereal disease, up 226 percent (now thirty-five thousand new cases per day!). Family divorce had declined for fifteen years; it then tripled each year since. SAT scores had previously been stable; now they've declined remarkably.

A recent statistical analysis by David Barton graphically illustrates how America has plummeted from righteous living, prosperity, and success in the last quarter-century. Consider the following chart compiled from his publication, *America: To Pray or Not to Pray*:

In 1962, the Court examined a simple twenty-two word prayer, first used to negate prayer in schools:

> "Almighty God, we acknowledge our dependence upon Thee, and we beg Thy blessings upon us, our parents, our teachers, and our country."

This simple prayer, said by children, acknowledged God. Americans' indifference allowed the removal of prayer from our schools. This is but one of the steps toward complete destruction of America's original Judeo-Christian educational system. This value-free environment has resulted in chaos. Since the 1962 removal of prayer:

- SAT scores have declined dramatically.
- Birth rates of unwed teens have increased
- Sexually transmitted diseases have increased
- Violent crime has greatly increased.
- The divorce rate has increased
- The incidence of couples living together has increased
- Abortions have become legal and frequent.

EDUCATION IN THE 1990S

Moving to the '90s educational systems, we see the tragic results of pagan education—immorality and illiteracy.

Don Feder explains in the Introduction of his book *A Jewish Conservative Looks at Pagan America*:

> By Pagan America, I mean this is no longer a Judeo-Christian Nation, animated by the ethical vision of the Bible, with its special emphasis on honesty, hard work, caring, and self discipline. Instead we are evolving into

"It seems like every time we have a school shooting or major incident involving a school, the first thing everybody wants to do is hold a prayer vigil. It seems to me that if you believe in the power of prayer post-disaster, you should believe in it pre-disaster,"
—Minister Kerry Hill

"when prayer was taken out of school guns started coming in."
—Jan Cook, Mother of four

Forbidding prayer establishes the religion of secularism, which characteristically shows no belief in God, God-given morals, prayer, or the Judgment Day.
—Anonymous
To Pray or Not to Pray, CollegeTermPapers.com

WHAT YOUR CHILD NEEDS TO KNOW WHEN

the type of Canaanite culture (unrestrained hedonism, ritual prostitution, child sacrifice and the civic virtue of Sodom), which my ancestors encountered at the dawn of moral history.

...The gods of the late twentieth century America include the doctrines of radical autonomy, of absolute rights divorced from responsibilities, of gender sameness, of self expression which acknowledges no higher purpose, of moral relativism and sexual indulgence. Their templates are courtrooms, legislative chambers, classrooms, news rooms, and the executive suites of entertainment conglomerates and publishing firms. We are one nation under God no more.

...Ideas have consequences. First the elite, then to a lesser extent the masses embrace certain toxic notions. The consequences fill our prisons, drug rehab centers, divorce courts, shelters for battered and abused, rape crises centers, mental hospitals, singles bars, and the roster of guests on the Oprah Winfrey Show.

Today we have enormous problems with illiteracy. Almost 72 million American adults are functional illiterates (*Education Week*, June 13, 1985, p. 28). People find that life is easier, and that they can get along without the "sweat" of reading, and so they choose instead to watch television and view cartoons. No one must read, except to fill out a form. We assume that today's people are far superior to those who lived before us; however, the literacy rate was much higher in early America than today. In the fifteenth, sixteenth, and seventeenth centuries there were more people who wanted to learn to read than there were people to teach them.

The right principles that made America great have been lost, not just among the lower classes, but in the highest offices in the land. There is no longer any connection between character and destiny. Moral teaching, proper standards, and respect for rules have been removed from our schools. Meaningless courses in "values clarification" and the tenets of secular humanism (classified as a religion by the Supreme Court in 1961) have been substituted. People claim that morals have changed. God makes morals, and He didn't change His mind. God hates wickedness.

The children from this background have now become the parents, teachers, political leaders, and news media of today. Ignorant of

"When you live in a society that turns its back on God and Godly answers to life, you will ultimately be left with ungodly, immoral behavior."
—Rev. Tom Geoffroy
Pastor, Christian Life Fellowship

"If you subsidize rice, you get more rice; if you subsidize wheat, you get more wheat. The state subsidizes irresponsible parenting and now we are reaping the whirlwind of this irresponsibility and dependence."
—Milton Friedman

"The Medieval classical approach to education emphasizes the ability of Christianity to use non-Biblical sources. Its problem lies in the willingness to use them too readily—even to the neglect of Scripture. In the delight at turning ancient philosophical methods to Christian use, the Biblical standards for education were neglected."
—David Mulligan, Far Above Rubies: Wisdom in the Christian Community

And if ye be Christ's, then are ye (also) Abraham's seed...
(GALATIANS 3:29)

For finding fault with them, He saith, Behold, the days come, saith the Lord, when I will make a new covenant with the house of Israel and with the house of Judah: Not according to the covenant that I made with their fathers (Moses and the Elders) in the day when I took them by the hand to lead them out of the land of Egypt ...
(HEBREWS 8:8-9)

"A growing awareness that the roots of our Christian faith are deeply embedded in the Soil of the Jewish faith is creating a virtual renaissance in Christian thinking and understanding. Concerned Christians universally are beginning to rethink the validity of many time-honored traditions and doctrinal concepts of conventional Christianity. There is a growing suspicion that, in many cases, we have been far too removed from our Hebraic origins."
—Robert S. Somerville, Director of Awareness Ministries

"An over-Hellenized, over-Latinized Christianity needs a re-Judaizing process to bring it back to its founding Jewish roots and RENEW it more in keeping with its own inherent ideals."
—Edward Flannery, The Anguish of the Jews

"The advantage of a classical education is that it enables you to despise the wealth which it prevents you from achieving."
—Russell Green

the great moral and religious strengths of our country, they were unable to impart these to the new generation.

RETURNING TO TRADITIONAL EDUCATION —WHAT TRADITION?

Today, there is a surge of interest in the secular world to return to Greek classical education. "We need to return to the traditional literary culture, the classical standards of the past," experts demand. Insistence on a "back to basics" of "reading, writing, and arithmetic," has again become popular. It is a desire to turn back to the fork where we took the wrong road.(See chart on page 39).

The classical method that was developed in ancient Greece and Rome and established in the middle ages, was used almost exclusively in the Western world until the 19th century. The main focus was reading the Greek and Roman classics. To be in touch with literary arts marked one as accomplished.

There can be no doubt that literary education is more whole, more human, and more satisfying than the scientific technological education. But is even literary education enough? Good literature—Scott, Milton, Vergil—promotes courage insight, high morality, and imagination, but it can never do what the Bible does.

Jacques Maritain of the University of Notre Dame explains,

> Greek wisdom is a wisdom of man, a wisdom of reason, it was turned toward created things to find the knowledge of the cosmos, not toward salvation, saintliness, eternal deliverance. Greek wisdom cannot be called a rational wisdom in a very modern sense of that term. Greek paganism had its roots in magical thought, which continued to furnish the subconscious atmosphere of Greek religion. Sacred traditions did not cease to form an undercurrent beneath Hellenic meditation. Ancient reason was a naturally religious reason. It operated in a climate of natural piety haunted by many terrors. Even at the time when it displayed the most intense rationalism, as in the Stoic school, the rationalism in question remained entirely different from our modern rationalism, and veered toward a kind of magical naturalism, conceiving Reason as a divine fire that permeated matter, and favoring all the pagan superstitions. Greek reason recognized good and bad fortune, believed in higher inspirations, in demonic influences; the idea of destiny, and of the jealousy of the gods, the superstitious fear of admitting happiness, the belief in omens and in divination, even the adoration of the divine similitudes scattered through nature, were evidence of a religious appreciation of the supra-human energies at work in the world and sustained a kind of sacred awe, or fear.

WHY GO BACK TO GREEK CLASSICAL WAYS —WHY NOT RETURN TO BIBLICAL METHODS?

The reaction against modern scientific educational failure creates a desire to return to traditional schooling. It is understandable that many well-meaning Christians, in search of a better way, have attempted to combine the Greeks' methods with the Bible. But there is a better way! Instead of returning to the ancient Greek ways, we need to return to the biblical model. The Hebrews did not follow the world's pattern for the education of their children. They refused to subject their children to the classical literature of their time but focused on God's Word. Our only hope for stable, ongoing, integrated culture is placing the Word of God at the center of our thinking, speaking, and acting.

Christian faith is divinely revealed and is securely anchored in the Bible. God breathed His Word into the minds of the biblical authors within a Hebrew cultural environment. We must, therefore, focus on the language and thought-patterns found in the Scriptures so that we can penetrate the mindset of the Hebrew people. The aim of education was ethical and religious. The education of youth was an obligation of the parents, and was deeply associated with ritual observances and learning the Mosaic law, both of which were regarded as essential.

The biblical model is comprised of three phases of learning 1) knowledge, 2) understanding, and 3) wisdom.

The Greek model is also comprised of three phases of learning: 1) grammar, 2) dialectic, and 3) rhetoric. The classical Greek approach is similar to the biblical model except for the main ingredient. True wisdom cannot be gained by unaided human reason. The Greeks wanted to conform to the good and natural things of the world. But without God, this is not possible.

Without knowledge, there can be no understanding or wisdom. Knowledge and understanding are likewise necessary if there is to be wisdom. The wise man is able to acquire even more knowledge and understanding, thus becoming wiser—he has learned how to learn.

This classical approach's primary focus is on literature, logic, and reasoning. Unfortunately, what the classical proponents call "The Great Books" are mainly works by ungodly men (Aristotle, Homer, Plato, Virgil, and Caesar) teaching ungodly ideas. Our primary focus should be on the 66 "Great Books" of the Bible. God's Word should temper our reasoning. *Trust in the LORD with all thine heart; and **lean not unto thine own***

"The phenomena of environment were depended on God alone (Psalms 104:27-30). Indeed, the Hebrews had no word for 'nature,' no conception of anything but the ultimate control of God, to whom all things were responsible (Hos. 2:21-22). Modern environmental sciences may be much clearer than the Hebrews were on the immediate creative and regulative physical powers operating in the physical world, but the Hebrews' recognition of God, as the ultimate agent of creation, gave them insight into a realm which science makes no pretense to know."
—J. M. Houston, Contributor
Pictorial Bible Atlas, 1981

"...some proponents of 'classical Christian education' seek to revive the writings of ancient pagans, Roman, Greek or otherwise, and present them to our children as possible sources of wisdom and true knowledge, we must strongly object. In the case of the Greeks, many of the 'great teachers' were not only idolaters, but sodomites and pedophiles with minds which were deeply affected by their perversions. This is precisely the type of reasoning and thinking from which God has redeemed us. We are to build our worldview exclusively on Holy Scripture, taking every thought captive to the obedience of Jesus Christ. To the extent that our mature children should study classical culture and writings, it is to identify the many false philosophies and intellectual strongholds which have infected Western civilization, and against which the Christian soldier is to wage war."
—Douglas W. Phillips, *Vision Forum*

"The biblical education structure is very simple. It is meant only to answer one question, 'why am I studying, such and such a thing?' There are four possible answers:
1. In order to know God's word.
2. In order to understand God's plan.
3. In order to better know his world or
4. In order to live more Godly in the Kingdom.

To know, why we are pursuing any study, brings us near, by leaps and bounds to the ultimate goal of education — 'wisdom.'"
—David Mulligan, *Far Above Rubies: Wisdom in the Christian Community*

understanding (Proverbs 3:5). The mind can be well trained in many things, but is worthless if the student does not have the mind of Christ.

Literature is a blessing, but should never be the purpose or center of learning. (See chart on page 39). When we return to Scripture-centered education, two things occur: 1. We can view language in its splendor without the danger of it replacing religion. We can appreciate it as God's gift to us. 2. Considering language as a skill, we can study it in a deeper way.

There is a long tradition in this country of resistance to the wisdom of the Greeks: Thomas Paine, Benjamin Franklin, and Noah Webster all judged the classics to be of scant use. ("Learning from the Greeks," *Commentary Magazine*, Valiunas, 1998)

The classical tradition of learning, with its emphasis on ancient authors and events, works. In learning completely the Greco-Roman world, the student learned to learn. He became a Historian, a Geographer and Orator, and a man of letters. This idea is sound, even if the subject matter is not. However, a Christian education must be centered in God's holy Word and must instruct in the ways of His Kingdom that differs from the world. **A biblical education refuses to limit God in an unofficial corner called "religion."** God is the source about reality, and His works are studied by all those who love Him. Unity exist between God's Word and His World. When the unity is disturbed, a breach opens between religion and learning. When this unity is destroyed, men are swallowed-up in either Theology or Science (Philosophy). Christian education must maintain the unity of knowledge between the supernatural and the natural ways of knowing. (Adapted from Mulligan's writings)

We need to be careful that we don't jump from the frying pan into the fire. The Bible warns against philosophies whose highest realities and concerns are atoms, energy, cosmic laws, or humanity—those founded on the basic principles of the world and not according to Christ. *Beware lest any man spoil you through philosophy and vain deceit, after the tradition of men, after the rudiments of the world, and not after Christ* (Colossians 2:8).

CHAPTER 4

HISTORY OF BIBLICAL EDUCATION
Solid Foundation

EDUCATION IN BIBLE TIMES

A Christian's roots are in the Bible, not in the Greeks' Hellenistic paganism. We need to look at the history of our patriarchs, Abraham, Isaac, and Jacob, the faithful followers of God, to find out how they taught their children the enduring, deep-rooted faith.

EDUCATION IN THE HOME

A study of education in Bible times can be very encouraging to home schoolers because the focus is on the home. The Hebrews called the Temple "miqdash." After the destruction of the Temple, they called the home "miqdash me`at." The root of *miqdash* is *qadash* (*Strong's* 4720, 6942) meaning "to be set apart," "a consecrated thing or place," "a sanctuary." The family home was put apart for something special. The Hebrew word *me`at* (meh-at´) (*Strong's* 4592) means "little" (Ezekiel 11:16). God made the home the "little sanctuary." The home was a house of prayer, worship, and study—all study—academics and spiritual.

Today's Christians have it backwards. The primary sphere of religious activity should be in the home, not the church. The dinner table was a place to gather—not just for food (Deuteronomy 8:3)—but also to study God's Word, pray, praise, and worship. The home was more important than the synagogue. The center of all training—religious, education, and family—was the home.

The Hebrew word for parent is similar to that for teacher. It is horeh, which is from the root word yarah, meaning "to cast, throw or shoot." The Bible commands the father, the priest of his little sanctuary, to instruct the children (Deuteronomy 6). The father is to impart wisdom and knowledge diligently to his children.

We can learn much from the weekly worship in the early church. The entire family prepared each week for the Sabbath. The Sabbath was a special day of worship, prayers, singing, and Bible reading. The men of the home went to the Temple (each man prepared to speak) for worship, prayer, and sacrifice, but then they returned home for worship with their families. The father blessed the children as he prayed for them one by one. I recently heard a very sad statement. The observation was made that, "One could walk into a Jewish unbeliever's home today and see the people's love for God, but what would one see in a believer's home?" Would we even be eating together around the table?

TEACHING THE WHOLE CHILD

Collier's Encyclopedia explains that education during Abraham's times taught the whole child:

The keynote of Jewish education appears as early as Gen. 18:19 in the revelation made to Abraham: "For I know him that he will command his children and his household after him, and they shall keep the way of the Lord, to do justice and judgment...." This same note runs throughout the Old Testament in various injunctions: "Train up a child in the way he should go; and when he is old, he will not depart from it" (Proverbs 22:6) and "Fear of the Lord is the beginning of wisdom" (Proverbs 9:10). The aim of education was ethical and religious. The education of youth was an obligation of the parents, and was intimately associated with the performance of ritual observances and with learning the Mosaic law, both of which were regarded as essential to the survival of the Jews as a people. In the educative process, both father and mother were equally concerned, and both were to be equally honored (the Fifth Commandment). The method of instruction in the home was for a long time oral, and learning by practice, and these methods were continued outside the home in gatherings and assemblies, held for both worship and instruction. Corporal punishment was regarded as an essential element in training.

"He that spareth the rod hateth his son: but he that loveth him chasteneth him betimes" (Proverbs 23:24) is a precept frequently repeated both in Proverbs and in Ecclesiastes. Visual aids, including monuments as records of history, were employed. The setting up of "great stones" with inscriptions on them implies an early knowledge of writing (Deuteronomy 27:2,3,8, and elsewhere). The scribes were not only copyists but also teachers and interpreters of the Law of Moses. There existed a knowledge of arithmetic and astronomy; music, dancing, games, and sports were cultivated, and moral instruction was an essential part of education.

STUDY AS WORSHIP

Marvin Wilson explains in *Our Father Abraham*:

People seek education for many worthy reasons: some desire to broaden horizons; others wish to develop skills; still others want to satisfy their intellectual curiosity. The Bible, however, teaches that study ought to be, above everything else, an act of worship, one of the highest ways by which a person can glorify God.

As a Pharisee, Paul was a learned product of Judaism, a man well versed in Jewish thought and biblical theology. (Philippians 3:4-6) Paul made no distinction between the so-called sacred and secular areas of life. He taught-as his Hebrew forebears did-that all of life was God's domain of activity. Every detail of life therefore, must be set aside and consecrated to the glory of God. So, Paul wrote to the Corinthians, "Whether therefore ye eat, or drink, or whatsoever ye do, do all to the glory of God." (1 Corinthians 10:31). He later wrote to the Colossians, "And whatsoever ye do in word or deed, do all in the name of the Lord Jesus, giving thanks to God and the Father by him." (3:17). As David Hubbard reminds us, "There is an intimate connection between work and worship. For to work is to give glory to God...We work with God's goods, and we use God's talents to perform the work, and we serve God's people through our work."

Wilson also explains in chapter 14:

Since the Bible period, Jews have considered the quest for knowledge to be one of the great desiderata [desires] of life (Philippians 3:4-11). Learning-learning-learning that is the secret of Jewish survival. (Hacker, ed. P.21.). ...So strongly did the early rabbis feel about the priority of education that they said it may not be interrupted even for the rebuilding of the Temple... Israel was to acknowledge the Lord's authority in every circumstance and turn of the way. (Psalms 16:8, Proverbs 3:5-6). The ultimate prophetic vision was that "all the peoples of the earth know that the Lord is God and there is no other." (1 Kings 8:60).

From early in history the center of education was the home. Both parents shared responsibility in this task (Proverbs. 1:8; 6:20), though the Father bore the chief responsibility for the instruction of the children (Deuteronomy 11:9).... In Bible times it was the Father-not textbooks, audiovisuals, or brightly colored classrooms-the main instruction was the learning process. As teacher of his children, the father served as a living dynamic communicator of divine truth. A Bible could not be substituted-there were no Bibles.

There is no shortcut method to a sound education. If someone wants to make spiritual training a priority, one must make a major commitment of time. Thus the Psalmist says, "...His delight is in the law [instruction] of the Lord; and in His law [instruction] doth he meditate day and night" (Psalms 1:2).

Ancient Israel had no formal system of schooling; however, learning and knowledge were considered one of the greatest goals of life.

A careful study of the Hebrew Bible will reveal what Martin Luther called a "special energy" in its vocabulary. Luther discovered what many Hebraists of the twentieth century have recently come to affirm with him: it is impossible to convey so much so

Would Jesus have been the head of his class if He had attended the Greek grammar school at Sephoris? What would He have done Homer, Herodotus, and Aeschylus? Or how would He have fared at the Academy of Plato or the Lyceum of Aristotle?
—David Mulligan, *Far Above Rubies: Wisdom in the Christian Community*

"The aim or purpose of Old Testament education is encapsulated within the revelation given to Abraham concerning the destruction of Sodom and Gomorrah. Here God bids Abraham to direct his children in 'the way of the Lord.'"
—Walter A. Elwell, *Baker's Evangelical Dictionary of Biblical Theology*

"Ultimately, biblical education is instruction in a lifestyle. For this reason, the apostle Paul reminded his pupil Timothy, 'you ... know all about my teaching, my way of life continue in what you learned' (2 Tim. 3:10,14). Not only is biblical education a lifestyle—it is a lifetime!"
—Andrew E Hill,

Four highlights of education
in ancient Israel:

1. It was very practical in
nature, often passed on in
the home by the parents or
acquired in guilds. It provided
basic instruction in crafts and
vocational pursuits (Exodus
35-36).

2. It gave guidance in worldly
wisdom. The wisdom literature (Proverbs, Job, and
Ecclesiastes) provides direction for coping with life, especially in social and economic
relations (Proverbs 1:2-3).

3. It provided instruction in an
ethical way of life. The
emphasis is often on learning
the law of the Lord (Exodus
20: 1-17).

4. It was a vehicle to pass on
the traditions that bind the
community together, give it a
common language, and pro-
vide the symbols for the celebration of a good and meaningful life. There is a special
emphasis on remembrance
of what God has done
(Deuteronomy 26:8-9).

—Duncan Ferguson,
Education, May 1998

briefly in any other language. Luther concluded the following: "The Hebrew language is the best language of all, with the richest vocabulary…. It has therefore been aptly said that the Hebrews drink from the spring, the Greeks from the stream that flows from it, and the Latins from a downstream pool" (Lapide p. x.).

EDUCATION DEFINED

The 1915 International Bible Encyclopedia gives this fascinating information about education during Bible times:

Religious education among ancient and modern peoples alike reveals clearly this twofold aspect of all education. The first aspect consists in the transmission of religious ideas and experience by means of imitation and example; each generation, by actually participating in the religious activities and ceremonies of the social group. Formal religious education begins with a systematic effort on the part of the mature members of a social group to teach the younger members by means of solemn rites and ceremonies, or patient training, or both.

All education is at first religious in the sense that religious motives and ideas predominate in the educational efforts of all peoples. The degree to which religion continues over in the educational system of a progressive nation depends upon the vitality of its religion and upon the measure of efficiency and success with which from the first that religion is instilled into the very bone and sinew of each succeeding generation. The secret of Israel's incomparable influence upon the religious and educational development of the world. The religion of Israel was a vital religion and it was a teaching religion. (Kent, GTJC)

EDUCATION IN EARLY ISRAEL

(from Patriarchal Times to the Exile)

The nomads and shepherds in the early Old Testament period held interests centered in the flocks and herds from which they gained a livelihood. The settlement of the Hebrew tribes in Palestine and their closer contact with Canaanitish culture resulted in changes in social and religious institutions. A permanent dwelling-place made possible, as the continual warfare of gradual conquest made necessary, a closer federation of the tribes, which ultimately resulted in the establishment of the monarchy under David. (Smith)

Education in Nomadic and Agricultural Periods

In these earliest cultural periods, there was no distinct separation between religion and ordinary life. The relation of the people to Yahweh [God's name in Hebrew] was conceived by them in simple fashion as involving on their part the obligation of obedience and loyalty, and on Yahweh's part reciprocal parental care over them as His people. The family was the social unit and its head the person in whom centered also religious authority and leadership, The tribal head or patriarch in turn joined in the functions which later were given to those of priest and prophet and king. Education was a matter of purely domestic interest and concern. The home was the only school and the parents the only teachers. But there was real instruction, all of which, moreover, was given in a spirit of devout religious earnestness and of reverence for the common religious ceremonies and beliefs, no matter whether the subject of instruction was the simple task of husbandry or of some useful art, or whether it was the sacred history and traditions of the tribe, or the actual performance of its religious rites.

According to Josephus (Ant, IV, viii, 12), Moses himself had commanded, "All boys shall learn the most important parts of the law since such knowledge is most valuable and the source of happiness"; and again he commanded (Apion, II, 25) to teach them the rudiments of learning (reading and writing) together with the laws and deeds of the ancestors, in order that they might not transgress or seem ignorant of the laws of their ancestors, but rather emulate their example. Certain it is that the earliest legislation, including the Decalogue, emphasized parental authority and their claim on the reverence of their children: "Honor thy father and thy mother, that thy days may be long in the land which Yahweh thy God giveth thee" (Exodus 20:12); "And he that smiteth his father, or his mother, shall be surely put to death. And he that curseth his father or his mother, shall surely be put to death" (Exodus 21:15,17); while every father was exhorted to explain to his son the origin and significance of the great Passover ceremony with its feast of unleavened bread: "And thou shalt tell thy son in that day, saying, It is because of that which Yahweh did for me when I came forth out of Egypt." (Exodus 13:8).

Education During the Monarchical Period

The period of conquest and settlement developed leaders who not only led the allied tribes in battle, but served as judges between their people. In time, sufficient cooperation was obtained to make possible the organization of strong intertribal union and, finally, the kingship. The establishment of the kingdom and the beginnings of city and commercial life were accompanied by more radical cultural changes, including the differentiation of religious from

"The Gospels consistently report that people were astonished or amazed at the teaching of Jesus (Mark 1:22; 11:18; Luke 4:32). What made Jesus a 'master teacher'? Granted he was God incarnate—a unique human being as the Son of Man. And yet, the approach, method, and content utilized by Jesus in his teaching continue to be paradigmatic for Christian education."
—Walter A. Elwell, *Baker's Evangelical Dictionary of Biblical Theology*

"A Teacher is one who makes himself progressively unnecessary."
—Thomas Carruthers

other social institutions, the organization of the priesthood, and the rise and development of prophecy.

Elijah, the Tishbite, Amos, the herdsman from Tekoa, and Isaiah, the son of Amoz, were all champions of a simple faith and ancient religious ideals as over against the worldly wise diplomacy and sensuous idolatry of the surrounding nations. Under the monarchy also a new religious symbolism developed. Yahweh was thought of as a king in whose hands actually lay the supreme guidance of the state: "Accordingly the organization of the state included provision for consulting His will and obtaining His direction in all weighty matters" (W. R. Smith, *Revue semitique*, 30). Under the teaching of the prophets, the ideal of personal and civic righteousness was moved to the very forefront of Hebrew religious thought, while the prophetic ideal of the future was that of a time when *the earth shall be full of the knowledge of Yahweh, as the waters cover the sea* (Isaiah 11:9), when all *from the least of them unto the greatest of them" shall know him* (Jeremiah 31:34). Concerning the so-called "schools of the prophets" which, in the days of Elijah, existed at Bethel, Jericho, and Gilgal (2 Kings 2:3,5; 4:38), and probably in other places, it should be noted that these were associations established for the purpose of mutual edification rather than education. The Bible does not use the word "schools" to designate these fraternities. Nevertheless, religious training occurred.

Deuteronomic Legislation

Shortly before the Babylonian captivity, King Josiah gave official recognition and sanction to the teachings of the prophets, while the Deuteronomic legislation of the same period strongly emphasized the responsibility of parents for the religious and moral instruction and training of their children. Concerning the words of the law Israel is admonished: *Thou shalt teach them diligently unto thy children, and shalt talk of them when thou sittest in thy house, and when thou walkest by the way, and when thou liest down, and when thou risest up* (Deuteronomy 6:7; 11:19). For the benefit of children as well as adults, the law was to be written "upon the door-posts" and "gates" (6:9; 11:20), and "very plainly" upon "great stones" set up for this purpose upon the hilltops and beside the altars (Deuteronomy 27:1-8). From the Deuteronomic period forward, religious training to the Jew became the synonym of education, while the word Torah, which originally denoted simply "Law" (Exodus 24:12; Leviticus 7:1; 26:46), came to mean "religious instruction or teaching," in which sense it is used in Deuteronomy 4:44; 5:1: *This is the law which Moses set before the children of Israel: ...Hear, O Israel, the statutes and the ordinances which I speak in your ears this day, that ye may learn them, and observe to do them*; and in Proverbs 6:23,

For the commandment is a lamp; and the law is light; And reproofs of instruction are the way of life.

READING AND WRITING

With the development and reorganization of the ritual, priests and Levites, as the guardians of the law, were the principal instructors of the people, while parents remained in charge of the training of the children. In families of the aristocracy, the place of the parents was sometimes taken by tutors, as appears from the case of the infant Solomon, whose training seems to have been entrusted to the prophet Nathan (2 Samuel 12:25). There is no way of determining to what extent the common people were able to read and write. Our judgment that these rudiments of formal education in the modern sense were not restricted to the higher classes is based upon such passages as Isaiah 29:11-12, which distinguishes between the man who "is learned" (literally, "knoweth letters") and the one who is "not learned," and Isaiah 10:19, referring to the ability of a child "to write," taken together with such facts as that the literary prophets Amos and Micah sprang from the ranks of the common people, and that "the workman who excavated the tunnel from the Virgin's Spring to the Pool of Siloam carved in the rock the manner of their work" (Kennedy in *Hastings, Dictionary of the Bible*). It should be added that the later Jewish tradition reflected in the Talm, Targum, and Midr, and which represents both public, elementary, and college education as highly developed even in patriarchal times, is generally regarded as altogether untrustworthy.

EDUCATION IN LATER ISRAEL

(from the Exile to the Birth of Christ)

The national disaster that befell the Hebrew people in the downfall of Jerusalem and the Babylonian captivity was not without its compensating, purifying, and stimulating influence upon the religious and educational development of the nation. Under the pressure of adverse external circumstances, the only source of comfort for the exiled people was in the law and covenant of Yahweh, while the shattering of all hope of immediate national greatness turned the thought and attention of the religious leaders away from the present toward the future. Two types of Messianic expectation characterized the religious development of the Exilic Period. The first is the priestly, material hope of return and restoration reflected in the prophecies of Ezekiel. The exiled tribes are to return again to Jerusalem; the temple is to be restored, its ritual and worship purified and exalted, the priestly ordinance and service elaborated. The second is the spiritualized and idealized Messianic expectation of the Second Isaiah, based on teachings of the earlier

According to Proverbs 1:7; and Ecclesiastes 12:13, the primary purpose of education in Bible times was to train the whole person for lifelong, obedient service in the knowledge of God.

"Education is a matter which rests primarily with the parent, with the father. The teacher is but a representative of the father, according to Jewish tradition. Thou shalt teach them diligently, not vicariously. Now parents act as they please—commercialism and vulgarity blare from the loudspeakers—and little children are expected to listen to the voice of the Spirit. Religious instruction, like charity, begins at home.
—Heschel, *The Insecurity of Freedom* (New York: Schocken Books, 1972), pp. 54-55.

"Study was considered in ancient times to be one of the highest forms of worship. In the Christian writings it is seen as a means of showing oneself approved of God (II Timothy 2:15). Study was pursued both day and night, as well as on the Sabbaths and holidays."
— Dr. Ron Moseley, "Jewish Education in Ancient Times," *Restore Magazine*

prophets. For the greatest of Hebrew prophets, Yahweh is the only God, and the God of all nations as well as of Israel. For him, Israel is Yahweh's servant, His instrument for revealing Himself to other nations, who, when they witness the redemption of Yahweh's suffering Servant, will bow down to Yahweh and acknowledge His rule. "Thus the trials of the nation lead to a comprehensive universalism within which the suffering Israel gains an elevated and ennobling explanation" (Ames, Hauck-Herzog, *Realencyklopadie fur protestantische Theologie und Kirche*, 185). In the prophetic vision of Ezekiel, we must seek the inspiration for the later development of Jewish ritual, as well as the basis of those eschatological hopes and expectations which find their fuller expression in the apocalypse of Daniel and the kindred literature of the later centuries. The prophecies of the Isaiahs and the Messianic hope which these kindled in the hearts of the faithful prepared the way for the teachings of Jesus concerning a Divine spiritual kingdom, based upon the personal, ethical character of the individual and the mutual, spiritual fellowship of believers.

Educational Significance of the Prophets

The educational significance of the prophetic writings of this as of the preceding periods is that the prophets themselves were the real religious leaders and representative men (Kulturtrager) of the nation. In advance of their age they were the heralds of Divine truth; the watchmen on the mountain tops whose clear insight into the future detected the significant elements in the social and religious conditions and tendencies about them, and whose keen intellect and lofty faith grasped the eternal principles which are the basis of all individual and national integrity and worth. These truths and principles they impressed upon the consciousness of their own and succeeding generations, thereby giving to future teachers of their race the essence of their message, and preparing the way for the larger and fuller interpretation of religion and life contained in the teachings of Jesus. The immediate influence of their teaching is explained in part by the variety and effectiveness of their teaching method, their marvelous simplicity and directness of speech, their dramatic emphasis upon essentials and their intelligent appreciation of social conditions and problems about them.

THE BOOK OF THE LAW

The immediate bond of union, as well as the textbook and program of religious instruction, during the period of the captivity and subsequently, was the Book of the Law, which the exiles carried with them to Babylon. When in 458 B.C. a company of exiles returned to Palestine, they, along with their poorer brethren who had not been carried away, restored the Jewish community at Jerusalem, and under the suzerainty of Persia, founded a new nationalism, based, even more than had been the earlier monarchy, upon the theocratic conception of Israel's relation to Yahweh. During this period it was that writings of poets, lawgivers, prophets, and sages were brought together into one sacred collection of scrolls, known later as the Old Testament canon, of which the Torah (the law) was educationally the most significant. The recognized teachers of this period included, in addition to the priests and Levites, the "wise men," or "sages" and the "scribes" or "copherim" (literally, "those learned in Scriptures").

WISE MEN OR SAGES

Whether or not the sages and scribes of the later post-exilic times are to be regarded as one and the same class, as an increasing number of scholars are inclined to believe, or thought of as distinct classes, the wise men clearly antedate, not only the copherim but in all probability all forms of book learning as well. Suggestions of their existence and function are met with in earliest times both in Israel and among other nations of the East. Isaiah 29:10, 2 Samuel 14:1-20, and 1 Kings 4:32 may be cited as illustrations of their pre-exilic existence. It is no lesser personage than King Solomon who, both by his contemporaries and later generations, was regarded as the greatest representative of this earlier group of teachers who uttered their wisdom in the form of clever, epigrammatic proverbs and shrewd sayings. The climax of Wisdom-teaching belongs, however, to the later post-exilic period. Of the wise men of this later day an excellent description is preserved for us in the Book of Ecclesiastes 39:3-4,8,10:

> He seeks out the hidden meaning of proverbs,
> And is conversant with the subtitles of parables,
> He serves among great men,
> And appears before him who rules;
> He travels through the land of strange nations;
> For he hath tried good things and evil among men.
> He shows forth the instruction which he has been taught,
> And glories in the law of the covenant of the Lord.
> Nations shall declare his wisdom,
> And the congregation shall tell out his praise.

THE BOOK OF PROVERBS

Of the instructional experience, wisdom, and learning of these sages, the Book of Proverbs forms the biblical compartment. Aside from the Torah, it is thus the oldest handbook of education. The wise men conceive of life itself as a discipline.

MY TIME WITH GOD

The child whispered, "God, speak to me." A meadowlark sang. But the child did not hear.

So the child yelled, "God, speak to me!" And the thunder rolled across the sky. But the child did not listen.

The child looked around and said, "God, let me see You." And a star shone brightly. But the child did not notice.

And the child shouted, "God, show me a miracle!" And a life was born. But the child did not know.

So the child cried out in despair, "God, touch me and let me know You here!" So, God reached down and touched the child. But the child brushed the butterfly away. And walked away unknowingly.

Author Unknown.

Parents are the natural instructors of their children:

My son, hear the instruction of thy father, And forsake not the law of thy mother (Proverbs 1:8).

The substance of such parental teaching is to be the "fear of Yahweh," which "is the beginning of wisdom"; and fidelity in the performance of this parental obligation has the promise of success:

Train up a child in the way he should go, And even when he is old he will not depart from it (Proverbs 22:6).

In their training of children, parents are to observe sternness, not hesitating to apply the rod of correction, when needed (compare 23:13,14), yet doing so with discretion, since wise reproof is better than "a hundred stripes" (17:10). Following the home training there is provision for further instruction at the hands of professional teachers for all who would really obtain "wisdom" and who can afford the time and expense of such special training. The teachers are none other than the wise men or sages whose words "heard in quiet" (Ecclesiastes 9:17) are "as goads, and as nails well fastened" (12:11). Their precepts teach diligence (Proverbs 6:6-11), chastity (7:5), charity (14:21), truthfulness (17:7), and temperance (21:17; 23:20-21,29-35); for the aim of all Wisdom-teaching is none other than *To give prudence to the simple, To the young man knowledge and discretion: That the wise man may hear, and increase in learning; And that the man of understanding may attain unto sound counsels* (Proverbs 1:4-5).

SCRIBES AND LEVITES

The copherim, or "men of book learning," were editors and interpreters as well as scribes or copyists of ancient and current writings. As a class, they did not become prominent until the wise men, as such, stepped into the background, nor until the exigencies of the situation demanded more teachers and teaching than the ranks of priests and Levites, charged with increasing ritualistic duties, could supply. Ezra was both a priest and a copher (Ezra 7:11; Nehemiah 8:1), concerning whom we read that he *set his heart to seek the law of Yahweh, and to do it, and to teach in Israel statutes and ordinances* (Ezra 7:10). Likewise the Levites often appear as teachers of the law, and we must think of the development of sopherism (scribism) as a distinct profession as proceeding very gradually. The same is true of the characteristic Jewish religious-educational institution, the synagogue, the origin and development of which fell within this same general period. The pupils of the copherim were the Pharisees (perushim, or "separatists") who during the Maccabean period came to be distinguished from the priestly party, or Sadducees.

"1. Scripture tells us that Solomon composed three thousand proverbs, and his wisdom was "greater than the wisdom of all the men of the East, and greater than all of the wisdom of Egypt" (I Kings 4:30). But the Gospels declare Jesus' wisdom, evident in His teachings and parables, to be greater than Solomon's (Luke 1:1-3:1; cf. I Corinthians 1:30).

2. The Hebrews never viewed wisdom as mere factual information or as purely cognitive. Rather, it was skill in applying knowledge to a specific area. Wisdom began with the ability to see and evaluate all of life from God's point of view (Proverbs 1:7). Wisdom had its seat in God.

3. The Hebrews tended to define wisdom empirically, in applied and rather concrete ways. That is, it usually implied the knack, know-how, or capacity to perform a particular task."

—Marvin Wilson, *Our Father Abraham*

"Happy is the man that findeth wisdom, and the man that getteth understanding. For the merchandise of it is better than the merchandise of silver, and the gain thereof than fine gold. She is more precious than rubies: and all the things thou canst desire are not to be compared unto her. 16 Length of days is in her right hand; and in her left hand riches and honour. Her ways are ways of pleasantness, and all her paths are peace. She is a tree of life to them that lay hold upon her: and happy is every one that retaineth her."

(PROVERBS 3:13-18)

GREEK AND ROMAN INFLUENCES

The conquest of Persia by Alexander (332 B.C.) marks the rise of Greek influence in Palestine. Alexander himself visited Palestine and perhaps Jerusalem (Josephus, Ant, X, i, 8), befriended the Jews and granted to them the privilege of self-government and the maintenance of their own social and religious customs, both at home and in Alexandria (the new center of Greek learning), in the founding of which many Jews participated. During the succeeding dynasty of the Ptolemies, Greek ideas and Greek culture penetrated to the very heart of Judaism at Jerusalem, and threatened the overthrow of Jewish social and religious institutions. The Maccabean revolt under Antiochus Epiphanes (174-164 B.C.) and the reestablishment of a purified temple ritual during the early part of the Maccabean period (161-63 B.C.) [the reason for the Hanukkah celebration today] were the natural reaction against the attempt of the Seleucidae forcibly to substitute the Greek gymnasium and theater for the Jewish synagogue and temple. (Felten, NZ, I, 83 f; compare 1 Macc. 1,3,9,13 and 2 Macc. 4-10)

The end of the Maccabean period found Phariseeism and strict Jewish orthodoxy in the ascendancy [power] with such Hellenic tendencies as had found permanent lodgment in Judaism reflected in the agnosticism of the aristocratic Sadducees. The establishment of Roman authority in Palestine (63 B.C.) introduced a new determining element into the conditions under which Judaism was to attain its final distinguishing characteristics. The genius of the Romans was practical, legalistic, and institutional. As organizers and administrators, they were preeminent. But their religion never inspired to any exalted view of life, and education to them meant always merely a preparation for life's practical duties. Hence, the influence of Roman authority upon Judaism was favorable to the development of a narrow individualistic Phariseeism, rather than to the fostering of Greek idealism and universalism. With the destruction of Jerusalem by the Romans a little more than a century later (A.D. 70) and the cessation of the temple worship, the Sadducees as a class disappeared from Judaism, which has ever since been represented by the Pharisees devoted to the study of the law. Outside of Jerusalem and Palestine, meanwhile, the Jewish communities at Alexandria and elsewhere were much more hospitable to Greek culture and learning, at the same time exerting a reciprocal, modifying influence upon Greek thought. It was, however, through its influence upon early Christian theology and education that the Hellenistic philosophy of the Alexandrian school left its deeper impression upon the substance and method of later Christian education.

"The goals of Jewish education may be broadly summed up:

(1) to transmit knowledge and skills from generation to generation;

(2) to increase knowledge and skills; and

(3) to concretize cultural values into accepted behavior. The three main orders of study in ancient Israel consisted of religious education, occupational skills and military training with the essence of all knowledge being the fear of the Lord (Psalms 111:10; Proverbs 1:7)."

— Dr. Ron Moseley, "Jewish Education in Ancient Times," *Restore Magazine*

EDUCATION IN NEW TESTAMENT TIMES

(from the birth of Christ to the end of the 1st century)

Elementary Schools

Jewish education in the time of Christ was of the orthodox traditional type and in the hands of scribes, Pharisees, and learned rabbis. The home was still the chief institution for the dispensation of
elementary instruction, although synagogues, with attached
schools for the young, were to be found in every important Jewish
community. Public elementary schools, other than those connected with the synagogues, were of slower growth and do not seem to
have been common until some time after Joshua ben Gamala,
high priest from A.D. 63-65, ordered that teachers be appointed in
every province and city to instruct children having attained the
age of six or seven years. In the synagogue schools, the chazzan, or
attendant, not infrequently served as schoolmaster.

Subject Matter of Instruction

As in earlier times the Torah, connoting now the sacred Old Testament writings as a whole, though with emphasis still upon the law,
furnished the subject matter of instruction. To this were added, in
the secondary schools (colleges) of the rabbis, the illustrative and
parabolical rabbinical interpretation of the law (the haggadhah)
and its application to daily life in the form of concise precept or rule
of conduct (the halakhah). Together the haggadhah and halakhah
furnish the content of the Talmud (or Talmuds), as the voluminous
collections of orthodox Jewish teachings of later centuries came to
be known.

METHOD AND AIMS

As regards teaching method, the scribes and rabbis of New Testament times did not improve much upon the practice of the copherim and sages of earlier centuries. Memorization, the exact reproduction by the pupil of the master's teaching, rather than general
knowledge or culture, was the main objective. Since the voice of
prophecy had become silent and the canon of revealed truth was
considered closed, the intellectual mastery and interpretation of
this sacred revelation of the past was the only aim that education
on its intellectual side could have. On its practical side it sought, as
formerly, the inculcation of habits of strict ritualistic observance,
obedience to the letter of the law as a condition of association and
fellowship with the selected company of true Israelites to which
scribes and Pharisees considered themselves to belong. The success with which the teachings of the scribes and rabbis were
accompanied is an evidence of their devotion to their work, and
more still of the psychological insight manifested by them in uti-

lizing every subtle means and method for securing and holding the attention of their pupils, and making their memories the trained and obedient servants of an educational ideal.

VALUABLE RESULTS OF HEBREW EDUCATION

Hebrew education achieved four valuable results:

1. It developed a taste for close, critical study.
2. It sharpened the wits.
3. It encouraged a reverence for law and produced desirable social conduct.
4. It formed a powerful bond of union among the Jewish people.

To these four points of excellence enumerated by Davidson must be added a fifth which, briefly stated, is this:

Jewish education by its consistent teaching of lofty monotheism, and its emphasis, sometimes incidental and sometimes outstanding, upon righteousness and holiness of life as a condition of participation in a future Messianic kingdom, prepared the way for the Christian view of God and the world, set forth in its original distinctness of outline and incomparable simplicity in the teachings of Jesus.

THE PREEMINENCE OF JESUS AS A TEACHER

Jesus was more than a teacher; but He was a teacher first. To His contemporaries He appeared as a Jewish rabbi of exceptional influence and popularity. He used the teaching methods of the rabbis; gathered about Him, as did they, a group of chosen disciples (learners) whom He trained and taught more explicitly with a view to perpetuating through them His own influence and work. His followers called Him Rabbi and Master, and the scribes and Pharisees conceded His popularity and power. He taught, as did the rabbis of His time, in the temple courts, in the synagogue, in private, and on the public highway as the exigencies of the case demanded. His textbook, so far as He used any, was the same as theirs; His form of speech (parable and connected discourse), manner of life, and methods of instruction were theirs. Yet into His message and method He put a new note of authority that challenged attention and inspired confidence.

Breaking with the traditions of the past, He substituted for devotion to the letter of the law an interest in men, with boundless sympathy for their misfortune, abiding faith in their worth and high destiny, and earnest solicitude for their regeneration and perfection. To say that Jesus was the world's greatest and foremost example as a teacher is to state a fact borne out by every inquiry, test, and comparison that modern educational science can apply to

Beware of false prophets, which come to you in sheep's clothing, but inwardly they are ravening wolves. Ye shall know them by their fruits. Do men gather grapes of thorns, or figs of thistles? Even so every good tree bringeth forth good fruit; but a corrupt tree bringeth forth evil fruit. A good tree cannot bring forth evil fruit, neither can a corrupt tree bring forth good fruit. Every tree that bringeth not forth good fruit is hewn down, and cast into the fire. Wherefore by their fruits ye shall know them.

(MATTHEW 7:15-20)

the work and influence of its great creative geniuses of the past. Where His contemporaries and even His own followers saw only "as in a glass, darkly," He saw clearly; and His view of God and the world, of human life and human destiny, has come down through the ages as a Divine revelation vouchsafed the world in Him. Viewed from the intellectual side, it was the life philosophy of Jesus that made His teachings imperishable; esthetically, it was the compassionate tenderness and solicitude of His message that drew the multitudes to Him; judged from the standpoint of will, it was the example of His life, its purpose, its purity, its helpfulness, that caused men to follow Him; and tested by its immediate and lasting social influence, it was the doctrine, the ideal and example of the human brotherliness and Divine sonship, that made Jesus the pattern of the great teachers of mankind in every age and generation. With a keen, penetrating insight into the ultimate meaning of life, He reached out, as it were, over the conflicting opinions of men and the mingling social and cultural currents of His time backward to the fundamental truths uttered by the ancient prophets of His race and forward to the ultimate goal of the race. Then with simple directness of speech He addressed Himself to the consciences and wills of men, setting before them the ideal of the higher life, and with infinite patience sought to lift them to the plane of fellowship with Himself in thought and action.

EDUCATIONAL WORK OF THE EARLY DISCIPLES

It remained for the disciples of Jesus to perpetuate His teaching ministry and to organize the new forces making for human betterment. In this work, which was distinctly religious-educational in character, some found a field of labor among their own Jewish kinsmen, and others, like Paul, among the needy Gentiles (Galatians 1:16; 2:7; 1 Timothy 2:7). As regards a division of labor in the apostolic church, we read of apostles, prophets, evangelists, pastors, and teachers (1 Corinthians 12:28; Ephesians 4:11). The apostles were the itinerant leaders and missionaries of the entire church. Their work was largely that of teaching; Paul insisting on calling himself a teacher as well as an apostle (2 Timothy 1:11; 1 Corinthians 4:17). The prophets were men with a special message like that of Agabus (Acts 21:10-11). The evangelists were itinerant preachers, as was Philippians (8:40), while the pastors, also called bishops, had permanent charge of individual churches.

The professional teachers included both laymen and those ordained by the laying on of hands. Their work was regarded with highest honor in the church and community. In contrast with the itinerant church officers, apostles and evangelists, they, like the pastors, resided permanently in local communities. With this class the author of the Epistle of James identifies himself, and there can be little doubt that the epistle which he wrote reflects both the content and form of the instruction which these earliest Christian teachers gave to their pupils. Before the close of the first century the religious educational work of the church had been organized into a more systematic form, out of which there developed gradually the catechumenate of the early post-apostolic period. In the Didache, or Teachings of the Apostles, there has been reserved for us a textbook of religious instruction from this earlier period (Kent, GTJC). Necessarily, the entire missionary and evangelistic work of the apostolic church was educational in character, and throughout this earliest period of church history we must think of the work of apostles, evangelists, and pastors, as well as that of professional teachers, as including a certain amount of systematic religious instruction.

Would Jesus have been the head of his class if He had attended the Greek grammar school at Sephoris? What would He have done Homer, Herodotus, and Aeschylus? Or how would He have fared at the Academy of Plato or the Lyceum of Aristotle?
—David Mulligan, *Far Above Rubies: Wisdom in the Christian Community*

"You cannot grow in grace in any high degree while you are conformed to the world."
—C.H. Spurgeon

While it is true that today we look upon Jesus as a miracle-worker, prophet, and preacher, He was foremost a teacher.

SECTION II
STATE ACHIEVEMENT TESTS

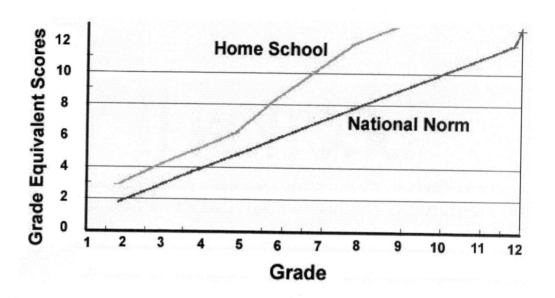

HOME SCHOOL STUDENTS COMPARED TO THE NATIONAL NORM GROUP IN GRADE EQUIVALENT UNITS

The grade equivalent score comparisons for home school students and the nation are shown in above. In grades one through four, the median ITBS/TAP composite scaled scores for home school students are a full grade above that of their public/private school peers. The gap starts to widen in grade five. By the time home school students reach grade 8, their median scores are almost 4 grade equivalents above their public/private school peers.

Report based on the results of the largest survey and testing program for students in home schools to date. In Spring 1998, 20,760 K-12 home school students in 11,930 families were administered either the Iowa Tests of Basic Skills (ITBS) or the Tests of Achievement and Proficiency (TAP), depending on their current grade. Information from Education Policy Analysis Archives by Dr. Rudner is with the College of Library and Information Services, University of Maryland, College Park.

CHAPTER 5

ACHIEVEMENT REQUIREMENTS
CONSTRUCTION MATERIALS

BASIC ACADEMIC REQUIREMENTS

We all need to seek God's Will in our lives, especially in regard to what we teach our children. This does not mean that we should not teach basic skills and school subjects. God forbid. We are stewards of what God has given us—our children. We are responsible for developing their minds to their fullest potential. We want our children to learn academics, but more importantly, to learn about life. We want them to be prepared to face the challenges of the world. We want them to learn all about God's great creations, not merely to pass a test, but for a greater motive.

We want our children to learn:

- Science—all about God's creation
- Math—about God's order
- History—about His-Story, His plan for the world and the redemption of His people. (With a strong focus on the Hebrews and their interactions with ancient civilizations.)
- Government—how God has established government for specific purposes
- Language Arts—how to tell others about God's truth (writing and speaking)
- Literature—how He has affected other lives
- Economics—to understand stewardship, God's rules
- Arts—to appreciate God's gifts of music, drama, dance, and art, as forms of worship to Him
- Health—about God's plan for nutrition and health

It is our personal responsibility to teach our children to read, study, research, and reason. We must teach them how to read, understand, analyze, and apply the Bible in a way that does not compromise or distort the intentions of the biblical author, or the real meaning of the biblical text. We, ourselves, must learn to ground our understanding of why we do what we do in a clear and sober analysis of what Scripture actually teaches, that we may teach our children to do the same. Otherwise, we will lack judgment, "blown about by every wind of doctrine."

WHY WORRY ABOUT THE STATE'S REQUIREMENTS?

Other subjects (besides Bible) can help us in our study of Scripture. It is a good reason, but it is doubtful whether that is the real reason that we include these subjects in the curriculum. We include them because they mean "school" to us—learning, education. That assumption—that we automatically know without pondering it—of what real education is constitutes the intellectual barrier we must traverse to arrive at a wisdom-centered curriculum.

We are not working for the school board or even for the children, but for God. Our first desires should be to inspire students to become "hearers and doers" of God's Word and to encourage students to search the Scriptures and apply them to everyday situations.

The Evaluation Check Lists in this book are intended to reflect common activities and expectations that are structured around developmentally appropriate activities, based on national curriculum standards.

The basic skill standards are generally non-biased. Facts such as math and spelling are safe. There is no opinion involved within establishing spelling rules. There are no secret messages in the rules of whether to add -es or -s to a word.

The achievement standards aren't all bad; it's how the State plans on enforcing the standards that concerns us.

It is one thing to write a set of goals, and quite another thing to write, design, and complete a series of lessons aimed at reaching those goals. Christians and non-believers can agree on basic academic goals, such as what to strive for: phonics, handwriting, grammar, the scientific method, arithmetic, and drawing. The problems arise when a secular curriculum twists the facts in order to be politically correct.

It is not the goals, but the content that is the problem. For instance, Christians and the state schools agree that children should understand the scientific method. The disagreement comes when the public school teaches that the scientific method can solve all of mankind's problems, or when the school twists the results from the scientific method to present a theory as fact, such as is the case with evolution.

Christians and the state schools agree that children should read a variety of classical literature. In fact, it is a wonderful standard! We should hope that all our children would read the classics. So what is the concern?

The state's (or the Greeks) definition of good classical literature and a Christian's view of good classical literature are quite different. Authors are teachers. They educate, motivate, touch the imagination, and indoctrinate students. What great literature do the state schools require? Would it be Henry Wadsworth Longfellow or Edgar Allen Poe? Ruth Norse wrote an article contrasting the lives of these two men. Look at just a portion:

> Henry Wadsworth Longfellow's work was for over fifty years considered classic. Today, Longfellow's work has been excluded from the required reading. Apparently, those who select great literature to be studied by students feel American literature must be filled more with passion and less with sentiment.
>
> Henry Wadsworth Longfellow was a man who pursued happiness in the traditional American way. He was born in Portland, Maine, in 1807, and became the best known and best loved American poet at home and abroad. His father was a Harvard graduate and attorney who would later be elected to the Massachusetts legislature and then to congress. The piety and patriotism of his mother, Zilpah, did honor to six Mayflower pilgrims named among her ancestors. Puritan and pilgrim faith merged in the shaping of the poet's character and worldview. Threads of truth from the King James Bible strengthen Longfellow's poetry. Frequent notations and commentaries on Sunday sermons are sprinkled through all the years of his letters and journals. They reflect his lifelong pursuit of reality in the practice of the Christian faith. Longfellow was freely enjoyed by American school children for 50 years.
>
> Edgar Allan Poe was born in Boston in 1809. Poe's articles appeared in the several magazines he wrote for or edited between 1835 and 1845. Poe was quoted as saying, "I love fame: I dote on it: I idolize it." And in another place, "My whole nature utterly revolts at the idea that there is any Being in the universe superior to myself!" The poet's mental and emotional state was displayed in several drunken sallies. He and his friends drank with such abandon that the sheriff was called to bring order to the campus. Most biographers tell us that he accumulated more than $2000 in gambling debts. One who knew him wrote: "He walked the streets, in madness or melancholy, with lips moving in indistinct curses, or with eyes upturned in passionate prayers, (never for himself, for he professed that he felt already damned), but for the happiness of those who were at the moment the object of his idolatry" (Nourse).

"Association for Childhood Education International (ACEI) strongly believes that no standardized testing should occur in the preschool and K-2 years. Further, ACEI strongly questions the need for testing every child in the remainder of the elementary years. The National Commission on Testing and Public Policy recently reached the same position. The National Association for the Education of Young Children has also called for an end to K-2 testing."
—Vito Perrone, "On Standardized Testing," in *Childhood Education*, 1991

"Authentic, performance-based assessment guarantees an increased understanding of the growth of individual children. Such an understanding reduces the need for currently used standardized testing programs."
—IBID

"What the schools on our list have in common is their recognition of the limitations of the SAT and ACT. Many of these colleges and universities have conducted their own studies which show that standardized tests do little to increase the ability of their admissions officers to predict success at their institutions."
—IBID

To which author—which teacher—would you have your child listen? The state schools require students to read literature by Edgar Allen Poe. Most Christians are offended by Poe's writings. A Christian standard for good literature is spelled out in God's Word: *Finally, brethren, whatsoever things are true, whatsoever things are honest, whatsoever things are just, whatsoever things are pure, whatsoever things are lovely, whatsoever things are of good report; if there be any virtue, and if there be any praise, think on these things. Those things, which ye have both learned, and received, and heard, and seen in me, do: and the God of peace shall be with you* (Philippians 4:8-9). Poe's books are anything but true, pure, virtuous, and lovely.

WHAT IS A STANDARDIZED ACHIEVEMENT TEST?

Standardized tests are usually created by commercial test publishers and are designed to give a common measure of students' performance. Because large numbers of students throughout the country take the same test, these tests are said to give educators a common yardstick or "standard" of measure. Educators use these standardized tests to measure how successful school programs are, or to give themselves a picture of the skills and abilities of today's students.

Standard—That which is established by sovereign power as rule or measure by which others are to be adjusted; that which is established as a rule or model, by the authority of public opinion, or by respectable opinions, or by general consent.

Achieve—To perform, or excite; to accomplish; to finish or to carry to a final close. To gain or obtain by means of exertion.

Test—To compare with a standard; to try; to prove strength or genius anything by experiment or by some fixed principle or standard.

Some popular tests include the California Achievement Tests (the CAT), the Stanford Achievement Test, the Iowa Test of Basic Skills (the ITBS), and the Stanford-Binet Intelligence Scale.

ARE STANDARDIZED TEST SCORES ACCURATE EVALUATIONS OF A CHILD'S SKILLS?

The use of standardized tests by schools is commonly criticized by parents, school teachers, and school officials because the tests do not necessarily confirm what students have learned, nor do they reveal what students have achieved. Critics have suggested that alternatives to standardized tests be developed and used for more effective student evaluation.

Tests are powerful only if we attach high value to them and relinquish our judgment about how to educate children (Meisels, 1992). Some tests are less informative than others, and some are hopelessly biased, narrow, or unrealistic; but any test can be misused, just as any idea can be distorted.

The pressure to demonstrate the effectiveness of education through children's performance on standardized tests not only changes how teachers teach and what children study, but it also seems to be changing our very understanding of the nature of learning and achievement (McGill-Franzen and Allington, 1993). The public schools are actually being pushed into functioning as test-preparation organizations.

Group-administered tests focus on the acquisition of simple facts, low-level skills, superficial memorization, and isolated evidence of achievement. These tests hold great power, and that power can be abused. Of greatest concern is that they rob teachers of their sense of judgment about how to help children develop to their optimal potential.

This loss of judgment is often observed in the use of readiness and early school achievement tests. The appropriateness of using standardized, group-administered achievement tests for children below third grade is highly dubious and questionable.

The content of these tests is generally abstract, verbally mediated, and potentially biased against children unfamiliar or uncomfortable with test-like activities and with middle-class manners and mores (Stallman and Pearson, 1990). Even more problematic is how little can be learned from the results of standardized tests administered to young children; the data may tell us a child's percentile ranking on a subtest, but it cannot tell us whether the child's performance reflects an inability to follow the complex test directions or whether the child did not have mastery of the information or skill.

HAVE THE ACHIEVEMENT TESTS HELPED

THE PUBLIC SCHOOL SYSTEM?

Standardized tests are problematic at all ages and levels of schooling. They are especially questionable in primary grades.The last thirty years have brought a dramatic decline in the quality of education in this country. In October, 1993, the U.S. Department of Education admitted that nearly 50 percent of all adults are "functionally illiterate" and cannot handle anything more than the simplest mathematical tasks. SAT scores have fallen almost 80 points since 1960. The achievement tests are being adjusted to change these scores, ensuring that less achievement will obtain higher scores. We are not increasing the knowledge required on these students' tests, but are lowering the results and

"Standardized testing has many faults currently. There are some solutions coming out now, as research continues. But in general, standardized testing has gone mad. There is too much emphasis on the tests, too many decisions based on them, and too many agencies producing them. In spite of all the evidence against the validity of standardized testing, their use is growing."
—Haney and Madaus, *Paper for the NAEP Study Group.* Center for the Study of Testing, Evaluation and Educational Policy, Sep. 1986

"What is needed is a return to the teaching side of school and less concentration on the evaluations. While evaluations can be useful to determine the effects of teaching, there are currently no evaluations that justify their interventions. I'm reminded of a phrase that I heard once from a farmer which is applicable to standardized testing: 'Cows grow faster when you feed them than when you weigh them.'"
—Stan Jones, *The Neutralization of Benefits in Standardized Testing*

expectations—with higher scores for equal or less knowledge.

Schools began handing out higher grades much more freely in the 1970s—at the same time standardized test results showed scholastic achievement was actually dropping. Often this has led to false security. In an extreme, but not an isolated case, a valedictorian of a school was denied admission to college because his SAT math test results were in the bottom 5 percent and SAT verbal test results were in the bottom 13 percent. After a repeat test (without a time limit), the admissions dean said, "My feeling is that a kid like this has been conned. He thinks he's a scholar. His parents think he's a scholar. He's been deluded into thinking he's gotten an education" (Adams).

The National Commission on Excellence in Education reported that "Each generation of Americans has outstripped its parents in education, in literacy, and in economic attainment. Now for the first time in the history of our country, the educational skills of one generation will not surpass, will not equal, will not even approach those of their parents."

HOME-EDUCATED STUDENTS SCORE HIGHER ON ACHIEVEMENT TESTS

A nationwide study (Ray, 1990) using a random sample of 1,516 families from one organization's membership, found home-educated students to be scoring, on average, at or above the 80th percentile in all areas on standardized achievement tests. (Note: The national average on standardized achievement tests is in the 50th percentile.)

Wartes (1989) found that home-school students in Washington consistently score at the 66th percentile on the Stanford Achievement Test, with their strongest scores in science, listening, vocabulary, and word reading.

Home-education students in Montana scored at the 72nd percentile on standardized achievement tests. (Ray, 1990)

The state of Tennessee (1988) reported that home-educated students in that state averaged about 83rd percentile in reading and about 77th percentile in math on standardized achievement tests.

The state of Oregon (1988) found that 73 percent of the home-school students in that state who were tested scored above average.

Dr. Howard Richman and his colleagues have found that the home-educated students in Pennsylvania score, on average, at the 86th percentile in reading and the 73rd percentile in math.

Repeatedly, across the nation, home-educated students score as well as or better than those in conventional schools.

Dr. Gary Knowles of the University of Michigan explored adults who were home educated. None were unemployed and none were on welfare. Ninety-four percent said that home education prepared them to be independent persons. Seventy-nine percent said that it helped them interact with individuals from different levels of society, and that they strongly supported the home-education method. (National Home Education Research Institute)

UNDERSTANDING ACHIEVEMENT TESTS SCORES

The percentile level equates scores to those contained in any other nationally validated test. When using it, we are comparing the student's performance to that of the national sample of students at that grade level who were used to standardize the test. In order to get the most accurate comparison to these national norms, the test is administered in April, since that is when the students in the national samples were tested. The percentile score shows where the student ranks relative to the rest of the population. For example, a percentile score of 70 means the student scored higher than 70 percent of the students in the tested population. The 50th percentile is often referred to as the national "norm" or "median."

SCORES ARE ESTIMATES

No score on any abilities or achievement test should be treated as a precise measure. Test scores are subject to measurement error; that is, if a student gave equal effort to two perfectly equivalent forms of the same test on successive days, corresponding scores would not likely be the same. Thus, we must recognize that differences of 5 to 10 percentile points or possibly more do not necessarily mean there are real differences in levels of achievement. This is true regardless of whether we are comparing scores for two students, the same student in different subject areas, or year-to-year scores in the same subject area. On the other hand, actual performance levels can differ by more than the percentile scores indicate.

A student's pattern of nationally referenced test scores over time is more revealing than a single set of scores. You should also consider other achievement measures such as the Writing Assessment, state tests, special projects, or performance assessments, as well as results of abilities tests in conjunction with achievement scores.

Nationally referenced test scores, particularly a single set, should never be the only criteria by which a student's educational progress is assessed.

"...no test can completely cover an issue, which leads to problems. If there is a certain bit of information on the tests, it shows up in the curriculum. The educators may do this in order to help students or their own marks. The rest of the curriculum has to fight to stay included. With standardized testing, a big line is drawn between the tested information and the non-tested information. Both students and educators begin to see this line as dividing relevant and non-relevant information."
—Haney and Madaus, *Paper for the NAEP Study Group*. Center for the Study of Testing, Evaluation and Educational Policy, Sep. 1986

"Pressuring everybody to do well on the tests makes people think that the tests are much more important than they really are. Most of these tests measure very narrow types of learning; there is a definite skill to answering multiple-choice questions that is independent of any useful education, and even the essays are very specifically formatted to see how well we can regurgitate the five-paragraph format drilled into our heads since grammar school."
—*Rethinking Schools*, Volume 13, No. 4, Summer 1999

NCE SCORES

Group averages are reported in normal-curve-equivalent (NCE) scores rather than percentile ranks. This is because percentile scores are unevenly spaced and cannot legitimately be averaged. NCE scores are more difficult to interpret, making them a poor choice for evaluating a student's scores.

GROUP SCORES

Average scores for classrooms or grade levels are much more stable than those for individual students. Assuming that a test has been administered under standard conditions to a fairly large group, we can be relatively confident that the average scores are fairly close to the group's actual achievement levels in areas measured by the test.

ABSOLUTE AND GAIN SCORES

When interpreting scores, two dimensions to be considered are (a) the absolute values of the scores and (b) any changes in the scores.

Consider the example of School A, in which eighth graders had an average NCE of 53, a drop of 3 points from the previous year's mean eighth-grade score of 56. In School B, the current year's average of 38 is 5 points above that of 33 for the past year's eighth graders. If other factors are fairly comparable, the results for School A are clearly superior to those for School B. Students in School A have an average slightly above the national median (NCE of 50), whereas those in School B are well below the national average, despite the gain of 5 NCEs.

However, other factors may warrant consideration. If School A served only gifted students, a mean score of 56 would not be impressive, and the further loss of 3 NCEs would reflect even more negatively on the results. If in School B, major reforms had been taken to address the previous poor performance of students, the gain of 5 NCEs may be viewed positively despite the fact that students are still achieving at less than desirable levels.

EXTREME SCORES

School administrators should investigate cases where either absolute or gain scores are extreme. Group gains or losses of 10-20 NCEs are possible, but unusual. Similarly, when a group of students show dramatic increases one year followed by sharp losses the following year, causes should be assessed. Consistently low scores (e.g., NCE under 30 or well below the general performance level for students at that school) should be a cause for concern. One general exception to score deviations is at the kindergarten level, where average scores tend to be higher than those at other grade levels. This appears to be a function of the test and/or its norms. Finally, the discussion of extreme scores does not imply that these are the only scores worthy of attention. The tests, combined with other sources of data, can be valuable tools for improving educational outcomes.

WHAT YOU CAN INFER FROM TEST SCORES

William A Mehrens, in his article "Preparing Students To Take Standardized Achievement Tests," states: "The only reasonable, direct inference you can make from a test score is the degree to which a student knows the content that the test samples. Any inference about why the student knows that content to that degree...is clearly a weaker inference...."

"Teaching to the test" alters what you can interpret from test scores because it involves teaching specific content. Therefore, it also weakens the direct inference that can be reasonably drawn about students' knowledge. Rarely should you limit your inference about knowledge to the specific questions asked in a specific format. Generally, you should make inferences about a broader domain of skills.

Further complicating matters, many people wish to use test scores to draw indirect inferences about why students score the way they do. Indirect inferences can lead to weaker and possibly incorrect interpretations about school programs.

Indirect inferences cannot possibly be accurate unless the direct inference of student achievement is made to the correct domain. Rarely should one limit the inference about knowledge to the specific questions in a test or even the specific objectives tested. For example, if parents want to infer how well their children will do in another school next year, they need to make inferences about the broader domain and not about the specific objectives that are tested on a particular standardized test. For that inference to be accurate, the instruction must not be limited to the narrow set of objectives of a given test. Thus, for the most typical inferences, the line demarking legitimate and illegitimate teaching of the test must be drawn between Points 3 and 4.

While, in my view, it is inappropriate to prepare students for standardized tests by focusing on the sample of objectives that happen to be tested, it is acceptable to undertake appropriate activities to prepare students to take standardized tests.

The tests are not perfect measures of what individual students can or cannot do, or of everything students learn. Also, your child's scores on a particular test may vary from day to day, depending on whether your child guesses, receives clear directions, follows the directions carefully, takes the test seriously, or is comfortable in taking the test.

How Can I Help My Child Do Well On Tests?

Spend some time teaching your children general test-taking skills. These skills will help students answer questions correctly if they have mastered the objectives. Without some level of test-taking skills, even knowledgeable students may miss an item (or a set of items) because they do not understand the mechanics of taking a test.

Veteran home-school mothers can tell you how each of their children will perform on an achievement test. They have been working with the children on a one-to-one basis for a while and know just what their strengths and weaknesses are. If a home-school mother tells me her son does not do well in math, odds are he'll score low in math. If for some reason, a mother says her child is an excellent reader and the child scores low in reading, I would look over the test to be sure there was not another reason for such a score. You can usually depend on the mother's observations more than the test results.

Test-preparation activities should not be additional activities, they should be incorporated into the regular, ongoing instructional activities such as:

- Immersing your children in a rich print and story environment by having a variety of books and magazines at home to encourage your child's curiosity;
- Using these books to find out any learning gaps;
- Making sure your child is well rested and eats a well-rounded diet;
- Not being anxious about test scores, but encouraging your child to take tests seriously;
- Memorizing Philippians 4:6 *(Be careful for nothing; but in every thing by prayer and supplication with thanksgiving let your requests be made known unto God)*.

States That Require Home-School Testing

Alaska	Nevada	Pennsylvania
Arkansas	New Mexico	South Carolina

Georgia	New York	South Dakota
Hawaii	North Dakota	Tennessee
Minnesota	Oregon	Virginia

TAKING THE ACHIEVEMENT TEST: AVOID TEST ANXIETY

It's good to be concerned about taking a test. It's not good to have "test anxiety." This is excessive worry about doing well on a test, and it can mean disaster for a student.

Students who suffer from test anxiety tend to worry about the future and are self critical. Instead of feeling challenged by the prospect of success, they become afraid of failure. This makes them anxious about tests and doubtful of their own abilities. Ultimately, they become so worked up that they feel incompetent about the subject matter or the test.

It does not help to tell the child to relax, to think about something else, or to stop worrying, but there are ways to reduce test anxiety.

Encourage your child to do these things:

- Space studying over days or weeks. (Real learning occurs through studying that takes place over a period of time.)

- Understand the information and relate it to what is already known. Review it more than once. (By doing this, the student should feel prepared at exam time.)

- Don't "cram" the night before—cramming increases anxiety, which interferes with clear thinking.

- Get a good night's sleep. Rest, exercise, and eating well are as important to test-taking as they are to other schoolwork.

- Read the directions carefully when the teacher hands out the test. If you don't understand them, ask the teacher to explain.

Look quickly at the entire examination to see what types of questions are included (multiple choice, matching, true/false, essay) and, if possible, the number of points for each. This will help with pacing the various parts of the test.

If you don't know the answer to a question, skip it and go on. Don't waste time worrying about it.

"Florida's move toward increased school accountability has fostered a lot of debate between lawmakers and educators over whether more testing leads to smarter kids. The two sides agree on one clear winner, though: the testing companies. ...'They all see this back-to-basics, educational standards movement as a gold mine—and it is,' said Gail Kalinoski, managing editor of the Educational Marketer, a trade publication that monitors the education publishing market....In 1996, the company reported $300-million in revenue. That figure more than doubled this year to $629-million, a figure boosted by the Florida contract, $69-million for three years, or $122-million for five years."
— "School Testing Companies Score It Big" *St. Petersburg* (FL) *Times*, 6/19/00

"The tests have become the focus of school, many complained. And teachers are teaching to the test. ...the high-stakes tests are not only responsible for a rash of cheating scandals in New York, Chicago and Texas as well as recent allegations at a Fairfax County middle school, they are redefining education across the country, fundamentally changing what goes on in classrooms every day."
— "Pressure to Perform," *Washington Post*, 6/11/00

Mark the question so you can identify it as unanswered. If you have time at the end of the exam, return to the unanswered question(s).

DO'S AND DON'TS

You can be a great help to your children if you will observe these do's and don'ts about tests and testing:

- Do encourage children. Praise them for the things they do well. If they feel good about themselves, they will do their best. Children who are afraid of failing are more likely to become anxious when taking tests, and more likely to make mistakes.
- Don't be too anxious about a child's test scores. If you put too much emphasis on test scores, this can upset a child.

The more effort and energy a child puts into learning, the more likely he or she will do well on tests.

Q. How Do I Find Out if My Child is Required to Take The Achievement Test?

A. Home-schooling laws regulate home schooling differently in each state. You should get a copy of your state's home-schooling law. Contact the Home School Legal Defense Association at (703) 338-5600, Box 159, Paeonian Springs, VA 22129, http://www.hslda.org.

Q. How Do I Know if I Am Meeting State Standards?

A. The second section of this book contains the Evaluation Check Lists. These check lists represent an overall picture of general content of the most widely used achievement tests according to category and grade level.

Q. How Do I Know If My Curriculum Covers Everything on the Test?

A. How do we know if the public school curriculum covers everything on the test? The American Federation of Teachers (AFT) reports that only 13 of 49 state standards are specific enough to be used effectively by teachers. Take a look at the public schools' scores—an average of 30 percentile points below the home-school scores. Currently, each of the fifty states has a different academic requirement for each grade. There are thousands of curriculum choices and dozens of teaching methods. No one curriculum covers everything on the achievement test, and no one test includes everything in any given curriculum. One curriculum covers an objective in the third grade that another curriculum covers in second grade. One curriculum taught by one teacher will focus on an entirely different aspect of the subject compared to that taught by another teacher. Some children are stuck in a drill-and-practice curriculum for basic skills, and other kids have an enriched literature-based curriculum, which will easily get them to the standards. Some children have teachers who care and who are well trained in the curriculum, while other teachers simply don't care.

One child, whose father was in the military, attended five different schools in six years. Because of the different state standards, she was never taught basic cursive writing. She had missed basic cursive in second grade in one school, went to third grade in a school that taught cursive in the fourth grade, then transferred to fourth grade in a school that taught cursive writing in second and third grades.

Home-schooling parents have the advantage of teaching their children an individual plan on different levels. The Evaluation Check Lists will guide you to any gaps, and you can take the time to get the basics mastered before going on to another level.

"The problem with standardized tests and the fixed curricula they engender is their tendency to kill off the kind of education that matters most. But who can blame a teacher or school for orienting the lesson toward helping students pass those tests with high marks? The temptation to teach students to do well on standardized tests is almost unavoidable when performance on such tests is how entire school systems are evaluated.

Schools believe they have an obligation to create standard curricula. Why should everyone know the same stuff? What a dull world it would be if everyone knew only the same material. Let children choose where they want to go, and with proper guidance they will choose well and create an alive and diverse society.

We really have to get over the idea that some stuff is just worth knowing even if you never do anything with it. Human memories happily erase stuff that has no purpose, so why try to fill up children's heads with such stuff? Concentrate on figuring out why someone would ever want to know something before you teach it, and teach the reason, in a way that can be believed, at the same time."
—Engines for Education, The Institute for the Learning Sciences, 1994

For more about the way the state teaches, see the books, *The Right Choice: The Incredible Failure of Public Education* and the *Rising Hope of Home Schooling* by Christopher J. Klicka, or the book by the New York Teacher of the Year, *Dumbing Us Down* by John Taylor Gatto.

Q. Shouldn't I Use Textbooks like the schools?

A. Textbooks don't work with all students. The public school achievement-test scores speak for themselves. Seventy-five percent of students using textbooks require more motivation (hands-on practice, presentations, etc.) to retain the material. (McCarthy)

The easiest way for the state to teach is to divide everything into subjects (from the Greeks' philosophy). They then divide each subject into 180 hours—thirty-six weeks of five days of forty-five to sixty minute classes. In this manner they can teach from textbooks, somewhere between thirty to fifty children at a time. Surprise! Not all children will learn a subject to the same degree in 180 hours. Some need much more time; others need much less. Some children can learn the material two to four times as fast using a different method. Instead of measuring 180 hours, we should be measuring the end result.

A few of my favorite books explaining alternatives to textbooks are: *You Can Teach Your Child Successfully* and *The Language Wars and Other Writings for Homeschoolers* by Ruth Beechick (anything written by Dr. Beechick is profitable), and *The Whole Hearted Child Home Education Handbook* by Clay and Sally Clarkson.

Home-schooling parents have the advantage of choosing the curriculum that suits their children. They can use a variety of approaches and levels if necessary.

These books are recommended to explain the different approaches and different materials available: *The Christian Home Educators Manual: Elementary Edition, The Christian Home Educators Manual: Jr. And Sr. High Edition*, and *The Big Book of Home Learning* by Mary Pride available in four manuals: *Getting Started, Elementary, Jr. Sr. High*, and *After School*.

Q. What About College?

A. Yes, a homeschooled student can get into college, including prestigious institutions such as Yale and Harvard, but do you really want them to go there? Getting into college is not a problem for most homeschoolers. Most colleges and universities have entrance exams, but many of them place much more weight on an individual student's ability and aptitude. Home-schooled students are welcomed at local community colleges, Ivy League universities, vocational institutes, or other avenues of higher education. Most of these institutions value ability and attitude over formal transcripts, diplomas, or GEDs. Home-schooled children have encountered little difficulty continuing their education.

Before you place extreme importance on a college education, however, remember that a college degree is worthless if one does not know Christ. It is of little value for our children to master chemistry and algebra if they don't know how to get along with their spouses or cannot learn how to discipline their children. It is of little value for one to be fluent in several foreign languages if he doesn't have tongue control. It is of little value for one to diagram a sentence if one cannot communicate true feelings. Are you sure college is God's plan for your child?

Efficient and economical college degree programs, with full regional accreditation, are now in full operation on the Internet. Bible-centered, higher education distance learning, as well as continuing adult education correspondence courses, all leading to external college degrees are accessible (for thousands of dollers less than traditional schools) from your computer monitor!

If you are planning for college or are interested in higher education alternatives, an excellent seminar by Inge Cannon will answer all your questions. The seminar titled *Apprenticeship Plus: Preparing Lives Unto Service* is available on tapes and in workbooks. This and many other excellent educational helps are available through Education Plus, P.O. Box 1029, Mauldin, SC 29662, (803) 281-9316. Call or write for a free brochure. Also see Cafi Cohen's excellent books *And What About College? How Homeschooling Leads To Admissions To The Best Colleges and Universities* (Holt Associates; ISBN: 0913677116), or *Homeschooling: The Teen Years* (Prima Publishing; ISBN: 0761520937), or *Homeschoolers' College Admissions Handbook: Preparing Your 12- to 18-Year-Old for a Smooth Transition* (Prima Publishing; ISBN: 0761527540).

Q. What About Algebra, Higher Math, and Lab Sciences?

A. With all the excellent self-teaching materials, manuals, CD Roms, and videos available, you can learn much of what is needed to teach as you prepare for each day, or even while your child learns. Home schoolers all over the country have formed

"If the primary purpose of college is educational, then something is amiss in the classroom. Simply put, research has shown that, for most subjects, tutorial instruction and guided independent study give superior results over classroom teaching. For example, in one study correspondence students consistently outperformed their classroom counterparts by more than ten percentage points on the final exam."
—John Thompson, College at Home, for the Glory of God, *Patriarch Magazine*

"Let father and mother lead a life marked by love to God and man; this is the atmosphere in which loving children can be trained. Let all the dealings with the children be in holy love. Cross words, sharp reproof, impatient answers are infectious. Love demands and fears not self-sacrifice; time and thoughtful attention and patient perseverance are needed to train our children aright."
—Andrew Murray *How to Raise Your Children for Christ*

small classes, hired tutors, and "swapped" teaching roles with experienced home schoolers for higher math and lab sciences. There are excellent self-teaching courses, videos, and other alternative teaching methods available to those who want to go beyond the basic skills.

Both *Senior High: A High School Formula* and *Lab Science* by Barb Shelton include an abundance of information for those interested in college-preparatory courses.

Q. How will Goals 2000, Outcome Based Education (OBE) and the new national standards affect the achievements tests?

A. The new government programs such as Goals 2000, National Standards, School-to-Work, and their successors should set off blaring alarms to all Christians. This question would take an entire book to answer, and thankfully these questions have been answered in Cathy Duffy's well-researched book *Government Nannies*. All parents should educate themselves concerning the new government educational reforms.

In the next few years, Goals 2000 will bring about major changes in the state standards. Eventually the tests will be rewritten to affect the national standards and other agendas from the government. The tests direct the curriculum. Parents have no control over the curriculum; therefore, no control over what their children are being taught. We can only wait and see the results.

Goals 2000 will greatly expand power of government over educational matters. To receive monies from the $400-million funds, each state must produce plans that conform to the national standards. This act will shift the control of the curriculum and management from local communities and states to the federal government. Goals 2000 appears to be more of an application for funds than an educational program.

Forty-three states used some sort of statewide assessment in 1994-96; most have not developed or adopted assessments that are connected to the new standards. One of the reasons most often cited by states is that the cost of developing these better forms of assessments is high. Reform requires a sustained, long-term commitment. As state standards are changed, there is the need to develop new materials, upgrade curricular materials, and provide teachers with training to update their knowledge bases and teaching skills. At the time of this writing (1997 edition), the national standards have not affected the conventional achievement tests. The Evaluation Check List will be revised to reflect the new tests, standards, subject categories, benchmarks, and frameworks as they change.

Q. How Do I Know if I am Teaching the Material that will Apply to My Child's Future?

A. Who decided the educational goals should consist of particular subjects, some of which are only used by a very small percentage of the population? You can't make everyone the same by forcing them all to learn the same thing. No one person can learn everything there is to know. God gave us all different gifts and talents. Jesus' whole story about the church being a part of the body illustrates this. Is the goal of education to make everyone the same?

Biology is a required subject because the student may choose a career in which he will need the skills taught in biology class. However, if the student chooses to become a businessman, many of the facts he spent time learning and memorizing in biology class [the ability to label the digestive system of a grasshopper] would probably be useless. Learning about any subject is always useful even if one is just learning to learn. However, most students are frustrated with learning and memorizing what they consider boring because it has no relevance to their lives.

The state's reasoning that children need to "learn skills for a possible goal" does not motivate learning. Students are told to learn algebra without ever being told when they may use algebra in real life. If the child doesn't know what the goal is, or if he will ever even be interested in such a goal, learning the skills is boring to the child. Adults learn the other way around—we choose a goal, then find out what skills are needed. When our eyes are on the goal, we are automatically motivated to learn the necessary skills.

Teaching all the children all the skills to prepare them for whatever path they may choose does not work. First of all, it is impossible to foresee all the pieces of knowledge a child will need in the future. Secondly, if a student is trying to be good at all the options, he will not have time enough to prepare for the specific path that God has chosen for him.

This story illustrates my point: Once a man had three horses: a racehorse, a plow horse, and a pony. The man made a schedule to get the most work out of his horses. On Mondays, Wednesdays, and Fridays, all three horses worked in the fields hooked to a plow. On Tuesdays and Thursdays, he took all three horses to the racetrack so each horse would learn to run fast. On the weekends, he used the three horses to give pony

"Education has always been considered to be a process whereby some essential body of knowledge is transmitted to students; schools have simply been places where that transmission officially takes place. The development of flexible, inquiring minds has rarely been the primary consideration in the design of educational systems. Making students into proper members of society has usually been of much greater concern than developing students who are creative thinkers.

Consider the most common classroom approach: one teacher standing in front of thirty children trying to get each one to be at the same place at the same time. This approach has the advantage of being relatively inexpensive, but it flies in the face of everything scientists have discovered about children's natural learning mechanisms, which are primarily experimentation and reflection. In other words, learning by doing. Consider also the concept of curriculum: that there is a particular body of knowledge everyone should know. This idea may comfort those who are concerned that our children know the "right stuff." Children, however, learn facts about the world because they feel the need to know them, often because these facts will help them do something they want to do. What is the right stuff for one may be the wrong or irrelevant stuff for another."
—Engines for Education, The Institute for the Learning Sciences, 1994

"How do we raise responsible, self-motivated learners? Some say rigorous, structured academics will teach our children self-discipline and perseverance. Others counsel us to turn children loose to follow their interests and eventually they will mature and become self-motivated.

From the time our children were tots we began to give them opportunities to learn to do a job well, pay attention to details, be faithful in the little things. We did this by both modeling the correct actions and attitudes and by allowing them to work beside us.

As they showed interest in learning new things, we taught them using relaxed, fun, and enjoyable methods. It was never "you have to do school now" but "you get to learn some new things now!". A big difference! We didn't have to bribe them —instead we allowed them at an early age to follow their own interests with regards to academics and we never pressured them. At the same time, we continued to teach them to be responsible and faithful in the small tasks we would require them to do around the house —mostly working right with us."

— Tamara Eaton,
Let's Get Motivated! Encouraging Self-Motivated Learners,
Christian Homeschool Forum, 1998

rides to children. At the end of the week the man complained that not one of the horses met his expectations.

The racehorse turned to the man and said, "I could not run properly when my back ached from plowing. If you had let me stay at the racetrack all week, I could have spent time doing and improving at what I do best."

The plow horse said, "If my feet were not so swollen from racing, I could have pulled the plow straighter and farther. If you had allowed me to stay in the fields all week, I could have spent time doing and improving at what I do best."

The pony said, "I have had it! If I didn't ache all over from doing things I am not made for, I wouldn't have been so grumpy to the children who rode me. If you had allowed me to give children rides all week, I could have spent time doing and improving at what I do best."

Christians should teach the skills established by God. The Bible does not command us to learn basic academic skills. It does not say "thou shall learn to read." Neither does the Bible tell us to learn to drive a car, but we know that anyone living in America in the '90's should know how to drive. Common sense tells us our children need to learn the three R's to function in this world. God's Word does tell us to teach our children His Word. His Word is full of wisdom for practical daily living. As children learn the Bible, they are learning how to learn. If we teach a child to study God's Word—reasoning, relating, researching, and recording—then he will know how to learn. When it is time, he will be prepared to learn the skills necessary to meet his goals. By the way, most of the higher-level critical thinking skills can be learned from reading, studying, and interpreting God's Word.

God knows more than the public school system! We can trust Him with our children's futures. God's Word promises that if we acknowledge God in all our ways, He will direct our paths. We know God has made each of our children for a specific purpose. If we teach them what He commands us to teach them, He will guide us to prepare them for the plan He has for them—knowingly or unknowingly. God can prepare us for the future in many ways. Just think about your life now. What happened in your past to prepare you for what God is calling you to do now? Did you learn it from school? From your parents? From church? From different situations? God uses all things for His good. Life is a classroom. He can and often does use bad situations to help us turn a weakness into a strength. Do you have an evaluation check list consisting of all the things that you have learned in your life to bring you to a place to do God's will? If you do, I venture it's a prayer list—not the state standards.

Q. How Do I Motivate an Unmotivated Child to Learn?

A. The answer to this question depends on the child. Is he not interested in the subject, not interested in learning, or not interested in obeying you—the parent?

If a Child Does Not Want to Obey

A child must be disciplined to learn. Depending on maturity levels, external discipline is necessary until he develops internal discipline. Younger children need supervision and guidance to complete projects until they are trained to work alone efficiently. Rules and consequences for breaking rules should be established in every home. If there is a discipline problem in the home, you may need to forgo school for a few days until the child understands who is in authority. If you need motivation or instruction in discipline, run, don't walk, to get *What the Bible Says about Child Training* by Richard Fugate (available in book, video, or audio forms).

If a Child Does Not Want to Learn Anything

Children love to learn naturally. Even children attending a traditional school setting enjoy learning—at first. Especially when a kindergarten class is full of neat things to learn about—goldfish, hamsters, seeds sprouting, math manipulatives, play areas, etc. Sometime around the second grade, when textbooks and workbooks are introduced and a child must sit in a one-square-foot desk area for six or more hours, most children decide that school is boring and their interest in learning declines. Many books are available describing different learning styles and methods to meet your child's needs. See the Internet site HomeschoolInformation.com, Cathy Duffy's book *The Christian Home School Curriculum Manual* or Mary Pride's *Big Books of Home Learning* for hundreds of suggestions.

Learning can be fun, but there are times when learning requires diligent work. These types of situations are also training in character. For example, children are not usually thrilled to memorize the multiplication tables. There are fun games to reinforce learning, but actual memorizing must be applied. Some learning is an opportunity to teach diligence, patience, longsuffering (no grumbling and complaining), kindness, etc.

"Those parents who say, 'Junior just refuses to ...,' or 'My child just won't put up with ...' have given up their authority and put their children in charge of their home. They have granted their children veto power and in doing so must follow their children's leadership. Needless to say, for those parents who have shared their authority with their children, parenting will be very difficult and unfruitful."

—Reb Bradley,
Child Training Tips

Correct thy son, and he shall give thee rest; yea, he shall give delight unto thy soul.
(Proverbs 29:17)

For it is God which worketh in you both to will and to do of his good pleasure. Do all things without murmurings and disputings: That ye may be blameless and harmless, the sons of God, without rebuke, in the midst of a crooked and perverse nation, among whom ye shine as lights in the world.
(Philippians 2:13 -15)

Being confident of this very thing, that he which hath begun a good work in you will perform it until the day of Jesus Christ.
(Philippians 1:6)

Children, obey your parents in all things.
(Colossians 3:20a)

So shall my word be that goeth forth out of my mouth; it shall not return unto me void, but it shall accomplish that which I please, and it shall prosper in the thing whereto I sent it.
(Isaiah 55:11)

If a Child Does Not Want to Learn a Specific Subject

Working with a child almost always gives a child incentive. Most children enjoy the attention of talking and sharing with their parents. Please don't throw workbooks at a young child, assign pages, and think learning has occurred. Workbooks are great—some of the time, but not all of the time. Children can be motivated by changing the instruction method. Some children are simply bored to tears working in textbooks. When's the last time you curled up by a fire with a good textbook? Provide "living books": historical novels, biographies, and classics that cover the material you want your children to know.

If you spend the time explaining why the child will need to know the material you are teaching, you will see a world of difference in your teaching. Examine your own learning motivations by answering the questions for each of the following scenarios:

1.   Your support group decides to go to on a field trip to a sheep farm in nearby Sheep Town. You have a large van, so you volunteer to drive. You are not familiar with Sheep Town. When you get home, you pull out your map to find out just where Sheep Town is. You call a friend who has been to Sheep Town to double check the directions. The day of the field trip, you drive to Sheep Town. After the field trip, you drive home. Even if you made a wrong turn, you eventually found your way to Sheep Town. On the way to and from the location, you observe new surroundings. You have learned the route from your home to Sheep Town. A month later someone asks directions to Sheep Town. You can accurately give him the directions to Sheep Town.

2.   You and your husband are at a support-group meeting. The group decides to go to Sheep Town. Your husband offers to drive and proceeds to get directions. You proceed to talk about curriculum with a friend. Your husband plans the trip to Sheep Town. You, your children, and friends all ride to Sheep Town together. You return home. A month later someone ask directions to Sheep Town. Can you give them the directions? You didn't pay much attention to the subject because you depended on someone else to know the directions.

3.   You are at a support-group meeting and someone asks you how to get to Sheep Town. You've never heard of the town and don't know the directions. Are you less intelligent than the person that does know the directions to Sheep Town? Of course not. You have never needed to know that information. Knowing information you will never use does not make you intelligent.

4.   You're in a support-group meeting. The leader announces a field trip to Sheep Town on Thursday. You have plans; your dentist is going to give you a root canal on Thursday. The leader asks anyone interested to stay after the meeting so she can show a map and explain the directions to Sheep Town. Would you stay after the meeting to learn the directions to Sheep Town? If you had no reason to have to know how to get there, you wouldn't stay.

5.   Suppose someone came to you during the support group meeting in the scenario above to tell you that all the stores in Sheep Town were having a 70-percent-off sale the week after your dental appointment. Would you reconsider staying after the meeting for directions? Most of the time, if we spend the time giving children a reason for having to know material, they respond favorably. Children, like adults, need to know that material they are learning is relevant to their lives.

6.   You are at home teaching your child. The geography book has a chapter titled "Sheep Town." You read this chapter to your child. Four months later, your child takes the achievement test. There is a question asking how far your town is from Sheep Town. Your child forgot what he learned about Sheep Town, so he guesses at the answer. How would you feel if he got the answer wrong? If he got the answer right?

If your child guessed wrong, does it mean you failed as a teacher? Does it mean your child is learning disabled? Are you both a success if he guessed right? Are you both wrong because he had to guess? If you are teaching your child, I will assume sometime before the fifth or sixth grade you will have taught him to read a map. Chances are your child will never have a question like "How far is it to Sheep Town?" unless a map of the area is provided. A nationwide achievement test will not evaluate specific things, like knowing where Sheep Town is, because children in other parts of the country will not be exposed to Sheep Town. Achievement tests evaluate basic skills such as map reading because it is a basic skill needed to get along in the world.

Q. What About Grades?

A. If a student is grade-oriented, he will spend more time and effort trying to find out the criteria for getting an A before he tries to learn the material. A college professor told me students frequently ask how long a term paper needs to be to get an A— as if it is graded by the pound. Are you grade-oriented? Do you teach your children to make sure they pass tests? If so, you are thinking like the majority of today's American parents, with a

"We must be prepared to be flexible in the way we try to tap into our children's innate interests. For instance, if children do not like the notion of doing dissection, they might instead find it fun to play-act the role of a white blood cell in a drama built around biology. Or, perhaps they will find using the analogy of biology practical when they are trying to design some mechanical structure. If one approach doesn't work, we should drop it and try another.

Good teachers should expose their students to enough situations that the students will become curious enough to take learning into their own hands.

If we abandon the idea of easy measurement of achievement, we can begin to talk about exciting learners with open-ended problems and we can begin to create educational goals such as learning to think for oneself."
—Engines for Education, The Institute for the Learning Sciences, 1994

"school mentality." The "school mentality" is a belief that making a high grade means learning, and that retention has taken place. You need to change your thinking. Change your goals to motivate children to learn and to enjoy learning—not to worry about grades and percentiles.

New home schoolers often fret over report cards and grades. This is another area in which we think that it must be profitable if the schools do it. Spend a moment and re-think these two issues—do home schoolers need report cards and grades? Could these items even be damaging? Are they scriptural? To determine if something is scriptural, look at the motives. Why do teachers give report cards?

- To tell parents how the children are progressing?
- So the teacher can keep everyone straight because she has thirty students?
- To brag about how well the child is doing or how well the teacher is instructing?
- To compare the child with the other children? (See Proverbs 16:18.)
- To keep a record of a child's progress?
- To evaluate the child?

You will know how your child is progressing by working with him daily. You evaluate the child by checking the work or listening to the child, not by giving the grade. What does God's Word say about comparing?

For we dare not make ourselves of the number, or compare ourselves with some that commend themselves: but they measuring themselves by themselves, and comparing themselves among themselves, are not wise. But we will not boast of things without our measure, but according to the measure of the rule which God hath distributed to us, a measure to reach even unto you (2 Corinthians 10:12-13).

We, as Christians, have a responsibility to do the best we can in all circumstances, not comparing ourselves to anyone but comparing only to the individual gifts and talents God has given to us.

Dr. George Reavis wrote a delightful story about an Animal School. It explains how we've been conditioned by yet another "school-mentality" concept, and it is an excellent illustration of the different gifts and talents of children.

THE ANIMAL SCHOOL

Once upon a time, the animals decided they must do something heroic to meet the problems of a "new world."
So they organized a school.

They adopted an activity curriculum consisting of running, climbing, swimming, and flying. To make it easier to administer the curriculum, ALL the animals took all the subjects.

The duck was excellent in swimming, in fact, better than his instructor, but he made only passing grades in flying and was very poor in running. Since he was slow at running, he had to stay after school, and drop swimming in order to practice running. This was kept up until his webbed feet were badly worn and he was only average in swimming. But average was acceptable in school so nobody worried about that
—except the duck.

The rabbit started at the top of the class in running, but had a nervous breakdown because of so much makeup work in swimming.

The squirrel was excellent in climbing until he developed frustration in the flying class, where his teacher made him start from the ground up instead of from the tree down. He also developed a charley horse from over-exertion, and then got a C in climbing and a D in running.

The eagle was a problem child and was disciplined severely. In the climbing class he beat all the others to the top of the tree, but insisted on using his own way to get there.

At the end of the year, an abnormal eel that could swim exceedingly well, and also run, climb, and fly a little, had the highest average, and was valedictorian.

Should you grade and give report cards? You decide. What are your motives? Be concerned about learning and retaining the material—not to get a letter grade on a paper. If letter grades are fun and motivational for your child, use them. If he doesn't know the material, keep teaching it until he does. If he was not applying himself, discipline measures should be taken.

Grading math quizzes and spelling tests is easy. If a child gets three out of ten wrong, then he reworks or reviews the problem word or lesson until he grasps the concept. Writing assignments and abstract work are more difficult to grade.

"The attributes of Christian love are expressed in I Corinthians 13:4-7 and Philippians 2:1-4 as being patient, kind, not easily provoked, merciful, and humble — all which Christian parents would desire to emulate. However, these attributes in no way nullify the equally important attributes of righteousness and justice. For example, a righteous government can not apply the attributes of patience, kindness, or mercy to law breakers. In the practice of proper government, justice can not be served by a tolerance of criminal activity. Governments must uphold righteous law for a stable condition to exist within a nation.

Likewise, parents are to provide for and comfort their children; but they are also required to set and enforce righteous standards for them. The practice of Christian love in parenting is exercised when parents combine the righteousness of setting legitimate standards for their children with the justice of fairly punishing for disobedience. It is in a child's best interest to learn right from wrong as well as to develop self-control over his self-centered nature. Loving parents will therefore train a child for his own benefit. This training process will require personal sacrifice on the parents' part, and that is even further demonstration of true Christian love in practice."

—Richard Fugate,
What the Bible Says About Child Training

Imagine that you have a set of twins. Twin 1 has a writing gift. He retains information easily, and expresses himself well. Twin 2, though a hard worker, consistently struggles with simple sentences. You assign both a passage to write about. Twin 1 glances at the books and haphazardly writes a few paragraphs. Twin 2 studies for several hours and struggles though each word, writing and re-writing his paragraphs. Twin 1's summary is written much better than Twin 2's. Do you reward 1 with an A, when you know he could do better work, and discourage 2 with a C when he obviously did his best?

Different Gifts and Talents

What if a child is unable to learn the material? Do you grade ability or effort? A special child that cannot grasp a certain concept or several concepts can try again next year or learn a method of getting along in the world without that concept. Should a child who learns easily receive a higher mark than a child who struggles with a subject?

The state of Louisiana has a strange law: If a child scores below a certain level on the achievement test for a certain time, he must go to public school. The irony is that many Louisiana public-schooled children score below the national norms—why don't they send the children home to school?

I know of a child who has struggled through spelling for many years. He doesn't get a grade. He and his mother both understand that spelling is a problem area, and continually work on it. What is the alternative? Should she give him an F and put him in public school? Should she keep him in the eighth grade for five years, giving D's in spelling? Should he fail because he has a weakness in spelling? This boy is so busy building and repairing computers, he hasn't had much time to work on spelling. By the way, who made these standards anyway? I wonder if they can put a computer together? Sometimes, it is OK for the duck to be an average runner, especially if he loves to swim. God made him that way.

Q. How do I really know if I'm doing enough?

A. The school system evaluates a student by grades. This is due to the belief that if a student makes a superior grade, it means that learning and retention have taken place. This mentality teaches that the way to get along in the world is to learn to play the game—understand and provide correct answers to the "authorities." There is the appearance of learning from filling in blanks in a workbook or making a high grade on a school test, but is the material retained? Can the student use the material?

Many things we know we have learned without trying to learn. Grammar is a good example. Most children can speak and carry on a conversation without knowing how to diagram a sentence. Should you teach your child diagramming? Will he need it? When was the last time you diagrammed a sentence? Children do not have to learn grammar to speak well. A child will speak correctly by reading good grammar, hearing the English language spoken correctly, and being corrected when he uses incorrect grammar. Memorizing vocabulary words usually has no purpose except to increase a test score. People use the words that they acquired naturally by being exposed to large vocabularies in books and conversations.

Pray for wisdom and ask God to show you what His Will is for your child. Observe your child's gifts and leanings. The Bible says: *Train up a child in the way he should go: and when he is old, he will not depart from it* (Proverbs. 22:6). "The way he should go" in Hebrew comes from the word peh, which means specific edge, portion, or side; with the preposition "according to," meaning according to the child's God-given gifts. It assuredly does not mean to train him up according to the secular, state standards.

Your child will learn more than enough if you will:
- Study God's Word daily (most important).
- Teach the basic skills—the three R's: Reading, wRiting, and aRithmetic.
- Teach how to do the three R's of learning: Research, Reason, and Record.
- Use the Evaluation Check Lists (in this book) to evaluate and plan.
- Instill a love for learning by making subjects interesting.
- Provide good literature (home library or library card).
- Find out your child's God-given gifts and his aspirations. Motivate him to follow those desires and supply the necessary provisions for him to find out more.

"When righteousness and justice are practiced according to God's principles in the training of children, there will be a balance for our responsive love; and then incorrect and unsuccessful extremes will be avoided. Parents can be firm in setting and enforcing righteous standards without being tyrannical or abusive. They can sacrificially give of themselves on behalf of their children, but still not give in to the demands of an immature child."
—Richard Fugate,
What the Bible Says About Child Training

The Purpose of Education

We must ask ourselves "what are our goals?" when educating our children. "The end of learning," wrote John Milton, "is to repair the ruin of our first parents by regaining to know God aright, and out of that knowledge to love Him, to imitate Him, to be like Him. If this be so—and the Bible says it is so—then the aim of American education is all wrong."

Gordon Clark explains in his book *A Christian Philosophy of Education:*

- The purpose of education is not to enable a student to earn a good income.
- The purpose of education is not to preserve our American system of government and political freedom.
- The purpose of education is not world unification.
- The purpose of education is not to teach young people a trade.
- The purpose of education is not to encourage the never-ending search of truth.
- The purpose of education is not to put the student in harmony with the cosmos.
- The purpose of education is not raise the consciousness of the students and train them for world revolution.
- The purpose of education is not to prepare the student for productive careers.
- The purpose of education is not the social adjustment of the child.
- The purpose of education is not to create good citizens.
- The purpose of education is far more noble than any of these things. The purpose of education is to make Christian men (and women), transformed by the renewing of their minds after the image of He who created them.
- The purpose of education is not for a job, diploma, or college. **Abraham, Elijah, Moses, John the Baptist, and Jesus received much of their training in the desert, not in a college.**

TESTS ARE NOT THE ONLY WAY TO EVALUATE YOUR CHILD

Think about the achievement test and the different ways children learn. Can we really believe that a child's intelligence, achievement, and competence can be represented adequately by standardized tests? Do we believe that any distribution curve is capable of classifying all children? Such beliefs would defy almost everything we understand about children's growth and responses to educational encounters.

Achievement testing is certainly not the best way to evaluate your child. We can evaluate our children using a variety of methods: by observing them, evaluating their day-to-day work, listening to them retell what they have learned, keeping records of how they mature throughout the year, and partially, by administering tests.

We must understand that standardized tests give only part of the picture of your child's strengths and weaknesses. The results of many methods will provide well-rounded insights into the skills, abilities, and knowledge of the child.

Studies by the educational systems show that evaluation is best made by working closely with the child, observing his reactions and work. Sound familiar? Home schooling is the ultimate way to evaluate your child. If you think about it, it is amazing that we home-school parents would place any value on an achievement test scores over our own experience (another sign of "school mentality"). You have been there with your child, side by side, through writing, math problems, and spelling quizzes. How could one achievement test tell you how your child is doing?

SHOULD MY CHILD TAKE THE ACHIEVEMENT TEST?

The home schoolers who test usually do so because their state requires testing. Testing is not necessary for evaluation purposes. If your state does not require testing, the Evaluation Check Lists in this book will give you the basics.

If you have been home schooling and your child is not doing well in a subject, you will know it—you don't need the test to tell you he's having trouble with fractions—you work with him daily. You know he's having trouble with fractions because you have been frustrated teaching him fractions. Or you know that you have not yet addressed fractions.

If your child is doing well in a subject and an achievement test score indicates he is doing poorly, chances are:

1. You haven't covered the material yet.
2. He misunderstood some questions in the form they were given.
3. He missed one question and was one question off for the rest of the answer sheet.
4. He was having a bad day.
5. He was intimidated by the unfamiliar environment.
6. The state's guidelines are different from your guidelines.
7. He was worried about test taking. (One little girl was so nervous she told her mother, "I hope Jesus comes back before I have to take that test.")
8. He doesn't do well with timed tests.
9. Someone or something was distracting him.
10. The teacher told the testing group that they could play on the playground as soon as they were finished. (This happened to my own son. I watched, in horror, as he filled in twenty circles in less than thirty seconds!)

DIAGNOSTIC TESTING

Diagnostic Testing can be beneficial before you start home schooling or if your child has a problem area (cannot learn the material). If you're bringing your child home to school in the beginning of fourth grade, you may want to find out if he is really ready for the fourth-grade material. He could be at fourth-grade-level math and at second-grade-level phonics. We have found that many children are promoted to the next grade level before they have mastered the basics. In these cases we recommend Diagnostic testing. Diagnostic testing is a one-on-one, un-timed test, presented verbally as well as written, that will reveal gaps much more accurately than achievement tests.

EVALUATION CHECK LISTS

Studies show that check lists are powerful substitutes for group-administered achievement tests. Research about this system shows that it provides teachers with reliable and valid data about children's academic performance (Meisels, Liaw, Dorfman, & Fails, in press). This system simultaneously informs, expands, and structures those perceptions while involving children and parents in the learning process. The check lists provide detailed, observation-based information about the child's skills, accomplishments, knowledge, and behavior.

Combining the "Evaluation Check Lists" with a cumulation of the child's work will give a great deal of information and evidence about children's activities and development that can be used to enhance instruction and to plan future goals.

The "Evaluation Check Lists" create a profile of children's individualized progress. Because of the common structure of the check lists from kindergarten through eighth grade, you can chart your children's progress over a wide span of time and develop or plan a curriculum that reflects individual growth and change.

PORTFOLIOS

Portfolios provide a cumulation of your child's work, made with the child's input, in an organized manner. Portfolios highlight and record aspects and progression of a child's quality work. A portfolio is a collection of samples of a child's interest, and evidence of his or her God-given abilities. A portfolio can show others more about your child's learning than any letter grade. Most children absolutely love building portfolios. The portfolios can center on your child, a thematic unit study, or a period of time. This method encourages children to be active learners, learning through a variety of means (living books, audios, videos, field trips, or writing). When children's experiences are rich and diverse, it invites them to display their initiative, and engages their curiosity. This performance assessment will help you learn about your child as you watch him learn about his world. Many schools now require portfolios for graduation requirements.

Portfolios include anything demonstrating what a student has learned from a subject (writing, science, etc.), course of study, Bible study, unit study, semester, or other time period of a school year. For example:

Art Work	Bible Studies	Book Reviews
Brochures	Computer Disks	Computer Printouts
Displays	Essays	Field Trip Reports
Formal Letters	Journal Entries	Maps
Photographs	Play Dialog	Poetry
Projects	Recipes	Research Papers
Songs	Writing Samples	

"Observational techniques are methods by which an individual or individuals gather firsthand data on programs, processes, or behaviors being studied. They provide evaluators with an opportunity to collect data on a wide range of behaviors, to capture a great variety of interactions, and to openly explore the evaluation topic. By directly observing operations and activities, the evaluator can develop a holistic perspective, i.e., an understanding of the context within which the project operates. This may be especially important where it is not the event that is of interest, but rather how that event may fit into, or be impacted by, a sequence of events. Observational approaches also allow the evaluator to learn about things the participants or staff may be unaware of or that they are unwilling or unable to discuss in an interview or focus group."
—User-Friendly Handbook for Mixed Method Evaluations, National Science Foundation (NSF)

What if you only had a month to live?

What would you teach your children?

The most important thing you can ever teach your child is the Gospel, the good news, the best that ever came from heaven to earth. If your child is too small to understand, stop now and write a letter to him explaining the plan of salvation. Do you know the plan of salvation well enough to explain it to your child? You must! God's Word commands it. If anything ever happens that you are separated, be sure he has this letter and God's Word. If your child is old enough to memorize, put God's Word in his heart so that he will always have it.

Teach your child that he is a sinner (Romans 3:10-12). The wages of sin is death (Romans 6:23), then hell. God provided a sacrifice for sinners, a gift—His only begotten, perfect son. Jesus took all your child's sins, your sins, and the sins of the world upon Himself. Jesus, God in the flesh, suffered and died that our sin would be paid for (Romans 5:8). But death could not conquer Him, and Jesus arose on the third day. He came to save us by pardoning us, that we might not die by the sentence of the law.

For God so loved the world, that he gave his only begotten Son, that whosoever believeth in him should not perish, but have everlasting life (John 3:16). God has given his love to the world: God so loved the world, so completely, so richly. Now we see that He loves us, and wishes us well. Behold, and wonder, that the great God should love such a worthless world! We can accept this gift from God by simply taking it.

And have put on the new man, which is renewed in knowledge after the image of Him that created him (Colossians 3:10).

Real growth and knowledge can only come from Jesus; in Him we become a new man, and only then can we follow Him and find our created purpose.

SECTION III
TEACHING WISDOM

The Heart of Wisdom Approach will teach you to:

- Develop a habit of daily Bible reading
- Read through the Bible with your family once a year
- Create a portfolio
- Create a Time Line Book
- Use Bible study tools (concordances, lexicons, and dictionaries)
- Know biblical history and geography
- Integrate writing and grammar skills with Bible studies
- Find the way to righteousness
- And more.

THE HEART OF WISDOM TEACHING APPROACH

The H.O.W. approach is a combination of the teaching methods listed below

Bible First	The Bible is the center of education, and all subordinate studies should be brought into the circle of light radiating from the Bible. Academics play an important part, but they are secondary. Students spend a large portion of the school day studying God's Word, and the other half studying God's world in the light of His Word.
A Return to Biblical Hebraic Education	The Bible outlines how we should teach our children. The ancient Hebraic aim of education was ethical and religious. Study is a form of worship. The method of instruction in the home was oral, and learning was accomplished by practice. The ancient Hebrew taught no distinction between sacred and secular areas of life. Every detail of life, therefore, must be set aside and consecrated to the glory of God. The primary purpose of education was to train the whole person for lifelong, obedient service in the knowledge of God (Prov.1:7; Eccl.12:13).
Living Books **Charlotte Mason's** **Philosophy**	Students should develop a love of learning by reading real books—literature—as opposed to twaddle, or "dumbed-down" literature. This method also incorporates copy work, narration (the assimilating of information), retelling (sorting, sequencing, selecting, connecting, rejecting, and classifying), creating a Time Line Book, and developing a "Nature Diary."
4 Step Lessons	These four steps are a cycle of instruction based on the Four Learning Styles developed by Dr. Bernice McCarthy. This system is an organized method of using all of the approaches listed on this page.
Integrated Unit Study	The "unit" or "theme" part of the name refers to the idea of studying a topic as a whole instead of as several "subjects." A unit study takes a topic and "lives" with it for a period of time, integrating science, social studies, language arts, and fine arts as they apply. This method is ideal for multi-level teaching.
Lifestyle of Learning	An approach outlined in *Wisdom's Way of Learning* by Marilyn Howshall. The emphasis is on parents relying on the Holy Spirit's guidance to provide the needed resources so that children can develop expertise in their fields of interest. Howshall explains how using these simple and natural tools (with the emphasis on the process of learning rather than the product of learning) will allow your children to begin to develop their own lifestyle of learning.
Delight-Directed Learning	Students acquire basic concepts of learning (reading, reasoning, writing, researching, etc.) during the process of examining the topic they are interested in. Education ought to be about building learners' abilities to do useful things. The focus is on the development of learning tools not gaining content.
Writing to Learn	Students think on paper—think to discover connections, describe processes, express emerging understandings, raise questions, and find answers; encouraging higher-level thinking skills. Students learn to Research, Reason, Relate, and Record.
Noteboook or Portfolio Method	Student create a Bible Portfolio, Unit Study Portfolios, and Time Line Books. As the family re-reads through the Bible every year, each student creates a new Bible portfolio. The Unit Study Portfolios reflect the students collecting, reading, writing and projects on specific topics. Each year, the portfolios will reflect changes in the student's ability, depth, focus, and spiritual growth.

Wisdom is the principal thing; therefore get wisdom:
and with all thy getting get understanding.
(Proverbs 4:7)

To teach true wisdom, a curriculum should spend a significant amount of time in God's Word. *For the word of God is quick, and powerful, and sharper than any two edged sword, piercing even to the dividing asunder of soul and spirit, and of the joints and marrow, and is a discerner of the thoughts and intents of the heart* (Hebrews 4:12).

The home-school movement has brought about (or restored) many superior, efficient, exciting teaching approaches. These methods verify, as explained in this book, that we need to renew our thinking concerning education. Not only must we renew our thinking about the context of what is taught but also about the method of what is taught (Joshua 24:23; Proverbs 3:5-6; Matthew 6:19-21; Romans 12:22).

David Mulligan explains the importance of Scripture-centered curriculum in a chapter of his book *Far Above Rubies: Wisdom in the Christian Community*. He also reveals the surprising hesitancy Christians feel about this approach to curriculum. He states:

> The idea of spending a lot of school time on the study of Scripture may at first be disturbing. We are so used to dividing "religious" activities from the rest of our time it seems as if Bible study just does not fit, except in a minor way, in our regular school day. We think of Bible study as suitable for family devotions, church services, Sunday school classes, and if the study gets "deep," in the seminary. How much Bible can children get without detracting from other studies?
>
> In asking this question we uncover in ourselves something of the tension that exists in the Western world between learning and religion. We know somehow that the question is not right; that we should be first giving place to Scripture, but can not quite let go of the other side of things. And rightly so! The other side, God's creation, is vastly important, but still Scripture should come first, and all other studies find their place in relation to it. We should turn the question around: "How many secular studies can a student pursue without detracting from his knowledge of God's Word?!"
>
> ...Christian education must be built upon a pattern that maintains Scripture at its center and bring all subordinate studies into the circle of light radiating from thence.

And these words, which I command thee this day, shall be in thine heart: And thou shalt teach them diligently unto thy children, and shalt talk of them when thou sittest in thine house, and when thou walkest by the way, and when thou liest down, and when thou risest up. And thou shalt bind them for a sign upon thine hand, and they shall be as frontlets between thine eyes. And thou shalt write them upon the posts of thy house, and on thy gates.

(Deuteronomy 6)

THE HEART OF WISDOM APPROACH

• The Bible is the main textbook.

• The portfolio is a chronicle of the lessons and concepts studied.

• Learning takes place as the portfolio is created.

• God's Word is the thematic focus out of which academics naturally flow.

• The lessons include several interrelated aspects:
  • spiritual training.
  • academic training.
  • character training.

The Bible passage home schoolers lean on, Deuteronomy 6, is not just a mandate to teach our children. It is a command to teach them God's Word. We also claim a wonderful promise in Malachi 4:6a: *And he shall turn the heart of the fathers to the children, and the heart of the children to their fathers…* but often forget that verse 4 tells us the promise will happen when we remember God's ways: *Remember ye the law of Moses my servant, which I commanded unto him in Horeb for all Israel, with the statutes and judgments.*

The ultimate desire for Christians should be for their children to have a heart of wisdom—true wisdom from God. The philosophy described throughout this book has progressed into a teaching approach called the Heart of Wisdom (H.O.W.) approach.

This chapter gives an overview of methods utilized by the Heart of Wisdom approach in an effort to motivate parents to make the Bible the main focus of the school day. The details of this philosophy will be explained in a book titled *The Heart of Wisdom Teaching Approach* (due to publish, Lord willing, before 2004). You can use this approach or adapt it to the methods and curriculum you are using. (This approach does not cover math.)

HEART OF WISDOM TEACHING APPROACH

The first goal of the Heart of Wisdom approach is to inspire students to become "hearers and doers" of God's Word and to encourage students to search the Scriptures and apply them to everyday situations. The second goal is to teach them a love of learning that will last a lifetime.

TWO-SIDED CURRICULUM BASE

There are, from man's point-of-view, two distinct areas or realms of study: God's Word and God's world. Since our criteria for education must flow from Scripture as the highest and most authoritative source of knowledge, the two realms are approached in different ways. All studies involved with increased understanding of God's Word are designated "direct studies." Since our knowledge of God's world must also be directed by Scripture and our principles of interpretation derive from God's Word, those courses that directly study God's world are designated "derived studies." This gives us a two-sided curriculum base.

In this approach, the Bible is the main focus and the core of the curriculum, with the secondary focus dedicated to developing academic skills. Students spend half the school day studying God's Word (direct Bible studies) and the other half studying God's world (derived studies—history, science, etc. using a unit study approach). Language arts are practiced throughout the day along with Bible and academic studies. Although we use the term "one half the school day," we don't mean 3 hours Bible followed by 3 hours academics, because students work in the Bible in all studies (hence half the school day).

To form a mental image of this approach, imagine four stacks of books: Stacks A, B, C, and D.

GOD'S WORD	GOD'S WORLD		
DIRECT STUDIES	DERIVED STUDIES		
BIBLE STUDY	GOD'S PLAN	GOD'S WORLD	GOD'S KINGDOM
	HISTORY, CULTURE	SCIENCE	THEOLOGY, LAW, HUSBANDRY, ECONOMICS
LANGUAGE ARTS			

✦ Stack A includes Bible, Bible tools (Bible dictionary, atlas, customs and manners reference, Lexicons, etc.) and a writing handbook.

✦ Stack B includes books related to a history theme (reference books and literature).

✦ Stack C contains books related to a science theme (reference books, textbooks, and science project books).

✦ Stack D includes books related to life skills (self-help, marriage, parenting, interior design, car repair, etc.).

You will use the books from Stack A (Bible) exclusively the first hour or two of the school day (depending on your students' ages). You will use Stacks A (Bible) and B (history) the second half of the school day for a number of weeks (or portion of the day). Then, Stack C (science) replaces Stack B for a number of weeks (or portion of the day). Stack D (life skills—used with Stack A) is not used until the high school years (when the school day is longer).

Writing, spelling, grammar, capitalization and punctuation, handwriting, vocabulary, phonics, and critical-thinking skills are not learned as separate subjects, but integrated into each study. Math is added at each students grade level.

BIBLE-FIRST PHILOSOPHY

The education system in the Bible arose as an instrument to pass on the people's relationship to God to each generation. The most important thing we can teach our children is that the Bible God's instruction book on how to live life — *a lamp unto my feet, and a light unto my path.* (Psalms 119:105). Par-

HEART OF WISDOM METHODS

1. Read the Bible daily.

2. Read through the Bible with the family once a year.

3. Develop the student's writing skills:
   a. context
   b. form
   c. mechanics
   d. editing and revision

4. Develop students' spelling skills by creating a personal spelling dictionary from student's writings.

5. Develop students' handwriting skills by practicing writing Bible verses.

6. Develop students' critical thinking skills:
   a. managing and using information to solve problems
   b. interrelating knowledge
   c. effectively communicating learning outcomes.

7. Reinforce phonics instruction using Bible storybooks (younger children).

8. Develop students' character through assignment completion:
   a. attentiveness
   b. commitment
   c. confidence
   d. decisiveness
   e. efficiency
   f. faithfulness
   g. perseverance
   h. promptness
   i. responsibility
   j. self-control

The Bible is the source of happiness and joy in our lives. The reason for this is that true joy in our hearts is inextricably bound up in our obedience to God. Our obedience is predicated on our knowledge of his requirements. Only when we exist in the sphere of obedience can we fully experience the joy and happiness God has for us.

"In the Biblical sense, wisdom is the 'ability to judge correctly and to follow the best course of action, based on knowledge and understanding'"
—Lockyer, *Nelson's Illustrated Bible Dictionary* (p. 1103).

The Wisdom teachings of the Bible follow from the two great themes:
1. Ten Commandments
2. The Greatest Commandments of Jesus: love God and our neighbor

SEVEN STEPS TO ACQUIRING WISDOM

1. Seek wisdom. Proverbs 2:4; 8:17.
2. Meditate upon God's Word. Proverbs 2:1; 3:1; 4:20.
3. Obey principles of Scripture. Obedience is essential for wisdom. Proverbs 2:7; 8:33; 10:8.
4. Pray for wisdom. Proverbs 11:2; James 3:5-6.
5. Observe how God works in His world. Proverbs 6:6; Matthew 6:26; Proverbs 14:16.
6. Heed godly counsel. Proverbs 12:15; 19:20; 15:31.
7. Associate with wise people. Proverbs 1:10.

ents need to reexamine the Word of God to discover what God has revealed regarding the education and training of children. Read 1 Timothy 1:3–7; 2 Timothy 1:13–14; and Titus 1:1–4 to develop a definition of education. Paul urged Timothy and Titus to be engaged in the kind of teaching that produces loving, trusting, and godly men and women. Paul, a Hebrew among Hebrews, taught character is a better indicator of a wise Christian than knowledge. (See The *Wisdom Unit Study* at http://homeschool-books.com for more on this topic.)

The core of the Heart of Wisdom Teaching Approach is learning to study and obey God's Word. This is done by reading the Bible through in one year and the creation of a Bible portfolio and a Time Line Book. Students learn basic Bible hermeneutics using several Bible study tools as well as learning about the culture and manners in Bible times. This teaching can be the most important undertaking in your child's entire life.

As Christians we are expected by God to be knowledgeable in the Word of God. For example, Paul told the Ephesians, *do not be unwise, but understand what the will of the Lord is* (Eph. 5:17). We should strive just as much as the first-century Christians did to find and know God's will for mankind.

With the Bible First Philosophy, parents and students of all ages are active in an ongoing project based on reading through the Bible, every year. The Bible is studied daily as students compile a chronicle of the concepts and beliefs. Student learn to use Bible study tools, enabling them to embark on their own search for truth, preparing them to follow the mandate in 2 Timothy 2:15 *Study to shew thyself approved unto God, a workman that needeth not to be ashamed, rightly dividing the word of truth.* This important foundation (often neglected for academic studies) is the ultimate preparation a student needs for life. Not only will God's Word renew their mind, it will teach them to confront the idols of our time, as Al Greene explains, "to discern and recognize idols such as statism, materialism, technicism, scientism, and all the other "isms" where faith is placed in something other than God."

As the family re-reads through the Bible every year, each student creates a new Bible portfolio and adds to their Bible Time Line Book. Each year, the portfolio will reflect changes in the student's ability, depth, and focus. The first year, a younger child's portfolio will contain drawings, handwriting samples, memory verses, dictated summary pages, photos of a play costume, pages from a Bible coloring book, etc., while older students' portfolios will contain character and event summaries, research papers, essays, computer printouts, time lines, maps, sketches, etc. (Language arts skills are practiced daily while completing assignments.)

Instead of looking at state standards when teaching your children, seek God and ask Him what He would have you teach your children. Listen to the Holy Spirit. God promises us wisdom if we ask for it. Following God's guidance will not only lead you in what to teach your unique, individual child; you will learn to walk a surrendered life, by faith. Scripture should come first, and all other studies find their place in relation to it. The H.O.W. approach leads progressively to a renewed mind and to a self-chosen commitment to a life of intellectual and moral integrity. After all, the Bible is instruction for life. All scripture is given by inspiration of God, and is profitable for doctrine, for reproof, for correction, for instruction in righteousness: *That the man of God may be perfect, thoroughly furnished unto all good works* (2 Timothy 3:16-17).

A RETURN TO BIBLICAL HEBRAIC EDUCATION

The frustrations of modern teaching methods have motivated Christian educators to return to better ways. Many have turned to the Greek classical methods—language and literature-focused studies. (Language and literature are important, but they should not be the foundation of life.) The Heart of Wisdom approach is also a return to better methods, but, like the Hebrews, we reject the Greek education model. Instead we desire a return to Hebraic teaching methods, which are Bible focused. Abraham Joshua Heschel summarized the differences between the two approaches by saying that

"The Greeks study in order to understand while the Hebrews study in order to revere."

Education for people in the biblical world was more than a simple matter of memorizing information and passing tests. It was the search for the hidden plan and presence of God. Educational goals in Scripture always involved the whole person—amoral intellectualism did not exist. The ancient Hebrews taught that education which does not begin with the fear of the Lord leads to foolishness. An old Hebrew saying states

**"One who aquires knowledge
but knows not what to do with it
is no more than a donkey carrying a load of books."**

William Barclay, in *Educational Ideals in the Ancient World* ,

Happy is the man that findeth wisdom, and the man that getteth understanding. For the merchandise of it is better than the merchandise of silver, and the gain thereof than fine gold. She is more precious than rubies: and all the things thou canst desire are not to be compared unto her. Length of days is in her right hand; and in her left hand riches and honour. Her ways are ways of pleasantness, and all her paths are peace. She is a tree of life to them that lay hold upon her: and happy is every one that retaineth her. The LORD by wisdom hath founded the earth; by understanding hath he established the heavens. By his knowledge the depths are broken up, and the clouds drop down the dew.
(PROVERBS 3:13-20)

"Proverbs is a book of godly wisdom. Someone once described Proverbs as 'the Ten Commandments in shoe leather.' It often contains the very practical and homespun wisdom of secular Proverbs, such as 'a stitch in time saves nine' or 'a fool and his money are soon parted.' But the wisdom of Proverbs goes far beyond mere worldly wisdom. It contains the revealed truth of God, Creator of heaven and earth."

—Bob Beasley,
The Wisdom of Proverbs

"Discovery after discovery has established the accuracy of innumerable details [in the Bible], and has brought increasing recognition to the value of the Bible as a source of history."
—W.F. Albright

explains that Hebrew education was very different from our notions of teaching and learning:

> The very basis of Judaism is to be found in the conception of holiness. "You shall be holy for I the Lord your God am holy." "And ye shall be holy unto Me: for I the Lord am holy, and have severed you from other people that ye might be Mine." That is to say, it was the destiny of the Jewish people to be different. Holiness means difference. And their whole educational system was directed to that end. It has been precisely that educational system which has kept the Jewish race in existence. The Jew is no longer a racial type; he is a person who follows a certain way of life, and who belongs to a certain faith. If Jewish religion had faltered, or altered, the Jews would have ceased to exist. First and foremost, the Jewish ideal of education is the ideal of holiness, of difference, of separation from all other peoples in order to belong to God. Their educational system was nothing less than the instrument by which their existence as a nation, and their fulfillment of their destiny, was ensured.

The Hebrew concept of education was not "to impart knowledge" or to "prepare oneself intellectually." It was to produce holiness and to impart a distinctive lifestyle. The primary purpose of education should be to train the whole person for life-long, obedient service in this knowledge just as it was in Bible times.

The Hebrews taught their children 613 commandments; 248 positive commands and 365 negative ones from the Torah (first five books of the Bible). These commands are instruction on how to live life; topics include: God, the poor, employers, employees, parents, children, animals, marriage, sex, family, food, business practices, holidays, judicial procedures, property, criminal laws, agriculture, taxes, worship, war, illness, etc. The 613 commands are instructions for life. (Not all 613 commands were for all people, some were specifically for priests, some for women, etc.)

> The aim of education in Biblical times was ethical and religious. The education of youth was an obligation of the parents, and was intimately associated with the performance of ritual observances and with learning the Mosaic Law. In the educative process, both father and mother were equally concerned, and both were to be

WHAT YOUR CHILD NEEDS TO KNOW WHEN

equally honored (the Fifth Commandment). The method of instruction in the home was for a long time oral, and learning by practice, and these methods were continued outside the home in gatherings and assemblies held for both worship and instruction. (Collier's Encyclopedia)

Like a typical first-century rabbi, Jesus did not deliver formal sermons, but as he traveled the country with his disciples he commented upon situations such as Martha's anxiety or the widow's contribution of two small coins (Lk. 21:1-2). Jesus typically used such incidents as springboards for his teaching, prefacing his remarks with "I tell you," and concluding with a pair of parables to illustrate and confirm the teaching. Jesus taught that only "one thing" is important. The "one thing" is to desire above all else God's rule and salvation in our lives and in the lives of those around us (Matthew 6:33, Luke 12:31). (Read more about Biblical Education in Chapter 4 and 9.)

The ancient Greek approach focuses on the Greek philosopher's writings (such as Homer, Thales. Socrates. Plato. Aristotle) as sources of wisdom and knowledge. The Greek thinkers, shunning God, came up with man-centered and mystical notions to define the world around them. The Greek approach tends to compartmentalize the student concentrating on his academic ability but the Bible views man as a unified whole.

**Under the Greek system learning begets goodness.
Under the Biblical system goodness begets learning.
All non-Biblical education assumes
man can become learned without God.
Biblical Education makes
knowledge the foundation of learning.**

Jesus, a Hebrew, used the Hebraic form of teaching. He taught using parables, role modeling, informal style, and in-depth discussions. Education research has now proven role modeling and interaction teaching methods are much better than the Greek impersonal, rhetoric-lecture style . During the fourth century, Greek oratorical skills replaced Hebrew role modeling and methods, the church lost the Hebraic practical application of biblical truth. Greek thought developed the pattern of opinions and theories about ethical questions instead of relying on God's Word. (Acts 17:21).

"Often our assumptions about teaching and learning create divisions of grade levels that make us miss extraordinary opportunities and applications for education, just because we believe that what works in kindergarten could never be valuable in college (and vice versa). We need to see teaching, as well as learning, as a layered process from kindergarten to college and from preschool to a mature age.

Layered learning is when we read, write, report, revise and draw ideas into words and images we begin the extraordinary work of interpreting and making sense of the world of information and ideas around us.

Drawing out ideas and connecting information through images makes the abstract and complex concrete and manageable. Composing ideas is what makes education matter. "

—Peter Elbow, *Explorations in Teaching and Learning*

In Hebrew, the word for "work" and "worship" has the same root meaning. Hebraic teaching was expected to point to practical truths that people could adopt and apply to their everyday lives..The Jesus of Hebraic society two thousand years ago would probably not be accepted by most theologians of modern America. His teachings were intended for man to live by, not to ponder.

—Restoration Ministries

"A little here, a little there" was a method used in teaching the Hebrew children, inculcating a little at a time. Doing the same in school time ensures that your children will understand that the Bible is not something meant just for church, but for daily living.

The Hebrews taught first by example. Your first obligation to your children is to let them observe you spending time in prayer and Bible study seeking God's truth. The Hebrew word for "work" and "worship" has the same root meaning. Hebraic teaching pointed to practical truths people could apply to their everyday lives. The influence of the teacher's character was of extream importance.

If we are to understand the Bible then we will have to understand it Hebraically, not Hellenistically. This will require a renewing of our minds intellectually and spiritually.

The world of ideas reflected in the Hebrew Bible is very different from that reflected in the Greek classics. The Hebrew language is verb oriented (verbs are used much more frequently then adjectives) while the Greek is noun and adjective oriented. The Greeks described what a person or object looked like physically while Hebrews described what the person or object was capable of. Its one of the reasons we don't have a physical description of Christ. Western Americans are much closer to focusing on the physical.

Hebrew logic is very different from Greek logic. Mike and Sue Dowgiewicz explain in *A Hebraic Perspective: The Foundational Thinking of the Early Church*:

> The Hebrews used "block logic". Each of their thoughts is able to stand alone; they don't necessarily fit together sequentially. If you view the Scripture as a form of block logic, it makes incredible sense. Each of their thoughts is able to stand alone; they don't necessarily fit together sequentially. If you view the Scripture as a form of block logic, it makes incredible sense. The Bible does not require a lot of the extra-scriptural explanation to which we in the West are so accustomed. Westerners attempt to piece together a lot of seemingly related scriptures in order to organize the Bible into a teachable format. Perhaps we feel we need this organization in order to meet our

Greek-oriented rational thinking processes. We even construct our doctrines so that they might be systematically understood, verse upon verse.

The Hebrew knows that he does not have all the answers; God does not require him to. He is willing to live at peace with God without being able to explain everything. Life is full of irreconcilable antitheses: a focus on the temporal as well as the eternal; a simultaneous love and fear of God; His nearness yet His transcendence. Westerners, however, feel a compelling need to rationalize biblical truths. God defies rational explanation. How can you explain a God Who is transcendent above the highest heavens yet indwells the spirit of His children? How can the same God Who has allowed His people Israel to undergo exiles, Inquisitions, and the Holocaust be the God of the resurrection to them that believe? Paul emphasized the unknowable mystery of God and marveled, *"Oh, the depth of the wisdom and knowledge of God*! How unsearchable his judgments, and his paths beyond tracing out! Who has known the mind of the Lord?"* (Romans 11:33-34).

Believers in the early Church knew that they did not want to "lean on their own understanding"; that is, they wanted revelation, not reason, to guide them. (See Acts 13:1-3)

William Barrett explains, in *Irrational Man,* the most fundamental differences between the Western, Hellenistic mind and the Hebrew mind is found in the area of knowing vs. doing:

> The distinction…arises from the difference between doing and knowing. The Hebrew is concerned with practice, the Greek with knowledge. Right conduct is the ultimate concern of the Hebrew, right thinking that of the Greek. Duty and strictness of conscience are the paramount things in life for the Hebrew; for the Greek, the spontaneous and luminous play of the intelligence. The Hebrew thus extols the moral virtues as the substance and meaning of life; the Greek subordinates them to the intellectual virtues…the contrast is between practice and theory, between the moral man and the theoretical or intellectual man.

You can purchase a blank *Book of the Centuries* published by Small Ventures Press, available through most home-school suppliers, or make your own with the instructions below.

TO SET UP YOUR
TIME LINE BOOK:

You will need:
-A three-ring notebook with a clear-plastic pocket cover
-Blank 8.5" x 11" pages
-Smaller lined pages (8.5 x 11 cut down to 8.5 x9)
-A three-hole punch
-Glue sticks

Decide upon the units of time you will use (decades, centuries, etc.) to divide your time line into segments. A time line documenting the period from Adam to the Messiah will begin with Creation (before 2000 B.C.) and end with the resurrection of Christ (c. A.D. 30). (The nice thing about the notebook-style time line is that it's cumulative; every year's study can be added in. You can continue this time line as you study later periods by adding pages.) As you study each period, there will be times when you will document decades on one page, and other times when you will document several centuries on one page. Place the appropriate section of the time line across the top of each 8.5" x 11" page to represent increments. The shorter lined pages will go in between these pages to hold notes. If there is not room on your time line to include all of your chronology, cull some of the dates or add pages with larger segments that leave more room.

PRAYING FOR WISDOM

Use this passage according to Ephesians 1:17-20. to pray for your children, spouse, or others needing wisdom:

"Dear God, Give unto _____ the spirit of wisdom and revelation in the knowledge. Let the eyes of _____ understanding being enlightened; that _____ may know what is the hope of his calling, and what the riches of the glory of his inheritance in the saints, And what is the exceeding greatness of his power to us-ward who believe, according to the working of his mighty power, Which he wrought in Christ, when he raised him from the dead, and set him at his own right hand in the heavenly places."

DELIGHT-DIRECTED LEARNING / LIFESTYLE OF LEARNING

The Bible instructs parents to recognize that each child is a unique individual, with a "way" already established that needs to be recognized, acknowledged, and reckoned with by means of the truth of Scripture.

Proverbs 22:6 says *Train up a child in the way he should go, Even when he is old he will not depart from it.* This verse shows us that a parent's training must be based on knowing his or her child. The Hebrew text is written with the personal pronoun attached to the noun "way." It reads, "his way" and not simply "in the way he should go." "Way" is the Hebrew derek, "way, road, journey, manner." Parents need to recognize the way each of their children is bent by the way God has designed each of them. If parents fail to recognize this, they may also fail to help launch their children into God's plan for their lives.

All children love to learn—at least all children love to learn before they go to school. Forced learning can destroy the natural love for learning that our children are born with. Children locked into studying something they find boring are no different than adults locked into boring, irrelevant meetings. If adults cannot see the relevance of the material covered in a meeting, they will "tune out" or "drop out." If children do not understand how the subject will help to address the concerns of their lives, they will tune out. Would you, for example, read this page if it were titled "Basic Plumbing Concepts"? You might if you had a kitchen-sink leak or a basement full of water. In the same way, students need to have an interest in the topic they are learning.

Delight-directed learning places students in charge of their own learning, helping them to find something that they want to accomplish. The Heart of Wisdom approach uses natural curiosity to motivate the student. The student acquires basic concepts of learning (reading, reasoning, writing, researching, etc.) during the process of examining the topic of interest. Less control can lead to more learning.

Marilyn Howshall's Lifestyle of Learning approach is based on leaning on the Holy Spirit and delight-directed learning. She explains,

> If the goal of your instruction is love from a pure heart (which will only come with an emptying of self) then you will provide a strong foundation of character in your children that will enable them with your help to acquire a

strong and unique, God-designed education which will include creative vocational purpose. If you want godly fruit, you have to know God and do things His way. You won't learn what His way is until you decide you want to know what it is and surrender your will to become completely teachable of the Holy Spirit.

MULTI-LEVEL UNIT STUDY

The Heart of Wisdom approach is designed for multi-level teaching. Students study the same topics, each on their individual level. The multi-level approach saves a tremendous amount of time in preparing, teaching, and correcting work.

A family of three using the traditional approach (textbooks and workbooks) must prepare, plan, teach, and correct work for 21 or more subjects (7 subjects for each child). This can be a nightmare for the teacher. In history, one child could be studying the American Revolution, another the Civil War, and another ancient Egypt. In science, one child could be studying animals, another planets, another physics. In Bible, one student could be studying the Ten Commandments, another the life of Christ, another creation.

With a multi-level unit study approach, all subjects except math and language arts can be taught together. Each child studies the topic at his or her own level. This saves over half of your teaching and preparing time. All children can go on field trips together, many projects can be done together, writing assignments and vocabulary words will be about the same topic, but on different levels. For example ,while studying animals, a younger child may be able to classify birds, mammals, and insects, while an older child would classify animals in much more detail (arachnids, crustaceans, etc). The older child learns and helps to teach the younger while the younger learns from the older.

Unit studies, sometimes called "thematic units" or "integrated studies," are very popular with homeschoolers. The child learns by actually experiencing or discovering through different methods and activities, rather than by simply reading a chapter from a textbook. A unit study takes a topic and "lives" with it for a period of time, integrating science, social studies, language arts, math, and fine arts as they apply.

The "unit" or "theme" refers to the idea of studying a topic as a whole instead of several "subjects." For example: most people think of water as a science subject. One way to look at water is as H2O—a chemistry subject—but, it is also art (a beautiful

"The wisdom tradition was swallowed up by the Greek standards for education and culture. 'Even Christian' education is essentially secular education, preparing one for success in the world, or in the more traditional schools, to be civilized, a polished gentleman of the Western world. The challenge fro Christian education is to replace and build on the tradition of Biblical wisdom, without destroying the good of western learning. That calls for a restructuring of the while model for education."
—David Mulligan, *Far Above Rubies: Wisdom in the Christian Community*

"If we abide by the principles taught in the Bible, our country will go on prospering and to prosper; but if we and our posterity neglect its instructions and authority, no man can tell how sudden a catastrophe may overwhelm us and bury our glory in profound obscurity."
—Daniel Webster

"Self-control is an everyday necessity. We need it every hour...children will not need arithmetic at all times in all places, but they will need this cardinal nature. It may be well for them to learn the bones of the human body, but it will be a vastly greater service for them to have their powers under complete control. They will need the latter, morning, noon and night, from this time until the close of life, while the former is used in certain times and places. It has been acclaimed that a man can govern a state more easily than himself. Self-control is an indispensable virtue."
—William M. Thayer, *Gaining Favor with God and Man*

waterfall), history (the Red Sea), economics (water bill), theology (baptism), language arts (babbling brook), geography (the location of bodies of water), etc. When one studies the "whole" he can see how it relates to the Creator.

LIVING BOOKS / CHARLOTTE MASON'S PHILOSOPHY

Charlotte Mason was an educator in England during the nineteenth century, and her methods are currently experiencing a rebirth among American home schools. Mason believed that children should be educated through a wide curriculum using a variety of real, living books. "Twaddle" and "living books" are terms coined by Mason. "Twaddle" refers to dumbed-down literature; absence of meaning. "Living books" refers to books that are well written and engaging—they absorb the reader, while the narrative and characters "come alive"; living books are the opposite of cold, dry textbooks. Charlotte Mason's concern was for students to develop a lifetime love of learning. She based her philosophy on the Latin word for education, educare, which means "to feed and nourish." This method focuses on the formation of good habits, reading a variety of books, narration, copying work, dictation, keeping a nature diary, keeping a spelling notebook, and preparing a time line book.

Narration

Narration is literally "telling back" what has been learned. Students are instructed to read a passage from the Bible, text from a suggested resource, or content from a Web site and "tell" what they have learned, either orally or in writing. This process involves sorting, sequencing, selecting, connecting, rejecting, and classifying. Narration increases the student's ability to remember, making review work unnecessary.

Time Line Book

Charlotte Mason's students created a Time Line Book (originally called a Museum Sketch Book; sometimes called a Book of the Centuries) to help them pull together seemingly unrelated information. As students learn historical facts, they make notes and sketches in their book on the appropriate page about famous people, important events, inventions, wars, etc. (See illustration on the next page).

Copy Work and Dictation

Copy work and dictation are underrated. Both provide ongoing practice for handwriting, spelling, grammar, etc. Both are also good exercises for teaching accuracy and attention to

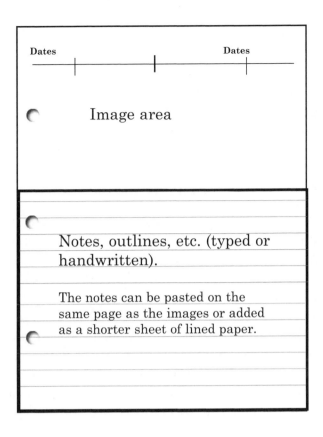

Dates ___|___|___ Dates

Image area

Notes, outlines, etc. (typed or handwritten).

The notes can be pasted on the same page as the images or added as a shorter sheet of lined paper.

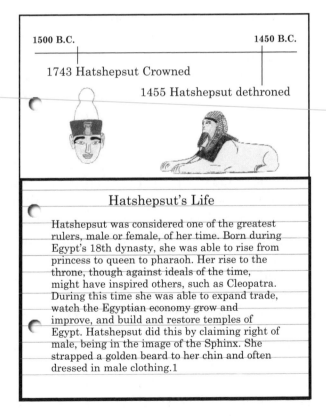

1500 B.C.   1450 B.C.

1743 Hatshepsut Crowned

1455 Hatshepsut dethroned

Hatshepsut's Life

Hatshepsut was considered one of the greatest rulers, male or female, of her time. Born during Egypt's 18th dynasty, she was able to rise from princess to queen to pharaoh. Her rise to the throne, though against ideals of the time, might have inspired others, such as Cleopatra. During this time she was able to expand trade, watch the Egyptian economy grow and improve, and build and restore temples of Egypt. Hatshepsut did this by claiming right of male, being in the image of the Sphinx. She strapped a golden beard to her chin and often dressed in male clothing.1

Sample page from a Time Line Book.

See another sample on page 144.

See another sample on page 144.

"Believe me, sir, never a night goes by, be I ever so tired, but I read the Word of God before I go to bed."
—Douglas MacArthur

"Almost every man who has by his life-work added to the sum of human achievement of which the race is proud, of which our people are proud; almost every such man has based his life-work largely upon the teachings of the Bible."
—Theodore Roosevelt

"We need not labor to get children to learn their lessons; that, if we would believe it, is a matter which nature takes care of. Let the lessons be of the right sort and children will learn them with delight. The call for strenuousness comes with the necessity of forming habits; but here again we are relieved. The intellectual habits of the good life form themselves in the following out of the due curriculum in the right way. As we have already urged, there is but one right way, that is, children must do the work for themselves. They must read the given pages and tell what they have read, they must perform, that is, what we may call *the act of knowing*. We are all aware, alas, what a monstrous quantity of printed matter has gone into the dustbin of our memories, because we have failed to perform that quite natural and spontaneous 'act of knowing,' as easy to a child as breathing and, if we would believe it, comparatively easy to ourselves. The reward is twofold: no intellectual habit is so valuable as that of attention; it is a mere habit but it is also the hallmark of an educated person."
— Charlotte Mason

The Hebrew position is one that acknowledges the need for objective leading from God. The mind of man without leading of God's spirit, has limitations. God provides the signals and our job is to read them properly. The Hebrews were free to use their reasoning abilities making decisions and determining direction in life but they were obligated to stay within the borders provided by God's Word. Reasoning without these borders leads to man's reliance on his own understanding.

Man's reasoning without God can man needs more than one wife because animals have more than one mate. Homosexuality is another example of man's reasoning without God.

Trust in the LORD with all thine heart; and lean not unto thine own understanding. Proverbs 3:5

Studying the Bible is the ultimate lesson in reasoning skills. Teaching students to think critically as they confront different information resources is the core of resource-based learning. Christians don't need expensive analogy workbooks. We have the depth of God's Word: the parables Jesus taught, the foreshadows in Bible holidays, the significance in numbers, the symbolism, the types, and passages such as Isaiah 53 revealing Christ.

detail. In copy work, students discover things about the text they are copying that they would be unlikely to notice otherwise. In dictation, the parent reads as the child writes. Students learn correct spelling, capitalization, punctuation, and other language mechanics when they compare their work to the original and correct mistakes.

LEARNING STYLES AND THE 4MAT SYSTEM

Scientific studies show that different people take in or perceive information differently and process information differently. The way we view the world is the way we perceive information. Some learners (1)need to "see" things concretely (through the five senses) to understand information. Other learners (2) can understand information abstractly (visually understand what cannot be seen). How we process what we learn is the way we use the information. Some learners (3) process reflectively while other learners (4) process actively. When you combine the ways in which one perceives and processes information, the results are four basic learning styles.

Studies show that 70 percent of children do not learn well the way the schools teach—lecture/textbook/test—most students need more. The 4Mat System, developed by Denise McCarthy, is a way to teach to all four of the learning styles described above. It does not isolate one type of learning but, instead, teaches in all ways so that students relate to the subject in the way that is the most comfortable for them and discover how to learn in other ways.

There are four basic steps to The 4Mat System. The amount of time necessary for each step will vary from a few minutes to a few days depending on the activities chosen. You can improve any Bible study, unit study, or even textbook curriculum by adapting it to these four steps, since the steps teach to all four learning styles and both brain hemispheres. Studies show that this four-step method motivates students to comprehend the material better and retain the information longer.

Step 1 Excite: (This is a critical step which is skipped in school.) Create an interest. Motivate students by making the lesson meaningful to their lives. Many students need to know why a topic is necessary to learn before they will learn it. When I asked a room of several hundred home-school parents (including several public school teachers) this question, "Why does your student need to know that proper nouns must be capitalized?" The only answer given was, "Because it's a rule."

If we first explain the reason that we capitalize proper nouns, students would remember the rule longer. We capitalize proper nouns to distinguish them from other words. For example, the word "mountain" refers to any mountain, but the "Rocky Mountains" are specific, so we use capital letters to show that they are a specific set of mountains. Therefore, in Step One of each lesson (Bible history, math, etc), discuss what the children may already know about the topic, why they should learn about it, and what they would like to find out. Use any of the following methods: Brainstorm, make lists, mindmap, outline, etc.

Step 2 Examine: Find out the facts. This is the traditional step used in schools with textbooks. We suggest several different resources (Bible, Bible reference books, Christian books, reference books, literature, living books, Internet sites, videos, etc.).

Step 3 Expand: Students do something with what was learned. The lesson is reinforced by completing an assignment or creating a project. Projects can be simple ten-minute activities or elaborate three-day endeavors. Studies show that students must do something with what is learned in order to retain the material.

Step 4 Excel: Pull everything together. The student shares what he has learned, through narration (verbally or in writing), a project, or sharing his time line or portfolio. When a student can teach someone else what he has learned, it is evident that he knows the subject.

WRITING TO LEARN

One of the best ways for a student to understand a topic is to write about it. Students must comprehend the material, restructure the new information, and then share their new understanding. "Writing to Learn" is much more than an accumulation of report writing; it helps students think and learn carefully and completely. Writing assignments are about creating both ideas and learning. During writing assignments, students learn how to assess information and determine its appropriateness, and to evaluate and compare, analyze and discern, add their own feelings, organize information, and communicate conclusions. Through these processes, students learn to manage and use information to solve problems, interrelate knowledge, and effectively communicate learning outcomes. Students develop excellence in achievement by producing the required quality assignments; they develop diligence

"The Bible is a book in comparison with which all others in my eyes are of minor importance."
—Robert E. Lee

"The first and almost only book deserving universal attention is the Bible. I speak as a man of the world and I say to you, 'Search the Scriptures.'"
—John Quincy Adams

In all things shewing thyself a pattern of good works: in doctrine shewing uncorruptness, gravity, sincerity, Sound speech, that cannot be condemned; that he that is of the contrary part may be ashamed, having no evil thing to say of you.
Titus 2:7-8

For I resolved to know nothing while I was with you except Jesus Christ and him crucified. I came to you in weakness and fear, and with much trembling. My message and my preaching were not with wise and persuasive words, but with a demonstration of the Spirit's power, so that your faith might not rest on men's wisdom, but on God's power.
1 Corinthians 2:2-5

by continually practicing clarity, accuracy, relevance, prioritizing, consistency, depth, and breadth through writing activities.

Charlotte Mason's narration methods for younger children involve "telling back" favorite stories read by parents. In later years, students progress to reading passages and "telling back" in verbal or written form what they have learned. "Talking it out," whether aloud or on paper, helps students think.

Often, teachers use writing as a way of testing. They use it to find out what students already know, rather than as a way of encouraging them to learn. But the active processes of seeking information, compiling notes, and evaluating, analyzing, and organizing content, as well as the processes of personal reflection, choosing and constructing words, and expressing ideas in writing, are valuable learning tools which students will use the rest of their lives.

Catherine Copley explains in *The Writer's Complex*:

> Writing provides food for thought-it enables you to knead small, half-baked words and sentences into great big loaves of satisfying thought that then lead to more thoughts. Developing ideas involves getting some ideas-in whatever form-onto paper or screen so you can see them, return to them, explore them, question them, share them, clarify them, change them, and grow them. It really is almost like growing plants or kneading bread and waiting for the results: plant the seed, start the process, and then let your mind, including your unconscious, take over. Go to sleep and let your dreaming continue to develop your ideas. Humans were born to think; it's almost impossible to stop us. Writing helps us to bring all that activity into consciousness, helps to clarify and direct our thinking, and generate more thinking. Writing, thinking, and learning are part of the same process.

With the H.O.W. approach parents correct spelling, capitalization, punctuation, grammar, sentence structure, subject/verb agreement, verb tense, and word usage in all writing by marking each error with a number that corresponds with a rule from a writing handbook. (We recommend any of the Write Source Handbooks: *Write One, Write Away, Writer Express, All Write*, or *Writers INC*—depending on grade level.)

SUGGESTED COURSE OF STUDY

The Heart of Wisdom approach includes a suggested course of study that can begin at any age and is then repeated every four years (see page 140). Students complete 5-7 history units and 4-6 science units per year. This suggested course of study can be easily adapted to fit different families' needs. The family with multiple ages will appreciate that they can jump in and start anytime. Students of all ages can study together in this setting, each studying the topic at his or her own level. The Bible is studied every year. History units are studied chronologically, and science units are studied in the order of creation. Practical life-skills studies are added during the high school years.

SUMMARY

The Heart of Wisdom teaching approach is for those who want to return to the biblical education method and make the Bible the focus of all learning. More details and resources for using this approach are available on our Web site and in the book *The Heart of Wisdom Teaching Approach*. The next chapter gives ideas on how to implement this approach.

Wisdom: An Internet-Linked Unit Study

This study is one of the most important things you will ever do with your children. Is your homeschooling on the right path? Are you headed in the right direction? Are you reaching for the right goal? It does not matter how hard you try or how diligent you are if you don't have the right directions.

Suppose you wanted to go to a city in Texas but you were given a map of Florida mislabeled Texas? Following the directions would not work—even if you tried harder or increased your speed. You would still be lost! The problem is not your attitude or effort—the problem is—you have the wrong map. Many homeschoolers are following the wrong map on their homeschool journey: they follow the state's standards, curriculum scope and sequence, or SAT benchmarks. This unique unit study is a map to true wisdom.

A map is not a territory, it is an explanation of certain aspects of a territory. In this study you will learn that true wisdom is understanding and knowing God. The moment we begin to understand and know God—we begin to see His holiness, we see His purposes, His love for men—we know who God is, so there's never any hesitation to obey Him.

There are two ways to live life—wisely or unwise. When we follow the path of wisdom the results are joy, peace, contentment, confidence in the presence of God. The results of living unwisely are conflict, discouragement, disappointment, disillusionment, and discontentment. Can you see this information is more important than any academics? Don't homeschool without including this important information! Ebook or paperback.

Lessons Teach:
- How to follow the wise path
- How to stay on it.
- How to stay off the worldly path
- How to set wise goals
- The importance of obedience
- How to pray for wisdom
- How to study God's Word
- How to make wise decisions
- How to choose friends wisely
- How to choose counsel wisely
- How to manage conflict wisely
- How to have the ultimate relationship with Christ
- And more!

A s discussed in the previous chapter, the H.O.W. approach has a two-sided curriculum base: God's Word (Bible studies) and God's world (academic studies). This chapter contains practical ideas for Bible study and a brief overview of the academic studies.

GOD'S WORD: BIBLE STUDIES

Using the H.O.W. approach, we show our children the importance of God's Word by making it the first priority of the day and continually referring to it throughout the day. The Bible was designed to be stimulating, interesting, delightful, challenging, comforting, and calming. Embarking on this path will provide you and your children with the wisdom all of you need for life.

The wise Solomon instructed us to search the Word of God for hidden treasure as we would seek after silver. In Matthew we read, *Seek ye first the kingdom of God, and his righteousness; and all these things shall be added unto you.* God wants us to diligently seek after His Word. Our desire is to be preferred over necessary food, raiment, or riches, (or state standards), or any enjoyment of life. We must make it first in importance. Everything else must give way before its demands.

Jesus said, "*Thou shalt love the Lord thy God with all thy heart, and with all thy soul, and with all thy mind*" (Matt. 22:37; also see Mark 12:30, Luke 10:27). To love God intellectually is to become a student of God—a student who takes a sincere interest in God. John Garr, founder of the Restoration Foundation, explains that study is the highest form of worship:

> The decision to study God's Word in order to do His Word is a meaningful act of submission and reverence-in short, it is worship. Study carried out with this motive is the very essence of Biblical learning. This is not study in order to understand; it is study in order to do.

> Study of God's Word in order to mold one's lifestyle to that Word is also worship in the truest sense of the English word worship, which means to "ascribe worth to." When we fully submit our lives to God's Word, when we study what he has said with complete devotion and intensity, we do, indeed, ascribe worth to Him: we worship Him.

The importance of studying the Word of God is seen in Paul's instructions to Timothy: "Study to show thyself approved unto God, a workman that needeth not to be ashamed, rightly dividing the word of truth. . . . from a child thou hast known the holy scriptures, which are able to make thee wise unto salvation through faith which is in Christ Jesus. All scripture is given by inspiration of God, and is profitable for doctrine, for reproof, for correction, for instruction in righteousness: that the man of God may be perfect, thoroughly furnished unto all good works" (II Timothy 2:15; 3:15-17).

Intense study is necessary to avoid the shame of inaccurately interpreting God's Word. This is in keeping with David's description of the righteous man: "His delight is in the law of the Lord; and in his law doth he meditate day and night" (Psalm 1:2). The meditation to which David refers is not East-ern Monism's meditation. It is the repeating over and over again, of the words of God until one so ingests the Word that it becomes a part of the very fiber of one's being.

The Bible is not just a valuable collection of ancient docu-ments. It is not just the annals of history. It is not just literary genius. It is not just an assemblage of entertaining stories. It is God's Word to us. Bible study is a transforming process. As we respond in obedience to what God speaks to us, then we will participate in the transformation whereby we become more and more like Jesus, our Lord.

READING THROUGH THE BIBLE EACH YEAR

It only takes fifteen to twenty minutes per day to read through the Bible in a year. We suggest that you set aside one to two hours each day (depending on your children's ages) for the Bible lessons. During these lessons, students will be learning to learn by referencing Bible tools. Having the tools on hand will make your studies more convenient and simple. Persever-ance, persistence, and dedication are important. Your attitude toward the studies serves to motivate and inspire your stu-dents.

Our goal in reading through the entire Bible is to grasp the whole picture. There is nothing special about the one-year (or fifty-two week) time frame. You should read the Bible at a pace you feel comfortable with; you may decide to spend two years or longer. The Bible Reading Check List in this book is simply a framework to get you started. Rely on the Holy Spirit to guide you through the readings. The most important thing for us to remember is not to focus upon the quantity of infor-mation we learn, but to remain faithful to whatever spiritual truth God has entrusted to our care. Your Bible study should be life changing, meaningful, and applicable to your daily struggles, tests, and challenges; it should not be just academic knowledge. An academic study of God's Word will produce little benefit apart from the Holy Spirit. Good study methods alone will not produce good Bible study. It takes a sincere heart with the right kind of attitude as well. The student who has a hunger and thirst for the Word of God will find that God will meet Him.

The Bible Reading Check List in Section IV arranges the Scriptures chronologically, in the order that the Bible events occurred. These portion divisions are from *The Narrated Bible: In Chronological Order*. *The Narrated Bible* is not a paraphrase or translation; the central text is composed entirely of Scripture using the New International Version. Narrative commentary is included in a separate and distinct typeface and color. Throughout the presentation of Scripture, chapter and verse designations are placed in the margin for easy reference. The narrative commentary is written in such a way as to be part of an unfolding story. The text in *The Narrated Bible* can be used for dictation and copying lessons (teaching handwriting, grammar, capitalization, and punctuation), because it is written in everyday English. Families with very young children may decide to use *God's Story* or Bible storybooks (explained later in this chapter). You can use any Bible version by referring to the chapters and verses listed in the Bible Reading Check List.

You Will Need:

- KJV Bible for Reference
- A chronological Bible to read aloud, such as *The Narrated Bible* (for younger children, *God's Story* or Bible storybooks)
- Write Source Handbook (proper age level)
- Spelling Notebook for each student (spiral-bound notebook divided alphabetically)
- Vocabulary Notebook for each student (spiral-bound notebook divided alphabetically)
- Art Portfolio for each student (Poster board stapled together to protect large artwork)
- Materials to make the Portfolio and Time Line Book (a three-ring notebook for each with a clear-plastic pocket cover, and a three-hole punch)
- A note book for the teacher to jot down ideas and thoughts
- Bible Tools
  - Bible Dictionary (Child or Adult)

STEP 1 EXCITE
- Brainstorm
- Mindmap
- Observe a video
- Discuss
- Make lists
- Draw tentative conclusions

STEP 2 EXAMINE
- Read the Bible
- Look up items and words in a Bible handbook
- Refer to a Commentary
- View Bible Maps
- Interview father or pastor

STEP 3 EXPAND
- Write a song
- Write poetry
- Make a poster
- Create illustrations
- Make a salt-dough model (lamp, menorah, etc.)
- Play interactive software
- Do a science experiment
- Create a puppet show
- Make a diorama from a shoe box
- Write a letter from a character
- Write a letter to a character
- Write a newspaper article about an event
- Trace a journey on a map
- Create a costumed play
- Make a booklet or pamphlet

STEP 4 EXCEL
Share and Explain a Project:
- Writing Activities
- Portfolio
- Artwork
- Oral Stories
- Recite poetry
- Sing a song

Reading the Bible each day causes children to come to you all day long with questions. This gives you an opportunity to do what God commands us to do in Deuteronomy 6:7: "And thou shalt teach them diligently unto thy children, and shalt talk of them when thou sittest in thine house, and when thou walkest by the way, and when thou liest down, and when thou risest up."

Bible Versions
We recommend the 1611 authorized King James Version Bible for Bible study, along with lexicons to look up Greek and Hebrew words. However, for daily Bible reading, we think of *The Narrated Bible* as a "story book" to read aloud, giving the children an overview of the entire Bible. It reads like a novel and is easy to understand.

- Bible Handbook (manners and customs)
- Bible Atlas (map book)
- *Strong's Reference Book*
- Hebrew Lexicon (older students)
- Greek Lexicon (older students)

The specific Bible resources we recommend are listed at the end of this chapter.

THE FOUR-STEP BIBLE LESSONS

There are four basic steps to the H.O.W. approach. The amount of time for each step will vary from a few minutes to a few hours depending on the activities chosen. These four steps teach to all four learning styles and both brain hemispheres. Studies show that this four-step method motivates students to comprehend the material better and retain the information longer. The steps will occasionally overlap each other; they are just a general outline to organize the lessons.

Explain to your children what a privilege it is for us to know God through Jesus, and how relationships are based on communication. God communicates with us through His Word; we communicate with God through prayer. Before beginning the school day, talk to God through prayer. Devote your day to Him and ask His blessings. During your studies, stop at any time you have difficulty with a passage. Remember that God promises us wisdom when we ask for it (James 1:5); therefore pray for wisdom. Prayer comes from a humble spirit that is willing to ask for assistance and acknowledge need. Praying shows that you recognize your dependence upon God (Proverbs 11:2; James 3:5-6).

STEP 1 EXCITE: CREATE AN INTEREST

Motivate students by making the lesson meaningful to their lives. (5-10 minutes)

Before Beginning a New Book of the Bible

Get a clear overview of the book as a whole before trying to dissect it into different minute parts. Discuss the author, time period, and overall theme. Refer to study tools such as: *What the Bible Is All About for Young Explorers* or the *Nelson Illustrated Encyclopedia of the Bible*; both include an outline and list of the main people in each book, helping you to see the contents of that book in a nutshell. They also include time lines that show you when events happened. You'll find summaries of sections within each book that show how each section fits

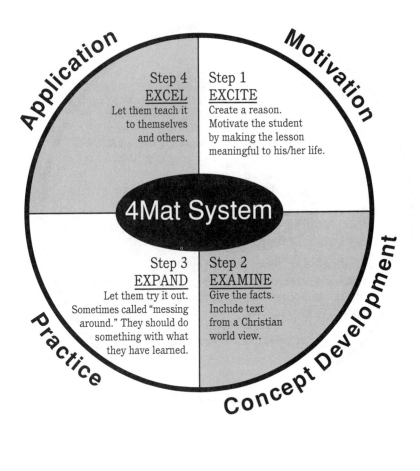

Application

Motivation

Step 4
EXCEL
Let them teach it
to themselves
and others.

Step 1
EXCITE
Create a reason.
Motivate the student
by making the lesson
meaningful to his/her life.

4Mat System

Step 3
EXPAND
Let them try it out.
Sometimes called "messing
around." They should do
something with what
they have learned.

Step 2
EXAMINE
Give the facts.
Include text
from a Christian
world view.

Practice

Concept Development

The 4MAT® model consists of four instructional goals:

1. Motivating students
2. Teaching ideas and facts
3. Experimenting with Concepts & Skills
4. Integrating new learning into real life

It addresses four styles of learners:

1. Those who learn by listening and sharing ideas
2. Those who learn by conceptualizing—integrating their observations into what is known
3. Those who learn by experimenting—testing theories in practice
4. Those who learn by creating—acting and then testing their new experience

The 4Mat lessons are designed so that all learning styles are addressed, in order that more than one type of student may be permitted to both "shine" and "stretch." Each lesson contains "something for everybody," so each student not only finds the mode of greatest comfort for him/her, but is challenged to adapt to other, less comfortable but equally valuable modes.

Step 4
He asked them to go
and tell others.
"Go ye therefore,
and teach all nations..."

Step 1
He took the people
where they were and
made the lesson mean-
ingful to their lives in some way.
He spoke to shepherds about
sheep, farmers about planting,
fishermen about fish, etc.

How Jesus Taught

Step 3
He asked them to do
something with what they
learned—to actively
respond—doing
and practice are vitally
connected with
knowing.

Step 2
He brought in the facts—
Scripture, "It is written,..."

For detailed instructions relating to copying and dictation methods, read chapters six through ten in Ruth Beechick's *You Can Teach Your Child Successfully.*

LISTENING TO BIBLE READINGS

If you are reading Bible text to older children, the toddlers may not seem to gain much from the reading time, but this period is an excellent opportunity to teach children to sit still and be quiet.

Sometimes we practice being still and sometimes, I provide a set of wood blocks or coloring books for younger children (only available to them during this reading time).

WRITING PROMPTS
-Write a newspaper article for an event that happened in the Bible story. Include who, what, where, why, when and how.
-Contrast the life of the people in the Bible story with your life today. How are they alike and different?
-Give examples of cause and effect in the event.
-Write about a character that displayed qualities of bravery. Tell what you would have done if you had been in that character's place.
-Write an editorial expressing your opinion about an event.
-Choose characters from the Bible reading and give a report on them.

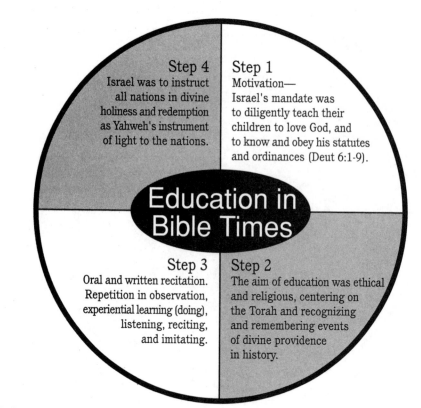

Modern-day science may have come up with the 4Mat System, but is it really a new way to teach or have we had this pattern all along?

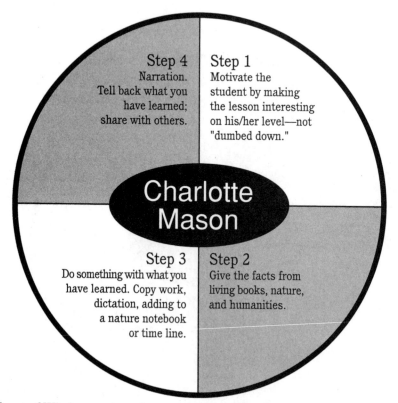

The Heart of Wisdom approach creates lesson plans using Charlotte Mason's methods and teaching to the four styles. Its a new, creative way to organize Charlotte Mason's unique methods.

into the big picture, illustrations that show events in detail, and maps that show you where it all happened.

Step 1 Suggestions:

- Brainstorm, ask questions, and discuss what the children may already know about the passage.
- Make a list of what they would like to find out.
- Share with them what the passage meant to you when you read it for the first time.
- Talk about the previous events (from previous day's readings).
- Have each student begin a mind map (see our Web site for samples— http://HomeschoolUnitStudies.com) which they will add to after the reading.
- Have each student begin an outline.

STEP 2 EXAMINE: READ THE PASSAGE AND USE BIBLE TOOLS

If you are using the Bible Reading Check List, the suggested readings contain several different stories. Example: One reading includes pages 23-30 in *The Narrated Bible*. These pages include the following stories:

1. The Call of Abram

2. Abram Dishonors Himself in Egypt

3. Separation of Abram and Lot

4. Defeat of the Kings

5. God's Covenant with Abram

It may be easier to complete one of the stories, using the Bible tools, then continue on to the next story.

Step 2 Suggestions

Each student may do one or several of the following:

- Look up the area where each story took place in a Bible atlas. *The Holman Atlas* or *Nelson's Illustrated Encyclopedia of the Bible* includes maps and historical text that will illuminate each story.
- Look up selected words in the Bible dictionary. Jot down unknown words for the next step.
- Look up manners and customs (such as circumcision) in a Manners & Customs book (*Nelson's Illustrated Encyclopedia of the Bible*).
- Use a Bible concordance to expand the study.
- Use a book like *Who's Who in the Bible* to learn about character and trials of a person's life.

Several Bible storybooks are available in Christian bookstores:

Hear Me Read Bible Storybooks are available on two levels. Each story consists of 15 to 25 words that are repeated often to help children develop a sight vocabulary. There are currently twenty-six books in the series.

The *Arch© Bible Storybooks* consists of a set of inexpensive, lively, rhyming poems, and colorful illustrations for children preschool to kindergarten. The books in this series published before in the 1980s, include realistic type illustrations. The newer illustrations are too "cartoony" for our family. There are over forty-four books in the series.

Now You Can Read Bible Stories are delightfully written and illustrated. The new series (from Thomas-Nelson) consists of nine books; however, we were able to find several books that used to be in this series (originally published by Rourke) from used book stores.

The *Biblearn* Series are good read-aloud hardback books with nice illustrations. Currently there are twenty-four books in this series. Books include several stories each.

-A large, sturdy three-ring notebook with a clear plastic front
(designed to slip a cover
sheet under the plastic) for
each child.
-Three-hole-punched plastic
protective covers (for photos,
artwork, and flat collections).
-Plastic photo pages (for photos of plays, large projects,
etc., in portfolio).
-Ten tabbed notebook dividers
labeled:
    1. Law/Instruction
    2. Historical
    3. Poetry
    4. Major Prophets
    5. Minor Prophets
    6. Gospels
    7. Acts
    8. Paul's Letters
    9. General Instruction
    10. Prophecy

Optional Supplies available at
Scrapbook Stores
  -Colored pencils and/or wash-
   able markers and/or crayons
  -Ruled and un-ruled paper
  -Decorative scissors
  -Die Cuts
  -Construction paper
  -Three-hole punch
  -Decorative paper
  -Decorative stamps
  -Scrapbook paper
  -Paper doll templates
  -Paper trimmers
  -Punches
  -Various art supplies (char-
   coal, paint, chalk, etc.)

• If the student is unclear about a certain passage, he should use a concordance to compare Scripture with Scripture. One passage will shed light on another as he cross-references with other verses and passages.

STEP 3 EXPAND: DO SOMETHING WITH WHAT WAS LEARNED

Ask each student which section of the reading spoke to him. Allow each student to choose the story or passage that he is the most interested in (delight-directed studies) to expand on in this step.

Step 3 Suggestions:

Each student may do one or several of the following:

• Rewrite the story in his own words.
• Narrate the story (tell back) to someone.
• Copy an important passage (the older the student, the longer the passage).
• Have you dictate the passage to him (the older the student the longer the passage).
• Dictate the story to you (younger students).
• Illustrate the story.
• Create a page for the Time Line Book (see next page)
• Illustrate the story.
• Create paper doll characters (see image on this page)
• act out the story using puppets.
• Make a salt-dough model of a map of the area.
• Create a diorama (a shoebox "scene").
• Create a scrapbook page (see samples on page 144).
• Create artwork on the computer (see sample on page 144).
• Create a lap book. (see our Web site for details).
• Write a song.
• Trace a journey on a map.
• Make a booklet.
• Make a poster.
• Write an essay
• Write a poem.
• Write a prayer.
• Write a letter.
• Make a newspaper article.

STEP 4 EXCEL: PULL EVERYTHING TOGETHER

In this step, the student shares his work with another person. This can be done at the end of the week or end of each day. The goal is for the student to prepare each assignment with the object of sharing in mind. When a student can teach some-one else what he has learned, it demonstrates that he knows the subject.

Step 4 Check List:

☐ Correct all written work to demonstrate correct spelling.

☐ Record any misspelled words in a Spelling Notebook.

☐ Correct all written work to demonstrate correct and effective use of grammar and punctuation.

☐ Add any new words or terms encountered to a Vocabulary Notebook

☐ Use each word or term in a sentence, either orally or in writing.

☐ Add corrected written work, maps, or any illustrations to a Portfolio.

☐ Add any important people or events to a Time Line Book.

☐ Share and explain what was learned with a friend or family member.

Heart of Wisdom Four-Year Plan

YEAR ONE

ANCIENT HISTORY	PHYSICAL SCIENCE
Adam to Abraham	Creation
Mesopotamia	Light
Ancient Egypt	Energy
Ancient Israel	Matter
Ancient Greece	Motion
Ancient Rome	Electricity
The Messiah	

YEAR TWO

WORLD HISTORY	EARTH SCIENCE AND BOTANY
Early Church	Weather
Vikings	Oceanography
Middle Ages	Botany
Renaissance	Geology
Reformation	Astronomy

YEAR THREE

EARLY AMERICAN HISTORY	THE ANIMAL WORLD
Age of Exploration	Marine Biology
Pilgrims to Colonies	Ornithology (Birds)
Colonies to Country	Entomology (Insects)
Civil War and Reconstruction	Earth Zoology
American West	

YEAR FOUR

INDUSTRIAL ERA–MODERN TIMES	ANATOMY
Industrial Era	Cell Design
World War I	Brain/Nervous System
The Depression	Skeletal/Muscular Systems
World War II	Respiratory/Digestive Systems
Holocaust	Heart/Circulatory System
Modern Times (1950 until Today)	Reproductive System

GOD'S WORLD: ACADEMIC STUDIES

The Heart of Wisdom course of study (see chart on the page140) is a logical structure of history and science unit studies (for grades K-12). For grades 7–12 we recommend you add life skill unit studies. The course is designed to be repeated every four years. History is taught chronologically and science is taught in the order of the days of creation. Literature, spelling, vocabulary, composition, character, and fine arts are taught, not as isolated subjects, but as interactive skills with each unit study theme. Math, grammar, and phonics are taught at grade level.

The Bible is studied every year. Students complete approximately five to seven history units and four to six science units per year. This suggested course of study can be easily adapted to fit different families' needs. The course does not have to be followed in order. You can rotate units according to the tastes of your children, or alter the course to the studies your child needs to complete his or her school year objectives.

The course of study can be followed as an outline to create your own unit studies, or as a guide to choosing preplanned studies. The book, *The Heart of Wisdom Teaching Approach* includes a section explaining the H.O.W. Bible-focused teaching philosophies and a section describing how you can make your own lessons following the course of study. The book also includes many outlines, resources (living books), and suggested activities. It's a how-to book for those desiring a Bible-focused, family-centered program to teach students a love of learning.

Preplanned unit studies (plants, Civil War, astronomy, etc.) by various publishers are available from several homeschool suppliers. Heart of Wisdom is in the process of publishing unit studies based on the philosophies outlined in Chapter 8 of this book. Each H.O.W. unit includes links to Internet sources. Each history volume includes five to seven units, while each science volume includes four to six units. Each unit includes: Overview, Objectives, Time Line, Vocabulary, Resource Lists, and approximatly twenty 4 Step Lessons (Excite, Examine, Expand, Excel).

See our Internet site at http://Homeschool-Books.com for publishing progress and sample lessons. The unit studies are available as EBooks (instant download to be read from your computer), individual books and combined volumes.

Step 3 Activities

-Tape-record a section of the Bible reading you especially liked. Tell why you chose this part. Add background music to fit the mood of the passage.

-Create a political cartoon, caricature, or cartoon strip for some event or character in the Bible reading.

-Create a mural, diorama, 3-dimensional figure, costume, or mobile to depict an event or person in the Bible reading.

-Make an acrostic using a character in the Bible reading. Tell about the character using each letter from the title.

-Make a time line for the events in the story.

-Create a travel brochure depicting points of interest in the Bible reading. Include transportation used, landforms, kinds of housing, natural beauty, etc.

*Ancient History:
Adam to Messiah*

Includes seven Ancient
History Unit Studies

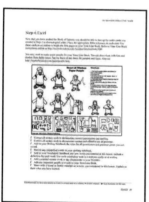

GETTING STARTED

HISTORY

We suggest the first year families get a good fundamental ovewrview of the Bible times, history, and culture of the ancient peoples by reading most of the Old Testament and the gospels, intertwined with ancient history studies by completing the the first seven unit studies: *Adam to Abraham, Mesopotamia, Ancient Egypt, Ancient Israel, Ancient Greece, Ancient Rome* and *The Messiah*. Available in the combined volume *Ancient History: Adam to Messiah*.

The entire family learns how God's people interacted with and lived among each of the world's civilizations. These lessons are an introduction to the Mesopotamian world of the patriarchs, the Egyptian world of the Exodus, the Babylonian world of Daniel, the Persian world of Esther, and the many Bible stories that show us not only the faithfulness of our God, and the greatness of our privileges, but also the marvelous wisdom of the plan of salvation. With these studies we can train our children to have a personal knowledge of God and His instruction telling us how to live. His Word reveals His will and spells out the kind of person He wants each of us to be. By obeying its commands, thinking as it tells us to think, and accepting the Savior it presents, we can learn how to live in our complex world. See the back of this book or our web site for more information.

SCIENCE

Heart of Wisdom first year set of science unit studies are in the order of the days of Creation: Creation (teaching evidence for a six day Creation and refuting evolution), Light, Energy, Matter, Motion, and Electricity.

The science unit studies are full of Bible illustrations. For example the unit on Light—this unit study reveals the mysteries of the light which God created for us. You begin with God's words, "Let there be light," then embark on a fascinating journey through the centuries, as your (and you!) children discover the physical properties of light while they come to understand that the character of God can be comprehended by observing what light is and what it does.

Light is a form of energy and may be produced in many different ways, not just by sun and stars. On the forth day of creation God caused the light of the sun to rule (govern) the day and the light of the moon and the stars to rule the night. Psalms 19:1 says, The heavens declare the glory of God; the

142

See the Wisdom Unit Study on page 130

skies proclaim the work of His hands. God's lights in skies unquestionably declare God's glory. The study of light helps us to understand and appreciate the world God has created.

HOW Unit Studies are also available as individual titles

Light has many applications in the Bible, physical, spiritual, moral or figurative. It is symbolic of Glory of God, of His purity, of His wisdom and His guidance. Moses saw the glory of God in the burning bush. Christ is our light the source of all wisdom and referred to as the Sun of righteousness. Light frequently signifies instruction, God's word a lamp unto our feet. Light symbolizes testimony.

John the Baptist, was called a "burning and a shining light." Saul of Tarsus had a dramatic encounter with the Light of God on the road to Damascus. The disciples were called "the light of the world." Believers are described as enlightened by Christ the light of the world who calls people "out of darkness into his marvelous light." Jesus said, "*I am the light of the world: he that followeth me shall not walk in darkness, but shall have the light of life.*" and "*As long as I am in the world, I am the light of the world.*" (John 8:12; 9:5).

In this science unit study together, you and your students will:

Learn about the physical characteristics of light as discovered by scientists throughout history

Learn how light is used in the Bible; how it is symbolic of the Glory of God, His purity, His wisdom, and guidance.

See how the creation and beauty of light reveal God, and that the physical properties of light are a picture of God: He is radiant or luminous energy which allows us to perform the functions of physical sight and spiritual sight;

Learn that apart from the light of the Word, we cannot see where we are or what we are doing, nor can we serve God effectively.

You don't need Heart of Wisdom Unit Studies to teach you these things. Sit down and dig into your Bible! Pray and ask God to lead you. He will show you the path He wants you to take.

SAMPLES OF STUDENT'S WORK

The following pages contain a few samples from HOW student's Creation and Ancient Egypt portfolios. We encourge student's to submit samples of their work to display on our Web site. You can see more samples at http://Homeschool-Books.com.

FROG PLAGUES

Paper doll characters

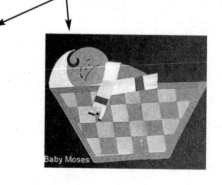

WHAT YOUR CHILD NEEDS TO KNOW WHEN

The images below are a good example of a family's Bible study with a wide age spread studying the same topic. The first Jonah page was created by a 4 year old with mom's help using scrapbook paper and stickers. (See our Web site for more information on "Scrapbooking to Learn." The second Jonah page was created by a teen learning an desk top publishing program on the computer.

Joanah's Prayer

Then Jonah prayed unto the Lord his God out of the fish's belly, And said, I cried by reason of mine affliction unto the Lord, and he heard me; out of the belly of hell cried I, and thou heardest my voice. For thou hadst cast me into the deep, in the midst of the seas; and the floods compassed me about: all thy billows and thy waves passed over me. Then I said, I am cast out of thy sight; yet I will look again toward thy holy temple. The waters compassed me about, even to the soul: the depth closed me round about, the weeds were wrapped about my head. I went down to the bottoms of the mountains; the earth with her bars was about me for ever: yet hast thou brought up my life from corruption, O Lord my God. When my soul fainted within me I remembered the LORD: and my prayer came in unto thee, into thine holy temple. They that observe lying vanities forsake their own mercy. But I will sacrifice unto thee with the voice of thanksgiving; I will pay that that I have vowed. Salvation is of the Lord.

And the Lord spake unto the fish, and it vomited out Jonah upon the dry land.
Jonah 2: 1 - 10

JONAH

"One of the single most instructive activities you and your child could participate in is writing short stories together.

Allow the child to dictate the story as you write down the words. It's fine to correct his language as you write as long as it is not done in a discouraging way. Say each word slowly, sound the letters or letter blends as you write, and then spell the word back before going to the next word. Frequently repeat the sentence as you are completing it so the child (and you) don't forget what you are writing. Read each sentence as it is finished, pointing out the word as you read. When you are finished with he story, allow the child to illustrate it, or work together to add some special "pizzazz." You will find that with practice, the child will be able to read the story himself. Encourage him by suggesting he read to any interested person that comes to visit."

—Mark B. Thogmartin,
*Teach a Child to Read
with Children's Books*

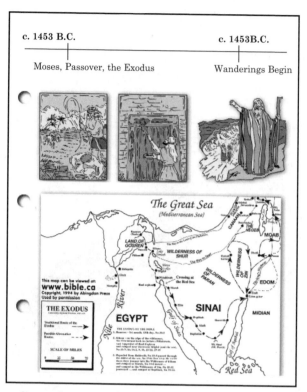

Sample page from a Bible Time Line Book

SECTION IV
EVALUATION CHECK LISTS

CHAPTER 10

BIBLE READING
The Solid Foundation

True learning, I believe, is learning something to the point at which it becomes second nature. Reading and math are good academic examples. Normally, we can read without thinking of how to sound out letters. Most of us know the multiplication tables without thinking. This applies to all areas of life.

Shouldn't our goal be to instill God's Word into our children, the way God instills the nurturing or protecting instinct into parents? Can we teach them, by word and deed, to the point that they would recognize evil—without thinking—and automatically turn away? Can we teach our precious ones to respond—automatically—in kindness to an unkind deed? Yes, we can.

PRIORITY: GOD'S WORD

If I could give only one piece of advice to a new home schooler, it would be this:

Do not get so wrapped up in academics that you leave out the most important thing. The Bible is the only book in which true wisdom is found. Teaching your children to apply God's truth will teach them to discern what's right or wrong, true or false, loving or cruel, profitable or foolish, noble or cowardly. Start every morning in God's Word! If you start with other subjects, Bible easily gets pushed out of the way.

Remember the saying that goes something like this: "Give a man a fish and you've fed him for a day, but teach a man to fish and you've fed him for life." The greatest gift you will ever give your child will be to teach him to develop the habit of purposefully reading, studying, and applying God's Word daily. It will affect every area of his life, every day of his life.

Don't believe that Bible study is not a legitimate subject—it is! the Bible is great literature, with many literary forms and devices—poetry, prose, allegory, epic, parable, history, even humor. The Bible is also regarded as a collection of materials for research into ancient history and culture. The books of the Old and New Testaments, are treated by many historians, in the same way as any other documents used for research into the history, religion, and culture of the ancient world. Old Testament scholarship is part of the study of the ancient Near East, and New Testament scholarship is part of the study of Graeco-Roman civilization.

Bible reading should be the highest priority in your child's studies. Students study literary forms and cultural background in the books of the Bible and apply the messages to their lives, to their relationships, and to the world. The Bible is the perfect textbook (2 Timothy 3:16-17).

J. I. Packard writes in the book *Knowing God*:

A study of the nature and character of God is the most practical project anyone can engage in. Knowing about God is crucially important for the living of our lives….We are cruel to ourselves if we try to live in the world without knowing about the God whose world it is and who runs it. The world becomes a strange, mad, painful place, and life disappointing and unpleasant business for those who do not know about God. Disregard the study of God and you sentence yourself to stumble and blunder through life blindfolded, as it were, with no sense of direction and no understanding of what surrounds you. This way you can waste your life and lose your soul.

USING THE CHECK LIST

The Check List in this chapter is based on reading the Bible through in one year, reading between thirty minutes to an hour (the amount of time for most television programs), five days a week. You may use the Check List according to the selected daily schedule, or ignore the suggested schedule and use your own. Both the verses and their corresponding *The Narrated Bible* page numbers are included in the Check List. (A Check List for seven daily readings is included in the back of *The Narrated Bible*.)

Please realize that this plan is only one option. Bible study is not measured in the number of verses we cover at one time, nor in the number of insights we are able to glean from one verse. Rather, the Bible is where we meet God to hear His Word. God opens our understanding when He sees fit. As always, God is in control. He knows the best time to reveal truth to us each individually.

You need to read the Bible at a pace you feel comfortable with. Our goal is to read though the Bible to get the whole picture. There's nothing special about the one-year (or 52-week) time frame. You can read though the Bible in two years or longer. This program is just a framework to get you started. Rely on the Holy Spirit to guide you through the readings. The most important thing for us to remember is not to focus upon the quantity of information we learn but to remain faithful to whatever spiritual truth God has entrusted to our care.

The previous chapter explains how the daily Bible readings can also be used to teach or reinforce language arts skills.

One Year through God's Word
Using *THE NARRATED BIBLE**

*THE NARRATED BIBLE IS A NARRATION BY F. LAGARD SMITH USING THE NEW INTERNATIONAL VERSION (NIV), PUBLISHED BY HARVEST HOUSE PUBLISHERS, EUGENE, OREGON 97402

WEEK ONE	NARRATED BIBLE	CHAPTER/VERSE
Beginnings of Early Mankind (Creation to ca. 2100 B.C.)		
The Beginnings	1	Genesis 1:1-2:4 ❑
Adam and Eve	3	Genesis 2:4-3:24 ❑
First Three Sons of Adam and Eve	6	Genesis 4:1-26 ❑
Descendants from Adam to Noah	8	Genesis 5:1-32 ❑
Mankind's Degeneration into Wickedness	11	Genesis 6:1-8 ❑
Noah and the Flood	12	Genesis 6:9-9:17 ❑
Human Condition Remains Sinful	16	Genesis 9:18-29 ❑
Dispersion of the Human Family	17	Genesis 11:1-9 ❑
Beginning of Nations	18	Genesis 10:1-32 ❑
Descendants from Shem to Abram	20	Genesis 11:10-26 ❑
Job, the Righteous Sufferer	22	The Book of Job ❑
Period of the Patriarchs (ca. 2100-1525 B.C.)		
The Call of Abram	23	Genesis 12:1-9 ❑
Abram Dishonors Himself in Egypt	24	Genesis 12:10-20 ❑
Separation of Abram and Lot	25	Genesis 13:1-18 ❑
Defeat of the Kings	27	Genesis 14:1-20 ❑
God's Covenant with Abram	29	Genesis 15:1-21 ❑
Birth of Ishmael Through Hagar	30	Genesis 16:1-16 ❑
Names and Circumcision as Signs of Covenant	32	Genesis 17:1-27 ❑
Appearance of Heavenly Visitors	34	Genesis 18:1-15 ❑
Destruction of Sodom and Gomorrah	35	Genesis 18:16-28 ❑
The Scheme of Lot's Daughters	38	Genesis 19:30-38 ❑

WEEK TWO		
Abraham Deceives Abimelech	39	Genesis 20:1-18 ❑
The Birth of Isaac	41	Genesis 21:1-7 ❑
Abraham and Abimelech Settle Dispute	42	Genesis 21:22-34 ❑
Expulsion of Hagar and Ishmael	43	Genesis 21:8-21 ❑
Abraham's Ultimate Test of Faith	44	Genesis 22:1-19 ❑
News Regarding Nahor's Family	45	Genesis 22:20-24 ❑
Sarah's Death and Burial	46	Genesis 23:1-20 ❑
Abraham Arranges Wife for Isaac	47	Genesis 24:1-67 ❑
Abraham Marries Keturah	50	Genesis 25:1-6 ❑
Death of Abraham	51	Genesis 25:7-10 ❑
Last Account of Ishmael	51	Genesis 25:12-18 ❑
Esau and Jacob	52	Genesis 25:11-28 ❑
A Birthright is Sold	53	Genesis 25:29-34 ❑
Isaac Follows in Abraham's Footsteps	53	Genesis 26:1-33 ❑
Trouble Between Jacob and Esau	55	Genesis 26:34-35; 27:1-41 ❑
Jacob Leaves for Haran	58	Genesis 27:42-46; 28:5-22 ❑
Jacob Marries and Has Children	59	Genesis 29:1-35 ❑
Laban and Jacob Outsmart Each Other	62	Genesis 30:25-43 ❑
Jacob Leaves Laban	63	Genesis 31:1-55 ❑
Jacob Returns to Canaan	66	Genesis 32:1-32 ❑

WEEK TEN

WEEK TWENTY-ONE

CHAPTER 11

CHARACTER EVALUATION
ERECTING THE BUILDING

It may be difficult, at first, reexamining our beliefs and attitudes about education. In doing so, it is essential that we compare our educational goals to God's Word. Education affects every area of human experience. The way we see our world, the values we hold important, the skills we feel are necessary, our opinions of the past, present, and future—all are clearly affected by our education and our educational philosophies. Education is a process of forming one for life.

We can teach a child self-control by using external force, until the child ultimately learns his own self-control by using his internal force. We can also teach a child to yield himself to God by giving up fleshly desires.

I beseech you therefore, brethren, by the mercies of God, that ye present your bodies a living sacrifice, holy, acceptable unto God, which is your reasonable service. And be not conformed to this world: but be ye transformed by the renewing of your mind, that ye may prove what is that good, and acceptable, and perfect, will of God (Romans 12:1-2).

All the virtues and holy tempers of Christianity are not ours unless they become the virtues and tempers of our ordinary life. In that Christianity is so far from leaving us to live in the common ways of life, conforming to the folly of customs, and gratifying the passions and tempers which the spirit of the world delights in, it is equally far from indulging us in any of these things. Its virtues, which it makes necessary to salvation, are only so many ways of living above and contrary to the world, in all the common actions of our lives. If our common life is not a common course of humility, self-denial, renunciation of the world, poverty of spirit, and heavenly affection, we do not live the lives of Christians.

The following story on the next page is an illustration of the fact that morals and values according to God's Word are far superior to the state's intellectual wisdom.

HIRING A QUALIFIED EMPLOYEE

You are the owner of a bakery store and you need to hire a manager. You have two people to choose from. Whom would you hire?

1. An expert baker with no morals and values.
2. An inexperienced person with godly morals and values.

Yes, it would be nice to hire an experienced baker with morals and values, but a number 3 is not available. Let's look at what could happen, over a period of time, if you hired Number 1 as opposed to Number 2.

Months 1-3

Hiring Number 1 would give you a jump-start in business. The expert baker could already plan recipes, bake, keep records, take care of all ordering and deliveries, deliver products on time, and answer customers' questions. How wonderful for you. You are able to leave the store and attend to other business with the security of knowing your new manager can take care of any problem. You are thinking of opening a second bakery.

Hiring Number 2 will require you to be present in the store to train your new employee. You will have to train him to follow all policies and procedures, to bake, keep records, take care of all ordering and deliveries, deliver products on time, and answer questions. Mistakes may be made and orders may be late. You may even encounter some angry customers who will not return. You cannot leave the store because the new employee may need you to handle a problem he has not yet encountered.

Month 4

Number 1 continues to produce good products, although he calls in sick frequently. You start questioning some of the record keeping. When you ask Number 1 about any problem, the replies seem inconsistent with accounts he is recording. Number 1 wants to do things his way, and you are aggravated because you want business handled differently. Two customers have complained about receiving the wrong change. You start staying at the store more because things just seem strange. You start praying for wisdom to handle this situation.

Number 2 learns well. He is caring, and has been very diligent, prompt, industrious, and hardworking in all areas. You can now leave the store and only call to check on things. Once in a while he makes a minor mistake but is willing to learn from mistakes and is very respectful.

Month 10

Your accountant calls to tell you that you are $xx.xx in the red. You look over the records and realize Number 1 has been fixing the records and probably skimming from the register. Number 1 has also been flirting with one of the female customers, and she is suing your business for sexual harassment. You have lost all profits made for the entire year. Number 2 is handling business just the way you like things to be done. You are able to leave the store and attend to other business with the security of knowing that your new manager can take care of any problem. The food is great and word of mouth about your bakery spreads. Business prospers and expands. You are thinking of opening a second bakery.

That may be an exaggerated account, but it is very possible. If you hire someone you can trust, you can always train him or her. If he or she is a Christian, striving to follow God's will, your employee should be diligent, honest, and respectful. The point is, academic skills are secondary. There are thousands of workers like our Number 1, but very few of the dependable kind of workers like the story's Number 2.

SAMPLES OF HOW TO USE THE CHARACTER TRAITS LIST

FOUR-STEP LESSON

Step 1. Introduction: Today we'll be doing a character study on being appreciative. Can you think of some examples of appreciation? Discuss and interact.

Step 2. Learn about the trait: Read the definition: Expressing, in words, actions, and thoughts, value to the actions of God and others the ways they have served me.

Read the Bible verse: God's Word says, *"In every thing give thanks: for this is the will of God in Christ Jesus concerning you"* (1 Thessalonians 5:18).

Step 3. Do something with what was learned: Students can copy or dictate the Bible verse and/or the definition (younger children can narrate the meaning orally). Or students can write or narrate a story about the character trait.

Step 4. Share with another: The purpose is to show appreciation sometime today. Share how you showed appreciation with your parents.

WATCH FOR A TEACHABLE MOMENT

Wait for a child to show a positive or negative character trait. Example: Susie won't share her toy with her younger brother. Take Susie into your lap and discuss generosity. Read the definition and Bible verse listed under "generous." Ask Susie how she can show generosity.

Reinforce positive behavior by pointing out positive character. Example: Johnny listens attentively to a lesson. Read the definition and Bible verse listed under "attentive." Congratulate Johnny for being attentive.

CHARACTER TRAITS

TRAIT WORD	DEFINITION	SCRIPTURE REFERENCE
APPRECIATIVE:	Expressing, in words, actions, and thoughts, value to the actions of God and others the ways they have served me.	1 Thessalonians 5:18—*In every thing give thanks: for this is the will of God in Christ Jesus concerning you.*
ATTENTIVE:	Being intent; observant; regarding a situation or person with care. Being attentive to the words, the manner, and matter of a speaker at the same time. Demonstrating that the person is worthy by giving genuine attention and consideration to God's Word or a person's words.	Hebrews 2:1—*Therefore we ought to give the more earnest heed to the things which we have heard, lest at any time we should let them slip.*
AVAILABLE:	Being accessible to others. Scheduling priorities to serve others in need.	Matthew 9:9—*And as Jesus passed forth from thence, he saw a man, named Matthew, sitting at the receipt of custom: and he saith unto him, Follow me. And he arose, and followed him.*
COMMITTED:	Giving in trust; putting into the hands or power of another.	2 Timothy 2—*The things thou hast heard of me, commit to faithful men.* Psalms 37:5—*Commit thy way unto the LORD; trust also in him; and he shall bring it to pass.*
COMPASSIONATE:	Giving of love and sorrow; at least some portion of love generally attends the pain or regret; to meet another's needs without experiencing anything in return.	Psalms 78—*He being full of compassion, forgave their iniquity.* Luke 15—*His father had compassion, and ran, and fell on his neck, and kissed him.* 1 Peter 3:8—*Finally, be ye all of one mind, having compassion one of another, love as brethren, be pitiful, be courteous:*
CONCERNED:	Regarding another with care. Bearing one another's burdens with tenderness and respect.	Galatians 6:2—*Bear ye one another's burdens, and so fulfill the law of Christ.*
CONFIDENT:	Having trust that whatever I say or do will benefit me and others.	Philippians 4:13—*I can do all things through Christ which strengtheneth me.*
CONSIDERATE:	Being thoughtful of others and their feelings.	Philippians 2:4—*Look not every man on his own things, but every man also on the things of others.*
CONSISTENT:	Being fixed or firm in mind, purpose, affection or principle; unshaken; unmoved. Being certain; steady; firm, and adherent to God's principles; diligent to purpose, or to duties.	1 Corinthians 15:58—*Therefore, my beloved brethren, be ye steadfast, unmoveable, always abounding in the work of the Lord, forasmuch as ye know that your labour is not in vain in the Lord.*
CONTENT:	Having rest or quietness of mind in the present condition; satisfaction which holds the mind in peace. Not having	Philippians 4:11—*Not that I speak in respect of want: for I have learned, in whatsoever state I am, therewith to be content.*

CHARACTER TRAITS

TRAIT WORD	DEFINITION	SCRIPTURE REFERENCE
	opposition, or further desire. Implying a degree of happiness in all situations because God will provide for all our needs.	1 Timothy 6—*Having food and raiment, let us be therewith content.*
COOPERATIVE:	Working with other Christians in harmony. Note: This is far different from what the state calls "cooperation."	Psalms 33:1—*Behold, how good and how pleasant it is for brethren to dwell together in unity!*
COURAGEOUS:	Realizing that God is giving us strength to endure any trial or danger. Being brave; having that quality of mind which enables men to encounter danger and difficulties with firmness, boldness, and resolution. Courage arises from a sense of duty; acts in a uniform manner.	Deuteronomy 31:6—*Be strong and of good courage, fear not, nor be afraid of them: for the LORD thy God, he it is that doth go with thee; he will not fail thee, nor forsake thee.*
CREATIVE:	Being able to perform a necessity or task from a different point of view.	Romans 12:2—*And be not conformed to this world: but be ye transformed by the renewing of your mind, that ye may prove what is that good, and acceptable, and perfect, will of God.*
DECISIVE:	Having the quality of determining a subject of deliberation or putting an end to a controversy by relying on the perfect will of God.	Joshua 24:15—*And if it seem evil unto you to serve the LORD, choose you this day whom ye will serve; whether the gods which your fathers served that were on the other side of the flood, or the gods of the Amorites, in whose land ye dwell: but as for me and my house, we will serve the LORD.*
DEPENDABLE	Being worthy of trust, to the point that someone can depend on you. Doing what you said you would do even if it means self-denial. We depend on God for existence; we depend on air for respiration; vegetation depends on heat and moisture; the peace of society depends on good laws and a faithful administration.	1 Timothy 6:20—*O Timothy, keep that which is committed to thy trust, avoiding profane and vain babblings, and oppositions of science falsely so called....*
DETERMINED:	Having a firm or fixed purpose, as a determined man; or manifesting a firm resolution, to accomplish God's will.	1 Corinthians 2:2—*For I determined not to know any thing among you, save Jesus Christ, and him crucified.*
DILIGENT:	Not just a trait—a command from God. Steady in application to business; not careless; constant in effort or exertion to accomplish what is undertaken; industrious; not idle or negligent; applied to persons.	Deuteronomy 6:17—*Ye shall diligently keep the commandments of the Lord your God.* Proverbs 22:29—*Seest thou a man diligent in his business? He shall stand before kings.* Colossians 3:23—*And whatsoever ye do, do it heartily, as to the Lord, and not unto men;*

CHARACTER TRAITS

TRAIT WORD	DEFINITION	SCRIPTURE REFERENCE
DISCERNING:	Having power to discern; capable of seeing, discriminating, knowing, and judging a difficult situation, and being able to make an accurate judgment.	Ezekiel 44:23—*And they shall teach my people the difference between the holy and profane, and cause them to discern between the unclean and the clean.*
DISCREET	Prudent; wise in avoiding errors or evil, and in selecting the best means to accomplish a purpose; circumspect; cautious. It is the discreet man, not the witty, nor the learned, nor the brave, who guides the conversation, and gives measures to society.	Genesis 41:33—*Let Pharaoh look out a man discreet and wise.* Psalms 112:5—*A good man showeth favour, and lendeth: he will guide his affairs with discretion.*
EFFICIENT:	Causing effects or producing. The efficient cause is that which produces; the final cause is that for which it is produced. Preparing yourself to accomplish the greatest productiveness.	Ephesians 5:16—*Redeeming the time, because the days are evil.*
EQUITABLE:	Being equal in regard to the rights of others; distributing equal justice; giving each his due; being just and impartial according to God's Law.	Proverbs 1:3—*To receive the instruction of wisdom, justice, and judgment, and equity.*
FAIR:	Honest; honorable; mild; opposed to insidious and compulsory actions. To be able to accomplish a thing by looking at everyone's side.	Matthew 7:12—*Therefore all things whatsoever ye would that men should do to you, do ye even so to them: for this is the law and the prophets.*
FAITHFUL:	Firmly adhering to duty; of true fidelity; loyal; true to allegiance; as a faithful subject. Being constant in the performance of duties or services and attending to commands of authority.	1 Corinthians 4:2—*Moreover it is required in stewards, that a man be found faithful.*
FEARLESS:	Facing danger boldly and with determination, for God gave us a spirit of power.	2 Timothy 1:7—*For God hath not given us the spirit of fear; but of power, and of love, and of a sound mind.*
FLEXIBLE:	Setting affections on things above, not on earthly things that can be changed by others.	Colossians 3:2—*Set your affection on things above, not on things on the earth.*
FORGIVING:	Overlooking one another's faults by means of expressing to them Christ's love (responding as if there were no faults)	Colossians 3:13—*Forbearing one another, and forgiving one another, if any man have a quarrel against any: even as Christ forgave you, so also do ye.*

CHARACTER TRAITS

FORTITUDE:	Having the strength or firmness of mind or soul which enables a person to encounter danger with coolness and courage, or to bear pain or adversity without murmuring, depression, or despondency. Fortitude is the basis or source of genuine courage or intrepidity in danger, of patience in suffering, of forbearance under injuries, and of magnanimity in all conditions of life. Having patience to bear continued suffering.	Romans 5:1-5—*Therefore being justified by faith, we have peace with God through our Lord Jesus Christ: By whom also we have access by faith into this grace wherein we stand, and rejoice in hope of the glory of God. And not only so, but we glory in tribulations also: knowing that tribulation worketh patience; And patience, experience; and experience, hope: And hope maketh not ashamed; because the love of God is shed abroad in our hearts by the Holy Ghost which is given unto us.*
FRIENDLY:	Having the temper and disposition of a friend; kind; favorable; disposed to promoting the good of another. Thou to mankind be good and friendly still, and oft return.	Proverbs 18:24—*A man that hath friends must show himself friendly: and there is a friend that sticketh closer than a brother.*
GENTLE:	Mild; meek; soft; bland; not rough, harsh, or severe; as a gentle nature, temper, or disposition; a gentle manner; a gentle address; a gentle voice.	Acts 20:35—*I have showed you all things, how that so labouring ye ought to support the weak, and to remember the words of the Lord Jesus, how he said, It is more blessed to give than to receive.*
HONEST:	Upright; just; fair in dealing with others; free from trickiness and fraud; acting and having the disposition to act at all times according to justice or correct moral principles; applied to persons.	2 Timothy 2:24—*And the servant of the Lord must not strive; but be gentle unto all men, apt to teach, patient.* 2 Corinthians 8:21—*Providing for honest things, not only in the sight of the Lord, but also in the sight of men.*
HUMBLE:	Modest; meek; submissive; as opposed to proud, haughty, arrogant or assuming. In an evangelical sense, having a low opinion of one's self, and a deep sense of unworthiness in the sight of God.	James 4—*God resisteth the proud, but giveth grace to the humble.* 1 Peter 5:5-6—*Likewise, ye younger, submit yourselves unto the elder. Yea, all of you be subject one to another, and be clothed with humility: for God resisteth the proud, and giveth grace to the humble. Humble yourselves therefore under the mighty hand of God, that he may exalt you in due time:*
JOYFUL:	Full of joy; very glad; exulting.	Ephesians 5:19—*Speaking to yourselves in psalms and hymns and spiritual songs, singing and making melody in your heart to the Lord;*
KIND:	Disposed to do good to others, and to make them happy by granting their requests, supplying their wants or assisting them in distress; having tenderness or goodness of nature; benevolent; benignant.	Ephesians 4:32—*And be ye kind one to another, tenderhearted, forgiving one another, even as God for Christ's sake hath forgiven you.*

CHARACTER TRAITS

TRAIT WORD	DEFINITION	SCRIPTURE REFERENCE
LOYAL:	Faithful to a friend or superior; true to plighted faith, duty, or love; not treacherous; used of subjects to their king, and of husband, wife, children.	John 15:13—*Greater love hath no man than this, that a man lay down his life for his friends.*
MEEK:	Mild of temper; soft; gentle; not easily provoked or irritated; yielding; given to forbearance under injuries. Appropriately humble, in an evangelical sense; submissive to the divine will; not proud, self-sufficient, or refractory; not peevish and apt to complain.	Numbers 12:3—*Now the man Moses was very meek, above all men.* Matthew 11:29—Christ says, "*Learn of me, for I am meek and lowly in heart, and ye shall find rest to your souls.*" Matthew 5:5—*Blessed are the meek, for they shall inherit the earth…*
MERCIFUL:	Compassionate; tender; disposed to pity offenders and to forgive their offenses; unwilling to punish for injuries; applied appropriately to the Supreme being.	Exodus 34:6—*The Lord passed before him and proclaimed, the Lord, the Lord God, merciful and gracious, long-suffering and abundant in goodness and truth.* Luke 6:36—*Be ye therefore merciful, as your Father also is merciful.*
OBSERVANT:	Taking notice; attentively viewing or noticing; as an observant spectator or traveler. Obedient; adhering to in practice, i.e. "He is very observant of the rules of his order."	Mark 14:38—*Watch ye and pray, lest ye enter into temptation. The spirit truly is ready, but the flesh is weak.*
OPTIMISTIC:	Concentrating on the best conditions of any situation.	Romans 8:25—*But if we hope for that we see not, then do we with patience wait for it.*
PATIENT:	Having the quality of enduring evils without murmuring or fretfulness; sustaining afflictions of body or mind with fortitude, calmness, or Christian submission to the divine will; as a patient person, or a person of patient temper.	Hebrews 12:1—*Wherefore seeing we also are compassed about with so great a cloud of witnesses, let us lay aside every weight, and the sin which doth so easily beset us, and let us run with patience the race that is set before us,*
PEACEFUL:	Quiet; undisturbed; not in a state of commotion; mild; calm; as peaceful words; a peaceful temper.	John 16:33—*These things I have spoken unto you, that in me ye might have peace. In the world ye shall have tribulation: but be of good cheer; I have overcome the world.*
PERSEVERANT:	Persistent in any thing undertaken; continuing pursuit or prosecution of business or enterprise begun.	Galatians 6:9—*And let us not be weary in well doing: for in due season we shall reap, if we faint not.*
PLEASING:	One that pleases or gratifies; one that courts favor by humoring or flattering compliance or a show of obedience.	1 Corinthians 10:33—*Even as I please all men in all things, not seeking mine own profit, but the profit of many, that they may be saved.*

CHARACTER TRAITS

TRAIT WORD	DEFINITION	SCRIPTURE REFERENCE
PRUDENT:	Cautious; circumspect; practically wise; careful of the consequences of enterprises, measures, or actions.	Proverbs 14:15—*The simple believeth every word: but the prudent man looketh well to his going.*
PUNCTUAL:	Having scrupulous regard to time, appointments, promises, or rules; as, to attend a meeting punctually; to pay debts or rent punctually; to observe punctually one's engagements.	Ecclesiastes 3:1—*To every thing there is a season, and a time to every purpose under the heaven:*
PURPOSEFUL:	By design; intentionally; with predetermination.	Psalms 119:2—*Blessed are they that keep his testimonies, and that seek him with the whole heart.*
RESOURCEFUL:	Efficient and willing to take upon oneself projects that others may overlook.	1 Thessalonians 4:11—*And that ye study to be quiet, and to do your own business, and to work with your own hands, as we commanded you…*
RESPECTFUL:	Viewing or considering others with a degree of reverence; esteeming as possessed of worth.	1 Thessalonians 5:12-13—*And we beseech you, brethren, to know them which labour among you, and are over you in the Lord, and admonish you; And to esteem them very highly in love for their work's sake. And be at peace among yourselves.*
RESPONSIBLE:	Governed by reason; being under the influence of reason; thinking, speaking, or acting rationally or according to the dictates of reason.	Romans 14:12—*So then every one of us shall give account of himself to God.*
SECURE:	Confident; not distrustful; having faith in God that He will work all things to His glory.	Job 11:18—*And thou shalt be secure, because there is hope; yea, thou shalt dig about thee, and thou shalt take thy rest in safety.*
SELF-CONTROLLED:	Checking; restraining; governing ones tongue, deeds, and actions. Having instant obedience to the Holy Spirit, developed through outward discipline.	(Galatians 5:24-25) Proverbs 25:28—*He that hath no rule over his own spirit is like a city that is broken down, and without walls.*
SINCERE:	Honest; with real purity of heart; without simulation or disguise.	Joshua 24:14—*Now therefore fear the LORD, and serve him in sincerity and in truth: and put away the gods which your fathers served on the other side of the flood, and in Egypt; and serve ye the LORD.*
SUBMISSIVE:	Cheerfully yielding to the will or power of another; obedient.	Hebrews 13:17—*Obey them that have the rule over you, and submit yourselves: for they watch for your souls, as they that must give account, that they may do it with joy, and not with grief: for that is unprofitable for you.*

CHARACTER TRAITS

TRAIT WORD	DEFINITION	SCRIPTURE REFERENCE
TACTFUL:	Saying and doing the right things with concern for others' feelings.	Colossians 4:6—*Let your speech be always with grace, seasoned with salt, that ye may know how ye ought to answer every man.*
THRIFTY:	Frugal; sparing; using economy and good management of property.	Proverbs 21:20 *There is treasure to be desired and oil in the dwelling of the wise; but a foolish man spendeth it up.*
TOLERANT:	Enduring; accepting others and willing to endure.	Romans 14:13—*Let us not therefore judge one another any more: but judge this rather, that no man put a stumbling block or an occasion to fall in his brother's way.*
TRUTHFUL:	Earning trust by reporting facts accurately.	Ephesians 4:25—*Wherefore putting away lying, speak every man truth with his neighbor: for we are members one of another.*
VIRTUOUS:	Morally good; abstaining from vice.	Philippians 4:8—*Finally, brethren, whatsoever things are true, whatsoever things are honest, whatsoever things are just, whatsoever things are pure, whatsoever things are lovely, whatsoever things are of good report; if there be any virtue, and if there be any praise, think on these things.*

Let no man despise thy youth; but be thou an example of the believers,
in the word, in conversation, in charity, in spirit, in faith, in purity.
Till I come, give attendance to reading, to exhortation, to doctrine.

1 Timothy 4:12-13

LANGUAGE ARTS

Language Mechanics • Language Expression • Spelling

• Study Skills • Reading

EVALUATION CHECK LIST FOR KINDERGARTEN

LANGUAGE ARTS

Kindergarten students should be able to do the following:

	CHILD'S NAME	CHILD'S NAME	CHILD'S NAME	CHILD'S NAME	CHILD'S NAME
Develop skill in gross motor functioning.	☐	☐	☐	☐	☐
Develop fine motor functioning.	☐	☐	☐	☐	☐
Develop hand-eye coordination.	☐	☐	☐	☐	☐
Recognize likenesses and differences of objects and pictures.	☐	☐	☐	☐	☐
Group objects and pictures into categories.	☐	☐	☐	☐	☐
Develop skill in auditory discrimination.	☐	☐	☐	☐	☐
Follow progression such as left-to-right, top-to-bottom and front-to-back.	☐	☐	☐	☐	☐
Position papers properly and hold a crayon or pencil correctly.	☐	☐	☐	☐	☐
Demonstrate basic handwriting strokes.	☐	☐	☐	☐	☐
Print own first name	☐	☐	☐	☐	☐
Recognize name when printed	☐	☐	☐	☐	☐
Recognize and name letters of the alphabet.	☐	☐	☐	☐	☐
Discriminate and identify upper-case and lower-case letters.	☐	☐	☐	☐	☐
Speak in complete sentences, most of the time.	☐	☐	☐	☐	☐
Complete sentences using context clues.	☐	☐	☐	☐	☐
Verbalize own experiences, needs, and wants.	☐	☐	☐	☐	☐
Make and describe observations.	☐	☐	☐	☐	☐
Ask questions.	☐	☐	☐	☐	☐
Describe the contents of a picture.	☐	☐	☐	☐	☐
Listen to a five-to ten-minute story.	☐	☐	☐	☐	☐
Retell a story.	☐	☐	☐	☐	☐
Listen to answer questions, predict an event or outcome, find the main idea or identify sequence.	☐	☐	☐	☐	☐
Repeat verses from memory.	☐	☐	☐	☐	☐
Use vocabulary necessary to describe self.	☐	☐	☐	☐	☐

EVALUATION CHECK LIST FOR KINDERGARTEN

LANGUAGE ARTS

Recognize rhyme, rhythm, and repetition in
   spoken words or literature............................. ☐ ☐ ☐ ☐ ☐

Identify colors. .... ☐ ☐ ☐ ☐ ☐

Name common objects. .... ☐ ☐ ☐ ☐ ☐

Speak clearly, properly, and politely. .... ☐ ☐ ☐ ☐ ☐

EVALUATION CHECK LIST FOR FIRST GRADE

LANGUAGE ARTS

First-grade students should be able to do the following:

	CHILD'S NAME	CHILD'S NAME	CHILD'S NAME	CHILD'S NAME	CHILD'S NAME

LANGUAGE MECHANICS AND EXPRESSION

	1	2	3	4	5
Alphabetize words through the first letter	☐	☐	☐	☐	☐
Identify correct capitalization of the pronoun "I."	☐	☐	☐	☐	☐
Recognize letters of the alphabet and the sounds they represent.	☐	☐	☐	☐	☐
Hold a pencil correctly, position the paper appropriately for left-or right-handedness, and sit in the correct writing position.	☐	☐	☐	☐	☐
Form all letters in manuscript, both upper and lower case.	☐	☐	☐	☐	☐
Print own name correctly.	☐	☐	☐	☐	☐
Copy simple sentences and/or short paragraphs.	☐	☐	☐	☐	☐
Use proper spacing between letters of a word and words of a sentence.	☐	☐	☐	☐	☐
Identify correct capitalization of the first word of a sentence.	☐	☐	☐	☐	☐
Identify the correct use of periods.	☐	☐	☐	☐	☐
Identify the correct use of question marks.	☐	☐	☐	☐	☐
Identify complete telling sentences.	☐	☐	☐	☐	☐
Identify complete asking sentences.	☐	☐	☐	☐	☐

SPELLING

	1	2	3	4	5
Spell words in isolation and in sentence dictation.	☐	☐	☐	☐	☐
Identify letter-sound associations for single initial consonants (excluding q and x).	☐	☐	☐	☐	☐
Substitute initial consonants to form new words					

EVALUATION CHECK LIST FOR FIRST GRADE

LANGUAGE ARTS

with the known word families (-*at*, -*ed*, -*it*, -*in*, -*ill*, -*ake*, -*ate*, -*an*, -*ax*, -*en*, *and* -*ing*)............... ❑ ❑ ❑ ❑ ❑

Identify letter-sound associations for single final consonants. .... ❑ ❑ ❑ ❑ ❑

Identify letter-sound associations for initial consonant digraphs (*ch*, *sh*, and "voiceless" *th*). .. ❑ ❑ ❑ ❑ ❑

Identify letter-sound associations for final consonant digraphs (*ch*, *sh*, *ck*). .... ❑ ❑ ❑ ❑ ❑

Identify letter-sound associations for initial consonant blends (consonant + *i* and consonant + *r* blends). .... ❑ ❑ ❑ ❑ ❑

Identify letter-sound associations for final consonant blends (*st*, *sk*)................................... ❑ ❑ ❑ ❑ ❑

Identify plural noun endings. .... ❑ ❑ ❑ ❑ ❑

Identify letter-sound associations for short vowels. .... ❑ ❑ ❑ ❑ ❑

Identify letter-sound associations for long vowels. .... ❑ ❑ ❑ ❑ ❑

Blend sounds together to form simple words. ❑ ❑ ❑ ❑ ❑

Recognize sight words................................... ❑ ❑ ❑ ❑ ❑

STUDY SKILLS

Demonstrate the ability to alphabetize words with different first letters .... ❑ ❑ ❑ ❑ ❑

LISTENING AND COMPREHENSION

Listen and respond to directions .... ❑ ❑ ❑ ❑ ❑

Listen for the purpose of answering simple questions. .... ❑ ❑ ❑ ❑ ❑

Listen to identify words that rhyme. .... ❑ ❑ ❑ ❑ ❑

EVALUATION CHECK LIST FOR FIRST GRADE

LANGUAGE ARTS

	CHILD'S NAME	CHILD'S NAME	CHILD'S NAME	CHILD'S NAME	CHILD'S NAME
Listen for the purpose of distinguishing like and unlike sounds.	☐	☐	☐	☐	☐
Listen to simple stories and retell in sequence.	☐	☐	☐	☐	☐
Use correct pronunciation in oral reading (period, question mark, comma and exclamation point).	☐	☐	☐	☐	☐
Use correct phrasing in oral reading.	☐	☐	☐	☐	☐
Recall what has been read silently or aloud.	☐	☐	☐	☐	☐
Participate in dramatization projects.	☐	☐	☐	☐	☐
Use details to identify story elements.	☐	☐	☐	☐	☐
Sequence events from a selection.	☐	☐	☐	☐	☐
Draw conclusions from given facts.	☐	☐	☐	☐	☐
Recognize words or phrases that tell who, what, when, where, why, or how.	☐	☐	☐	☐	☐
Answer simple questions after listening to a reading selection.	☐	☐	☐	☐	☐
Participate in a discussion by making relevant contribution to a specific topic.	☐	☐	☐	☐	☐
Communicate thoughts and feelings orally.	☐	☐	☐	☐	☐
Pronounce the basic 220 Dolch sight words (see page 300).	☐	☐	☐	☐	☐

EVALUATION CHECK LIST FOR SECOND GRADE

LANGUAGE ARTS

Second-grade students should be able to do the following:

LANGUAGE MECHANICS AND EXPRESSION

	CHILD'S NAME	CHILD'S NAME	CHILD'S NAME	CHILD'S NAME	CHILD'S NAME
Print legibly and neatly.	❑	❑	❑	❑	❑
Copy simple sentences using proper spacing between words within words and between sentences.	❑	❑	❑	❑	❑
Write simple sentences from dictation.	❑	❑	❑	❑	❑
Arrange words in logical order to form sentences.	❑	❑	❑	❑	❑
Identify correct capitalization of the first word of a sentence.	❑	❑	❑	❑	❑
Identify correct capitalization of the pronoun "I."	❑	❑	❑	❑	❑
Identify correct capitalization of proper nouns.	❑	❑	❑	❑	❑
Identify correct use of periods.	❑	❑	❑	❑	❑
Identify correct use of question marks.	❑	❑	❑	❑	❑
Identify complete telling sentences.	❑	❑	❑	❑	❑
Identify complete asking sentences.	❑	❑	❑	❑	❑
Identify common and proper nouns.	❑	❑	❑	❑	❑
Identify the two parts of a simple sentence.	❑	❑	❑	❑	❑
Verbalize own experiences, needs, and wants.	❑	❑	❑	❑	❑
Speak in complete and connected sentences.	❑	❑	❑	❑	❑
Use appropriate manner of speaking and control of voice in a given situation.	❑	❑	❑	❑	❑
Participate in conversation and discussion.	❑	❑	❑	❑	❑

SPELLING

	CHILD'S NAME	CHILD'S NAME	CHILD'S NAME	CHILD'S NAME	CHILD'S NAME
Spell words in isolation and from sentence dictation.	❑	❑	❑	❑	❑
Identify and complete rhymes.	❑	❑	❑	❑	❑
Identify correctly spelled words.	❑	❑	❑	❑	❑
Identify and form compound words.	❑	❑	❑	❑	❑

EVALUATION CHECK LIST FOR SECOND GRADE

LANGUAGE ARTS

Identify the base words in those formed with the following endings: -s, -es,-d, -ed, -ing, -ly, -er, -est. ☐ ☐ ☐ ☐ ☐

Divide words into syllables using the VC/CV rule. .... ☐ ☐ ☐ ☐ ☐

Recognize sight words....................................... ☐ ☐ ☐ ☐ ☐

Identify contractions. .... ☐ ☐ ☐ ☐ ☐

Identify letter-sound associations for consonants in the medial position. .... ☐ ☐ ☐ ☐ ☐

Identify letter-sound associations for initial consonant blends..................................... ☐ ☐ ☐ ☐ ☐

Identify letter-sound associations for final consonant blends.. ☐ ☐ ☐ ☐ ☐

Recognize letter-sound associations for consonant digraphs (ch, sh, wh, th, ck, ng, nk). .... ☐ ☐ ☐ ☐ ☐

Recognize letter-sound associations for long vowels. .... ☐ ☐ ☐ ☐ ☐

Recognize letter-sound associations for vowel digraphs. .... ☐ ☐ ☐ ☐ ☐

Identify letter-sound associations for short vowels. .... ☐ ☐ ☐ ☐ ☐

Use spelling patterns as clues to vowel sounds associated with the following rules. .... ☐ ☐ ☐ ☐ ☐

A word with a single vowel is usually short (cap, hop, cup). .... ☐ ☐ ☐ ☐ ☐

An e at the end of a one-syllable word usually makes the preceding vowel long (like, hope, make). If two vowels are together in a one-syllable word, the first is usually long and the second is silent (goat, keep, pie). .... ☐ ☐ ☐ ☐ ☐

Vowels followed by an r in one-syllable words are pronounced as ar and er (her, first, fur,

EVALUATION CHECK LIST FOR SECOND GRADE

LANGUAGE ARTS

car and *horn*). .... ☐ ☐ ☐ ☐ ☐

Identify word pairs that are synonyms,

antonym, and homonym......................... ☐ ☐ ☐ ☐ ☐

STUDY SKILLS

Perform a task by following simple, oral direc-

tions.. ☐ ☐ ☐ ☐ ☐

Alphabetize words through the second letter.. ☐ ☐ ☐ ☐ ☐

Use a primary picture dictionary. .... ☐ ☐ ☐ ☐ ☐

Group words and objects into categories. .... ☐ ☐ ☐ ☐ ☐

LISTENING AND COMPREHENSION

Select a title for a selection. .... ☐ ☐ ☐ ☐ ☐

Read to find the answer to a specific question. .. ☐ ☐ ☐ ☐ ☐

Read to verify a statement. .... ☐ ☐ ☐ ☐ ☐

Read silently to answer specific questions and/or

gain information. .... ☐ ☐ ☐ ☐ ☐

Read selected material to:

predict outcomes...................................... ☐ ☐ ☐ ☐ ☐

draw conclusions. .... ☐ ☐ ☐ ☐ ☐

sequence events. .... ☐ ☐ ☐ ☐ ☐

distinguish between fact and fiction

(reality and fantasy). .... ☐ ☐ ☐ ☐ ☐

identify cause and effect. .... ☐ ☐ ☐ ☐ ☐

identify the main idea (stated). .... ☐ ☐ ☐ ☐ ☐

identify story details. .... ☐ ☐ ☐ ☐ ☐

Select a title. .... ☐ ☐ ☐ ☐ ☐

Compose a thank-you note............................. ☐ ☐ ☐ ☐ ☐

EVALUATION CHECK LIST FOR THIRD GRADE

LANGUAGE ARTS

Third-grade students should be able to do the following:

LANGUAGE MECHANICS AND EXPRESSION

	CHILD'S NAME	CHILD'S NAME	CHILD'S NAME	CHILD'S NAME	CHILD'S NAME
Improve use of manuscript in the first six weeks...	☐	☐	☐	☐	☐
Use basic strokes of cursive style to form letters and words legibly and neatly.	☐	☐	☐	☐	☐
Identify complete sentences.	☐	☐	☐	☐	☐
Arrange words in logical order to form sentences.	☐	☐	☐	☐	☐
Identify correct use of periods.	☐	☐	☐	☐	☐
Identify correct use of question marks.	☐	☐	☐	☐	☐
Identify correct use of exclamation marks.	☐	☐	☐	☐	☐
Identify correct use of commas in dates, cities, and states.	☐	☐	☐	☐	☐
Use the apostrophe to form contractions and possessives.	☐	☐	☐	☐	☐
Identify correct use of singular and plural nouns.	☐	☐	☐	☐	☐
Identify correct capitalization of proper nouns, the first word of a sentence, the pronoun "I," addresses and dates.	☐	☐	☐	☐	☐
Recognize the simple subject of a sentence.	☐	☐	☐	☐	☐
Recognize the simple predicate of a sentence.	☐	☐	☐	☐	☐
Recognize and use correct forms of regular verbs (present and past tense).	☐	☐	☐	☐	☐
Select words that add detail to sentences.	☐	☐	☐	☐	☐
Compose a simple, original paragraph.	☐	☐	☐	☐	☐
Recognize parts of a friendly letter.	☐	☐	☐	☐	☐
Write abbreviations of commonly used words.	☐	☐	☐	☐	☐
Write creatively about selected subjects.	☐	☐	☐	☐	☐

EVALUATION CHECK LIST FOR THIRD GRADE
LANGUAGE ARTS

SPELLING

	CHILD'S NAME	CHILD'S NAME	CHILD'S NAME	CHILD'S NAME	CHILD'S NAME
Spell words in isolation and in sentence dictation.	☐	☐	☐	☐	☐
Spell the basic Dolch sight words (pg 300).	☐	☐	☐	☐	☐
Use the following basic study steps to master spelling words:					
look at the word.	☐	☐	☐	☐	☐
sound the word.	☐	☐	☐	☐	☐
spell the word.	☐	☐	☐	☐	☐
write the word.	☐	☐	☐	☐	☐
Recognize correctly spelled words using sound or symbol relationships (consonant blends, long and short vowels, vowel diphthongs)...	☐	☐	☐	☐	☐
Recognize sight words.	☐	☐	☐	☐	☐
Identify unknown records through context clues.	☐	☐	☐	☐	☐
Know and use antonym, synonyms, homonym, and words that rhyme.	☐	☐	☐	☐	☐
Identify the base word from words containing the following prefixes and suffixes: *a, al, be, un, in, ful, less*.	☐	☐	☐	☐	☐
Identify correctly spelled affixes including prefixes *re* and *un* and suffixes s and *ed* and base words.	☐	☐	☐	☐	☐
Form new words using prefixes and suffixes.	☐	☐	☐	☐	☐
Identify correctly spelled contractions.	☐	☐	☐	☐	☐
Recognize letter-sound relationships for long vowels.	☐	☐	☐	☐	☐
Recognize letter-sound relationships for two-letter consonant blends in the initial and final position (*sc, sp, sk, sm, sn, st*).	☐	☐	☐	☐	☐

Evaluation Check List for Third Grade

LANGUAGE ARTS

	CHILD'S NAME	CHILD'S NAME	CHILD'S NAME	CHILD'S NAME	CHILD'S NAME
Recognize letter-sound relationship for three-letter consonant blends in the initial position (*spl, str, spr, scr*).	❑	❑	❑	❑	❑
Recognize letter-sound associations for consonant digraphs (*ng, nk, wh, th, ph*).	❑	❑	❑	❑	❑
Recognize letter-sound associations for vowel digraphs (*ai, ay, ee, ea*).	❑	❑	❑	❑	❑
Recognize letter-sound associations for vowel diphthongs (*oi, oy, oo*).	❑	❑	❑	❑	❑
Use spelling patterns as clues to vowel sounds in words.	❑	❑	❑	❑	❑
Differentiate between hard and soft sounds of *c* and *g*.	❑	❑	❑	❑	❑
Divide two-syllable words into syllables using the *VC/CV* rule.	❑	❑	❑	❑	❑

STUDY SKILLS

Use guide words to find words and entries in a dictionary.	❑	❑	❑	❑	❑
Locate the page on which a story begins by using the table of contents.	❑	❑	❑	❑	❑
Arrange words in alphabetical order to the second letter.	❑	❑	❑	❑	❑
Use a glossary.	❑	❑	❑	❑	❑
Classify and categorize words.	❑	❑	❑	❑	❑
Locate the title, author and illustrator on the title page.	❑	❑	❑	❑	❑

LISTENING AND COMPREHENSION

Read for the following specific purposes: to gain pleasure.	❑	❑	❑	❑	❑

EVALUATION CHECK LIST FOR THIRD GRADE

LANGUAGE ARTS

	CHILD'S NAME	CHILD'S NAME	CHILD'S NAME	CHILD'S NAME	CHILD'S NAME
to answer questions.	❑	❑	❑	❑	❑
to predict outcomes.	❑	❑	❑	❑	❑
Recall story details of material read.	❑	❑	❑	❑	❑
Respond to questions on who, what, when, where, or why after reading a selection.	❑	❑	❑	❑	❑
Identify and describe the characters of stories.	❑	❑	❑	❑	❑
Predict events in a story.	❑	❑	❑	❑	❑
Identify relevant and irrelevant information in a paragraph.	❑	❑	❑	❑	❑
Differentiate between possible and impossible situations.	❑	❑	❑	❑	❑
Compare or contrast items.	❑	❑	❑	❑	❑
Read selected material to:					
use context to select from given predictions.	❑	❑	❑	❑	❑
use context to select from possible conclusions.	❑	❑	❑	❑	❑
distinguish between fact and fiction.	❑	❑	❑	❑	❑
identify cause and effect.	❑	❑	❑	❑	❑
sequence events.	❑	❑	❑	❑	❑
identify the main idea (stated).	❑	❑	❑	❑	❑

Evaluation Check List for Fourth Grade

Language Arts

Fourth-grade students should be able to do the following:

CHILD'S NAME | CHILD'S NAME | CHILD'S NAME | CHILD'S NAME | CHILD'S NAME

Language Mechanics and Expression

Write legibly in cursive style. .... ❑ ❑ ❑ ❑ ❑

Identify complete sentences. .... ❑ ❑ ❑ ❑ ❑

Classify sentences according to type. .... ❑ ❑ ❑ ❑ ❑

Identify subject and predicate (simple). .... ❑ ❑ ❑ ❑ ❑

Identify correct use of subject-predicate agreement (natural order). .... ❑ ❑ ❑ ❑ ❑

Identify correct use of nouns (common/proper, singular/plural). .... ❑ ❑ ❑ ❑ ❑

Form plurals and possessives of nouns. .... ❑ ❑ ❑ ❑ ❑

Identify use of regular verbs (present and past tense). .... ❑ ❑ ❑ ❑ ❑

Identify correct use of adjectives. .... ❑ ❑ ❑ ❑ ❑

Identify correct use of adverbs. .... ❑ ❑ ❑ ❑ ❑

Identify correct capitalization of the first word of sentences, addresses, titles, dates, the pronoun *I*, and proper nouns. .... ❑ ❑ ❑ ❑ ❑

Write abbreviations of commonly used words. ❑ ❑ ❑ ❑ ❑

Identify correct capitalization and periods in abbreviations, including titles and initials. ❑ ❑ ❑ ❑ ❑

Identify correct use of ending punctuation marks, including: periods, question marks, and exclamation points. .... ❑ ❑ ❑ ❑ ❑

Identify correct use of commas in friendly letters, words in a series, dates, and addresses. ❑ ❑ ❑ ❑ ❑

Identify correct use of subject pronouns. .... ❑ ❑ ❑ ❑ ❑

Identify parts of a paragraph (topic sentence, indented first line and supporting detail sentences). .... ❑ ❑ ❑ ❑ ❑

Evaluation Check List for Fourth Grade

LANGUAGE ARTS

	CHILD'S NAME	CHILD'S NAME	CHILD'S NAME	CHILD'S NAME	CHILD'S NAME
Identify relevant and irrelevant information in a paragraph.	❏	❏	❏	❏	❏
Identify parts of friendly letters and envelopes.					
Compose an invitation.	❏	❏	❏	❏	❏

SPELLING

	CHILD'S NAME	CHILD'S NAME	CHILD'S NAME	CHILD'S NAME	CHILD'S NAME
Recognize sight words (including the complete Dolch word list pg 300).	❏	❏	❏	❏	❏
Spell words in isolation and in sentence dictation.	❏	❏	❏	❏	❏
Recognize letter-sound associations for vowel digraphs (*ea, ee ei*).	❏	❏	❏	❏	❏
Recognize letter-sound associations for vowel diphthongs (*ou, aw, au*).	❏	❏	❏	❏	❏
Recognize correctly spelled words using sound/symbol relationships (consonant blends, long vowels, vowel diphthong and digraphs).	❏	❏	❏	❏	❏
Identify silent consonants in words.	❏	❏	❏	❏	❏
Apply letter-sound association for the two sounds of *c* and *g*.	❏	❏	❏	❏	❏
Identify correctly spelled words containing affixes (prefixes *in, un, dis,* and *re,* and suffixes *s, ed, er, est* and *ilu*).	❏	❏	❏	❏	❏
Identify contractions and their meanings.	❏	❏	❏	❏	❏
Proofread for errors (letter sequence, letter omission).	❏	❏	❏	❏	❏
Recognize syllable patterns (*VC/CV, V/CV, VC/V*).	❏	❏	❏	❏	❏
Divide polysyllabic words using syllabication rules.	❏	❏	❏	❏	❏
Speak in a manner appropriate to the occasion.	❏	❏	❏	❏	❏

EVALUATION CHECK LIST FOR FOURTH GRADE

LANGUAGE ARTS

	CHILD'S NAME	CHILD'S NAME	CHILD'S NAME	CHILD'S NAME	CHILD'S NAME
Pronounce words clearly and correctly.............	❏	❏	❏	❏	❏
Demonstrate following directions (oral and written)..	❏	❏	❏	❏	❏

LISTENING AND COMPREHENSION

Give oral directions.	❏	❏	❏	❏	❏
Listen to answer specific questions..................	❏	❏	❏	❏	❏
Listen to restate main ideas.............................	❏	❏	❏	❏	❏
Read for specific purpose:					
to gain pleasure.	❏	❏	❏	❏	❏
to answer questions.	❏	❏	❏	❏	❏
to predict outcomes.......................................	❏	❏	❏	❏	❏

STUDY SKILLS

Select the appropriate reference material (encyclopedia, dictionary, etc.).	❏	❏	❏	❏	❏
Arrange library cards in alphabetical order. ..	❏	❏	❏	❏	❏
Identify and use parts of books (glossary, table of contents, chapter headings, and index). ..	❏	❏	❏	❏	❏
Use context to identify new words, determine the meaning of known words, verify predictions and verify conclusions..........................	❏	❏	❏	❏	❏
Read selected material to:					
identify story details...................................	❏	❏	❏	❏	❏
sequence events..	❏	❏	❏	❏	❏
identify main idea (stated)...........................	❏	❏	❏	❏	❏
identify central message.	❏	❏	❏	❏	❏
recognize author's purpose.	❏	❏	❏	❏	❏
recognize first- and third-person narratives (point of view).	❏	❏	❏	❏	❏

EVALUATION CHECK LIST FOR FOURTH GRADE

LANGUAGE ARTS

	CHILD'S NAME	CHILD'S NAME	CHILD'S NAME	CHILD'S NAME	CHILD'S NAME
identify basic conflicts and solutions	☐	☐	☐	☐	☐
classify statements of evidence.	☐	☐	☐	☐	☐
distinguish between fact and opinion.	☐	☐	☐	☐	☐
distinguish reality and fantasy.	☐	☐	☐	☐	☐
distinguish fiction from nonfiction.	☐	☐	☐	☐	☐
identify idioms.	☐	☐	☐	☐	☐
identify cause and effect relationships.	☐	☐	☐	☐	☐
make comparisons from given information.	☐	☐	☐	☐	☐
interpret the feeling and behavior of characters.	☐	☐	☐	☐	☐
select from possible conclusions.	☐	☐	☐	☐	☐
select from given predictions.	☐	☐	☐	☐	☐

EVALUATION CHECK LIST FOR FIFTH GRADE

LANGUAGE ARTS

Fifth-grade students should be able to do the following:

CHILD'S NAME CHILD'S NAME CHILD'S NAME CHILD'S NAME CHILD'S NAME

LANGUAGE MECHANICS AND EXPRESSION

Write legibly in cursive style. .... ❏ ❏ ❏ ❏ ❏

Use manuscript skills for labeling, graphing, and identification. .... ❏ ❏ ❏ ❏ ❏

Recognize complete sentences in spoken and written language. .... ❏ ❏ ❏ ❏ ❏

Write complete sentences using correct capitalization and punctuation. .... ❏ ❏ ❏ ❏ ❏

Identify correct capitalization of words in titles, addresses, and dates. .... ❏ ❏ ❏ ❏ ❏

Identify correct capitalization and use of periods in abbreviations, including initials and titles. .... ❏ ❏ ❏ ❏ ❏

Identify correct use of ending punctuation. .... ❏ ❏ ❏ ❏ ❏

Identify correct use of commas in friendly letters, words in a series, dates, addresses, and between the quoted words of a speaker and the rest of the sentence. .... ❏ ❏ ❏ ❏ ❏

Use commas in introductory expressions and direct address. .... ❏ ❏ ❏ ❏ ❏

Classify sentences according to type. .... ❏ ❏ ❏ ❏ ❏

Distinguish between complete and incomplete sentences. .... ❏ ❏ ❏ ❏ ❏

Identify subject and predicate (simple and compound). .... ❏ ❏ ❏ ❏ ❏

Form compound sentences. .... ❏ ❏ ❏ ❏ ❏

Within the context of phrase(s), sentence(s) or a short paragraph, identify correct use of the following:

Evaluation Check List for Fifth Grade

LANGUAGE ARTS

	CHILD'S NAME	CHILD'S NAME	CHILD'S NAME	CHILD'S NAME	CHILD'S NAME
nouns (common/proper, singular/plural).....	❏	❏	❏	❏	❏
principal parts of regular verbs....................	❏	❏	❏	❏	❏
verb tense (present, past, and future).	❏	❏	❏	❏	❏
linking and auxiliary verbs.	❏	❏	❏	❏	❏
pronouns (case usage).	❏	❏	❏	❏	❏
possessive pronouns.	❏	❏	❏	❏	❏
adjectives.	❏	❏	❏	❏	❏
adverbs.	❏	❏	❏	❏	❏
articles.	❏	❏	❏	❏	❏
subject-predicate agreement (natural order).	❏	❏	❏	❏	❏

SPELLING

Spell words in isolation or in sentence dictation.					
Recognize sight words.....................................	❏	❏	❏	❏	❏
Identify and form compound words.	❏	❏	❏	❏	❏
Recognize correctly spelled words using sound/ symbol relationships (controlled vowels, schwa sound).	❏	❏	❏	❏	❏
Use base words with suffixes and prefixes.	❏	❏	❏	❏	❏
Proofread for errors (letter sequence, letter omission).	❏	❏	❏	❏	❏
Recognize syllable patterns (V/C, V/CV, VC/V).	❏	❏	❏	❏	❏
Recognize correct spelling of contractions.	❏	❏	❏	❏	❏
Recognize correct spelling of possessives (nouns/pronouns).	❏	❏	❏	❏	❏
Identify correct spelling of plural nouns...........	❏	❏	❏	❏	❏
Identify stressed and unstressed syllables.	❏	❏	❏	❏	❏
Identify synonyms, given the context of sentence(s) or a short paragraph.	❏	❏	❏	❏	❏

A downloadable version of this book.is available for purchase at **http://Homeschool-Books.com**. With it you can search for text and and print the pages from your computer.

EVALUATION CHECK LIST FOR FIFTH GRADE

LANGUAGE ARTS

	CHILD'S NAME	CHILD'S NAME	CHILD'S NAME	CHILD'S NAME	CHILD'S NAME
Identify antonym, given the context of sentence(s) or a short paragraph.	☐	☐	☐	☐	☐
Decode words by applying rules for syllabication.	☐	☐	☐	☐	☐
Unlock the meanings of words through use of the following:					
base words, prefixes and suffixes.	☐	☐	☐	☐	☐
contextual clues.	☐	☐	☐	☐	☐
homonym and heteronyms.	☐	☐	☐	☐	☐
Apply basic word attack skills.	☐	☐	☐	☐	☐
Utilize a written and oral vocabulary appropriate to the grade level.	☐	☐	☐	☐	☐
Arrange sentences in logical order to form a paragraph.	☐	☐	☐	☐	☐
Develop simple, original paragraphs.	☐	☐	☐	☐	☐
Identify parts of friendly letters and envelopes.	☐	☐	☐	☐	☐

STUDY SKILLS

Use the dictionary as a guide for alphabetizing, finding definitions, spelling, syllabication and pronunciation.	☐	☐	☐	☐	☐
Interpret diacritical marks.	☐	☐	☐	☐	☐
Determine the appropriate meaning of a word using the dictionary.	☐	☐	☐	☐	☐
Select and use the appropriate reference material (dictionary, encyclopedia, etc).	☐	☐	☐	☐	☐
Identify and use parts of books.	☐	☐	☐	☐	☐
Be able to find the following parts of books:					
table of contents.	☐	☐	☐	☐	☐
index.	☐	☐	☐	☐	☐
glossary.	☐	☐	☐	☐	☐

Evaluation Check List for Fifth Grade

LANGUAGE ARTS

title page... ❏ ❏ ❏ ❏ ❏

Use the table of contents and index to find on
what page certain information can be found. ❏ ❏ ❏ ❏ ❏

Be able to identify what is in a chapter from
the table of contents. .... ❏ ❏ ❏ ❏ ❏

Identify the following information on cards by
using the card catalog:

author. .... ❏ ❏ ❏ ❏ ❏

title. .... ❏ ❏ ❏ ❏ ❏

subject.. ❏ ❏ ❏ ❏ ❏

publisher. .... ❏ ❏ ❏ ❏ ❏

call number. .... ❏ ❏ ❏ ❏ ❏

Be able to look up a specific person's telephone
number and address in the telephone direc-
tory. .... ❏ ❏ ❏ ❏ ❏

Be able to organize topic words in an outline
form.. ❏ ❏ ❏ ❏ ❏

Understand main heading and subheadings. ❏ ❏ ❏ ❏ ❏

LISTENING AND COMPREHENSION

Demonstrate following directions in emer-
gency situations....................................... ❏ ❏ ❏ ❏ ❏

Interpret graphs, charts, tables, maps and dia-
grams. .... ❏ ❏ ❏ ❏ ❏

Follow oral and written directions. .... ❏ ❏ ❏ ❏ ❏

Use recall, sequence, and order in expressing
written and oral ideas. .... ❏ ❏ ❏ ❏ ❏

Speak with inflections, pauses, and the necessary intonations to express punctuation and
give meaning to sentences. .... ❏ ❏ ❏ ❏ ❏

Form accurate oral descriptions in discussion. ❏ ❏ ❏ ❏ ❏

EVALUATION CHECK LIST FOR FIFTH GRADE

LANGUAGE ARTS

	CHILD'S NAME	CHILD'S NAME	CHILD'S NAME	CHILD'S NAME	CHILD'S NAME
Write brief reports using notes and pertinent data.	☐	☐	☐	☐	☐
Read selected material to:					
select from given predictions.	☐	☐	☐	☐	☐
select from possible conclusions.	☐	☐	☐	☐	☐
identify cause and effect relationships.	☐	☐	☐	☐	☐
recognize author's purpose.	☐	☐	☐	☐	☐
identify the main idea (stated).	☐	☐	☐	☐	☐
identify story details.	☐	☐	☐	☐	☐
sequence events from a selection.	☐	☐	☐	☐	☐
distinguish fact from opinion.	☐	☐	☐	☐	☐
classify statements of evidence.	☐	☐	☐	☐	☐
recognize conflicts and their solutions.	☐	☐	☐	☐	☐
Identify the theme or central message of a selection.	☐	☐	☐	☐	☐
Identify figurative language.	☐	☐	☐	☐	☐
Recognize time and place relationships (setting).	☐	☐	☐	☐	☐
Recognize the following types of literature:					
autobiography.	☐	☐	☐	☐	☐
biography.	☐	☐	☐	☐	☐
folk and fairy tales.	☐	☐	☐	☐	☐
historical fiction.	☐	☐	☐	☐	☐
informative articles.	☐	☐	☐	☐	☐
myths and legends.	☐	☐	☐	☐	☐
Use context clues to formulate ideas.	☐	☐	☐	☐	☐

EVALUATION CHECK LIST FOR SIXTH GRADE

LANGUAGE ARTS

Sixth-grade students should be able to do the following:

LANGUAGE MECHANICS AND EXPRESSION

Improve speed while maintaining accuracy and legibility in handwriting......................... ❑ ❑ ❑ ❑ ❑

Identify correct capitalization of words in titles of books, songs, magazines, newspapers, appropriate words in outlines, and of proper nouns and adjectives. .... ❑ ❑ ❑ ❑ ❑

Identify correct use of ending punctuation including periods, question marks and exclamation marks. .... ❑ ❑ ❑ ❑ ❑

Identify correct use of capitalization and periods in abbreviations, including initials and titles. .... ❑ ❑ ❑ ❑ ❑

Identify correct use of capitalization in the name of a historical period............................ ❑ ❑ ❑ ❑ ❑

Identify correct use of commas:

    in dates. .... ❑ ❑ ❑ ❑ ❑

    in addresses. .... ❑ ❑ ❑ ❑ ❑

    in words in a series. .... ❑ ❑ ❑ ❑ ❑

    in letters. .... ❑ ❑ ❑ ❑ ❑

    between the quoted words of a speaker and the rest of the sentence. .... ❑ ❑ ❑ ❑ ❑

    to set off an introductory phrase.................. ❑ ❑ ❑ ❑ ❑

    to set off an appositive phrase....................... ❑ ❑ ❑ ❑ ❑

    after closing of a friendly letter. .... ❑ ❑ ❑ ❑ ❑

    to set off a name in direct address. .... ❑ ❑ ❑ ❑ ❑

Distinguish between simple and compound sentences. .... ❑ ❑ ❑ ❑ ❑

Distinguish between simple and complete sub-

LANGUAGE ARTS

CHILD'S NAME | CHILD'S NAME | CHILD'S NAME | CHILD'S NAME | CHILD'S NAME

...jects and predicates. ....

Identify simple and compound subjects and predicates (natural order). .... ❑ ❑ ❑ ❑ ❑

Within the context of phrase(s), sentence(s) or a short paragraph, identify correct use of the following: ❑ ❑ ❑ ❑ ❑

nouns (common/proper, singular/plural, and possessive). .... ❑ ❑ ❑ ❑ ❑

subject-predicate agreement. .... ❑ ❑ ❑ ❑ ❑

case usage of pronouns (nominative, objective, possessive). .... ❑ ❑ ❑ ❑ ❑

principal parts of regular verbs.................... ❑ ❑ ❑ ❑ ❑

demonstrative adjectives. .... ❑ ❑ ❑ ❑ ❑

comparative and superlative forms of adjectives. .... ❑ ❑ ❑ ❑ ❑

verb tense (present, past, and future). .... ❑ ❑ ❑ ❑ ❑

conjunctions... ❑ ❑ ❑ ❑ ❑

prepositions. .... ❑ ❑ ❑ ❑ ❑

negative words. .... ❑ ❑ ❑ ❑ ❑

"good" and "well." .... ❑ ❑ ❑ ❑ ❑

SPELLING

Spell words in isolation and in sentence dictation. ❑ ❑ ❑ ❑ ❑

Recognize sight words..................................... ❑ ❑ ❑ ❑ ❑

Identify base words and correct spelling of affixed words. .... ❑ ❑ ❑ ❑ ❑

Recognize correct spelling of possessives (nouns/pronouns)... ❑ ❑ ❑ ❑ ❑

Identify correct spelling of homophones........... ❑ ❑ ❑ ❑ ❑

Recognize correct spelling of plurals of nouns. ❑ ❑ ❑ ❑ ❑

Distinguish compound words from polysyl-

EVALUATION CHECK LIST FOR SIXTH GRADE

LANGUAGE ARTS

CHILD'S NAME | CHILD'S NAME | CHILD'S NAME | CHILD'S NAME | CHILD'S NAME

labic words in sentences, paragraphs or standing alone. .... ❑ ❑ ❑ ❑ ❑

Divide polysyllabic words into syllables. .... ❑ ❑ ❑ ❑ ❑

Use context as a clue to the meanings of unfamiliar words (synonyms, antonym, definition, restatement, example). .... ❑ ❑ ❑ ❑ ❑

Apply basic word attack skills. .... ❑ ❑ ❑ ❑ ❑

STUDY SKILLS

Use the dictionary. .... ❑ ❑ ❑ ❑ ❑

Choose the appropriate reference book to find specific information (telephone directory, encyclopedia, dictionary). .... ❑ ❑ ❑ ❑ ❑

Demonstrate following written or graphic (map) directions. .... ❑ ❑ ❑ ❑ ❑

Write directions. .... ❑ ❑ ❑ ❑ ❑

Identify and use parts of a book. .... ❑ ❑ ❑ ❑ ❑

Identify the following information on cards by:

    using the card catalog. .... ❑ ❑ ❑ ❑ ❑

    author. .... ❑ ❑ ❑ ❑ ❑

    title. .... ❑ ❑ ❑ ❑ ❑

    subject. .... ❑ ❑ ❑ ❑ ❑

    publisher. .... ❑ ❑ ❑ ❑ ❑

    call number. .... ❑ ❑ ❑ ❑ ❑

    year of publication. .... ❑ ❑ ❑ ❑ ❑

Use the encyclopedia. .... ❑ ❑ ❑ ❑ ❑

Use an atlas. .... ❑ ❑ ❑ ❑ ❑

Use radio and television schedules. .... ❑ ❑ ❑ ❑ ❑

Use a telephone directory. .... ❑ ❑ ❑ ❑ ❑

Use a newspaper to find certain information. .... ❑ ❑ ❑ ❑ ❑

Calculate the number of sections in a news-

EVALUATION CHECK LIST FOR SIXTH GRADE

LANGUAGE ARTS

	CHILD'S NAME	CHILD'S NAME	CHILD'S NAME	CHILD'S NAME	CHILD'S NAME
paper.	❑	❑	❑	❑	❑
Interpret graphs, maps, charts, tables, and diagrams.	❑	❑	❑	❑	❑
Sequence sentences correctly in a paragraph.	❑	❑	❑	❑	❑
Construct a paragraph with appropriate title, indentation, margins, punctuation, and spelling.	❑	❑	❑	❑	❑
Identify parts of letters and envelopes.	❑	❑	❑	❑	❑
Compose a business letter and address appropriate envelope.	❑	❑	❑	❑	❑
Develop simple outlines.	❑	❑	❑	❑	❑
Understand main heading and subheadings.	❑	❑	❑	❑	❑
Present an oral report.	❑	❑	❑	❑	❑
Make formal and informal introductions.	❑	❑	❑	❑	❑
Participate in a discussion by making relevant contributions to a specific topic.	❑	❑	❑	❑	❑
Make oral and written summaries of any material read.	❑	❑	❑	❑	❑
Given the organizing principle of a list, determine the order in which the topics should appear.	❑	❑	❑	❑	❑

LISTENING AND COMPREHENSION

	CHILD'S NAME	CHILD'S NAME	CHILD'S NAME	CHILD'S NAME	CHILD'S NAME
Locate facts to support the main idea.	❑	❑	❑	❑	❑
Use simple outline skills to demonstrate comprehension.	❑	❑	❑	❑	❑
Skim for specific information.	❑	❑	❑	❑	❑
Identify the central message of a selection.	❑	❑	❑	❑	❑
Read selected material to identify the main idea (stated):					
identify story details.	❑	❑	❑	❑	❑

EVALUATION CHECK LIST FOR SIXTH GRADE

LANGUAGE ARTS

	CHILD'S NAME	CHILD'S NAME	CHILD'S NAME	CHILD'S NAME	CHILD'S NAME
sequence events from a selection.	☐	☐	☐	☐	☐
select from possible inferences and conclusions.	☐	☐	☐	☐	☐
make inferences based on statements of evidence.	☐	☐	☐	☐	☐
select from given predictions.	☐	☐	☐	☐	☐
identify cause and effect relationship.	☐	☐	☐	☐	☐
distinguish fact from opinion.	☐	☐	☐	☐	☐
distinguish fiction from nonfiction.	☐	☐	☐	☐	☐
Identify the various forms of fiction and non-	☐	☐	☐	☐	☐
fiction.	☐	☐	☐	☐	☐
Distinguish literal from figurative language (idioms, hyperboles, similes, and metaphors).	☐	☐	☐	☐	☐
Recognize sound devices (alliteration).	☐	☐	☐	☐	☐

EVALUATION CHECK LIST FOR SEVENTH GRADE

LANGUAGE ARTS

Seventh-grade students should be able to do the following:

CHILD'S NAME | CHILD'S NAME | CHILD'S NAME | CHILD'S NAME | CHILD'S NAME

LANGUAGE MECHANICS AND EXPRESSION

Assess cursive writing for legibility. .... ❑ ❑ ❑ ❑ ❑

Identify correct capitalization of proper nouns, the first word in a direct quotation, greetings and closing of letters and appropriate words in outlines. .... ❑ ❑ ❑ ❑ ❑

Understand correct capitalization of a direction used as the name of a region and use lower case when used as a direction (South Carolina, he went south). .... ❑ ❑ ❑ ❑ ❑

Identify correct use of commas in dates, addresses, words in a series, in letters, between quoted words of a speaker and the rest of the sentence, in compound sentences, and after introductory phrases. .... ❑ ❑ ❑ ❑ ❑

Use an apostrophe to form the possessive of a singular noun or to form the possessive of a plural noun. .... ❑ ❑ ❑ ❑ ❑

Use semicolon and colon correctly. .... ❑ ❑ ❑ ❑ ❑

Differentiate between complete and incomplete sentences. .... ❑ ❑ ❑ ❑ ❑

Identify simple and compound sentences. ...... ❑ ❑ ❑ ❑ ❑

Recognize complex sentences. .... ❑ ❑ ❑ ❑ ❑

Identify simple and compound subjects and predicates. .... ❑ ❑ ❑ ❑ ❑

Within the context of phrase(s), sentence(s) or a short paragraph, identify correct use of the following:

subject-predicate agreement. .... ❑ ❑ ❑ ❑ ❑

Evaluation Check List for Seventh Grade

Language Arts

	CHILD'S NAME	CHILD'S NAME	CHILD'S NAME	CHILD'S NAME	CHILD'S NAME
agreement of pronoun and antecedent.	❑	❑	❑	❑	❑
comparative and superlative forms of adjectives and adverbs.	❑	❑	❑	❑	❑
case usage of pronouns.	❑	❑	❑	❑	❑
types of pronouns (possessive, reflexive, interrogative, relative, demonstrative, and indefinite).	❑	❑	❑	❑	❑
principal parts of regular and irregular verbs.	❑	❑	❑	❑	❑
verb tense (present, past, and future).	❑	❑	❑	❑	❑
conjunctions.	❑	❑	❑	❑	❑
prepositions and prepositional phrases.	❑	❑	❑	❑	❑
negative words.	❑	❑	❑	❑	❑
Distinguish between common/proper nouns, concrete/abstract nouns, and collective nouns.					
Use possessive forms of nouns.	❑	❑	❑	❑	❑
Use apostrophes correctly.	❑	❑	❑	❑	❑
Distinguish between transitive and intransitive verbs.	❑	❑	❑	❑	❑
Recognize and use direct and indirect objects.					
Recognize and use predicate nominatives and predicate adjectives.	❑	❑	❑	❑	❑
Combine sentences using adjectives, adverbs, and conjunctions.	❑	❑	❑	❑	❑
Identify run-on sentences.	❑	❑	❑	❑	❑
Distinguish between relevant and irrelevant information in a paragraph.	❑	❑	❑	❑	❑
Sequence sentences in a paragraph.	❑	❑	❑	❑	❑

EVALUATION CHECK LIST FOR SEVENTH GRADE

LANGUAGE ARTS

The five columns are headed: CHILD'S NAME, CHILD'S NAME, CHILD'S NAME, CHILD'S NAME, CHILD'S NAME

SPELLING

Use sound/symbol relationships to spell words.

Recognize correctly spelled affixed and base words... ❑ ❑ ❑ ❑ ❑

Recognize correct spelling of contractions. ...... ❑ ❑ ❑ ❑ ❑

Recognize correct spelling of possessives (nouns/pronouns). .... ❑ ❑ ❑ ❑ ❑

Identify correctly spelled homophones within the context of sentences or phrases. .... ❑ ❑ ❑ ❑ ❑

Recognize correct spelling of plurals of nouns.

Recognize sight words.................................. ❑ ❑ ❑ ❑ ❑

Distinguish compound words from polysyllabic words. .... ❑ ❑ ❑ ❑ ❑

Divide polysyllabic words into syllables........... ❑ ❑ ❑ ❑ ❑

Use context as a clue to the meaning of unfamiliar words... ❑ ❑ ❑ ❑ ❑

STUDY SKILLS

Use the dictionary as a spelling aid. .... ❑ ❑ ❑ ❑ ❑

Apply dictionary skills by:

    using guide words. .... ❑ ❑ ❑ ❑ ❑

    identifying parts of speech.......................... ❑ ❑ ❑ ❑ ❑

    identifying accented syllable. .... ❑ ❑ ❑ ❑ ❑

    interpreting diacritical marks...................... ❑ ❑ ❑ ❑ ❑

    interpreting the derivation of a word. .... ❑ ❑ ❑ ❑ ❑

    determining meaning................................. ❑ ❑ ❑ ❑ ❑

Identify the following information on cards by using the card catalog:

    author.. ❑ ❑ ❑ ❑ ❑

    title. .... ❑ ❑ ❑ ❑ ❑

    subject.. ❑ ❑ ❑ ❑ ❑

EVALUATION CHECK LIST FOR SEVENTH GRADE

LANGUAGE ARTS

	CHILD'S NAME	CHILD'S NAME	CHILD'S NAME	CHILD'S NAME	CHILD'S NAME
publisher.	☐	☐	☐	☐	☐
call number.	☐	☐	☐	☐	☐
year of publication.	☐	☐	☐	☐	☐
illustrator	☐	☐	☐	☐	☐
Locate information in an encyclopedia.	☐	☐	☐	☐	☐
Use various reference materials:					
atlas.	☐	☐	☐	☐	☐
thesaurus.	☐	☐	☐	☐	☐
Use parts of a book to find:					
copyright.	☐	☐	☐	☐	☐
information in a specific chapter.	☐	☐	☐	☐	☐
meaning of a word.	☐	☐	☐	☐	☐
category of the book.	☐	☐	☐	☐	☐
Locate information in telephone directories.	☐	☐	☐	☐	☐
Use radio and television schedules.	☐	☐	☐	☐	☐
Demonstrate following written or graphic (map) directions.	☐	☐	☐	☐	☐
Identify parts of business letters and envelopes.	☐	☐	☐	☐	☐
Use note-taking skills.	☐	☐	☐	☐	☐
Identify correct outline form.	☐	☐	☐	☐	☐
Write reports.	☐	☐	☐	☐	☐
Proofread and revise writing.	☐	☐	☐	☐	☐

LISTENING AND COMPREHENSION

Use expanded vocabulary to enhance oral communication.	☐	☐	☐	☐	☐
Make comparisons and contrasts.	☐	☐	☐	☐	☐
Identify inconsistencies in logic.	☐	☐	☐	☐	☐
Use analogies to describe relationships.	☐	☐	☐	☐	☐
Prepare and give an oral presentation.	☐	☐	☐	☐	☐

EVALUATION CHECK LIST FOR SEVENTH GRADE

LANGUAGE ARTS

CHILD'S NAME | CHILD'S NAME | CHILD'S NAME | CHILD'S NAME | CHILD'S NAME

Read selected material to:

identify the main idea (stated). .... ❏ ❏ ❏ ❏ ❏

identify story details. .... ❏ ❏ ❏ ❏ ❏

sequence events from a selection. .... ❏ ❏ ❏ ❏ ❏

select from possible conclusions. .... ❏ ❏ ❏ ❏ ❏

make inferences based on statements of

evidence. .... ❏ ❏ ❏ ❏ ❏

select from given predictions. .... ❏ ❏ ❏ ❏ ❏

identify cause and effect relationships. .... ❏ ❏ ❏ ❏ ❏

distinguish fact from opinion. .... ❏ ❏ ❏ ❏ ❏

identify author's choice of form or purpose. ❏ ❏ ❏ ❏ ❏

identify foreshadowing. .... ❏ ❏ ❏ ❏ ❏

recognize first-and third-person narratives

(point of view). .... ❏ ❏ ❏ ❏ ❏

Distinguish and interpret figurative language. ❏ ❏ ❏ ❏ ❏

Distinguish types of sensory language. .... ❏ ❏ ❏ ❏ ❏

Identify the theme or central message. .... ❏ ❏ ❏ ❏ ❏

Identify forms of literature such as fables, tall

tales, novels, short stories, essays, drama

and poetry. .... ❏ ❏ ❏ ❏ ❏

Describe plot development in a literary selec-

tion. .... ❏ ❏ ❏ ❏ ❏

Make critical evaluations. .... ❏ ❏ ❏ ❏ ❏

EVALUATION CHECK LIST FOR EIGHTH GRADE

LANGUAGE ARTS

Eighth-grade students should be able to do the following:

LANGUAGE MECHANICS AND EXPRESSION

Produce legible cursive handwriting. .... ❑ ❑ ❑ ❑ ❑

Identify correct capitalization in:

    dates. .... ❑ ❑ ❑ ❑ ❑

    addresses. .... ❑ ❑ ❑ ❑ ❑

    letter parts. .... ❑ ❑ ❑ ❑ ❑

    proper nouns. .... ❑ ❑ ❑ ❑ ❑

    proper adjectives. .... ❑ ❑ ❑ ❑ ❑

    titles. .... ❑ ❑ ❑ ❑ ❑

    outlines. .... ❑ ❑ ❑ ❑ ❑

    quotations. .... ❑ ❑ ❑ ❑ ❑

Identify correct use of standard punctuation. ❑ ❑ ❑ ❑ ❑

Recognize errors in sentence structure (fragment, run-on, etc.). .... ❑ ❑ ❑ ❑ ❑

Combine sentences, avoiding run-ons and comma splices, to form a correctly structured new sentence. .... ❑ ❑ ❑ ❑ ❑

Analyze sentence structure (simple, compound, complex). .... ❑ ❑ ❑ ❑ ❑

Identify simple and compound subjects and predicates (natural and inverted order, interrogative, intervening phrases). .... ❑ ❑ ❑ ❑ ❑

Within the context of phrase(s), sentence(s), or a short paragraph, identify correct use of the following:

    agreement (between subject/verb and pronoun/antecedent). .... ❑ ❑ ❑ ❑ ❑

    comparative and superlative forms of adjectives and adverbs. .... ❑ ❑ ❑ ❑ ❑

Evaluation Check List for Eighth Grade

Language Arts

	CHILD'S NAME	CHILD'S NAME	CHILD'S NAME	CHILD'S NAME	CHILD'S NAME
case usage of pronouns.	☐	☐	☐	☐	☐
types of pronouns (possessive, reflexive, interrogative, demonstrative and indefinite).	☐	☐	☐	☐	☐
noun forms (singular, plural, possessive).	☐	☐	☐	☐	☐
principal parts of verbs (regular, irregular, troublesome).	☐	☐	☐	☐	☐
verb tense.	☐	☐	☐	☐	☐
prepositional phrases as modifiers.	☐	☐	☐	☐	☐
negative words.	☐	☐	☐	☐	☐
conjunctions.	☐	☐	☐	☐	☐
interjections.	☐	☐	☐	☐	☐
Identify and use participles and participial phrases.	☐	☐	☐	☐	☐
Identify and use gerunds and gerund phrases.					
Identify and use infinitives and infinitive phrases.	☐	☐	☐	☐	☐

Spelling

Use sound/symbol relationships to spell words.					
Recognize correctly spelled affixed and base words.	☐	☐	☐	☐	☐
Recognize correct spelling of contractions.	☐	☐	☐	☐	☐
Identify correct forms of possessives (nouns/pronouns).	☐	☐	☐	☐	☐
Identify correctly spelled homophones within the context of sentences or phrases.	☐	☐	☐	☐	☐
Recognize correct spelling of plurals of nouns.	☐	☐	☐	☐	☐
Define and spell compound words.	☐	☐	☐	☐	☐
Recognize multiple meanings of words.	☐	☐	☐	☐	☐
Recognize sight words.	☐	☐	☐	☐	☐
Divide polysyllabic words into syllables.	☐	☐	☐	☐	☐

EVALUATION CHECK LIST FOR EIGHTH GRADE

LANGUAGE ARTS

Use context as a clue to determine word meanings. ☐ ☐ ☐ ☐ ☐

STUDY SKILLS

Locate information from various sources......... ☐ ☐ ☐ ☐ ☐

Use parts of a book to find:

    copyright... ☐ ☐ ☐ ☐ ☐

    information in a specific chapter. .... ☐ ☐ ☐ ☐ ☐

    meaning of a word... ☐ ☐ ☐ ☐ ☐

    category of the book. .... ☐ ☐ ☐ ☐ ☐

Demonstrate following written or graphic (map) directions.. ☐ ☐ ☐ ☐ ☐

Identify parts of friendly or business letters and envelopes. .... ☐ ☐ ☐ ☐ ☐

LISTENING AND COMPREHENSION

Demonstrate effective oral communication skills. .... ☐ ☐ ☐ ☐ ☐

Elaborate on an idea. .... ☐ ☐ ☐ ☐ ☐

Recognize logical fallacies (faulty reasoning, generalization, rationalization, etc.). .... ☐ ☐ ☐ ☐ ☐

Recognize and define propaganda techniques. ☐ ☐ ☐ ☐ ☐

Write and evaluate paragraphs with respect to unity, arrangement of details and effective use of language. .... ☐ ☐ ☐ ☐ ☐

Proofread and revise writing. .... ☐ ☐ ☐ ☐ ☐

Identify correct outline form. .... ☐ ☐ ☐ ☐ ☐

Write a report.. ☐ ☐ ☐ ☐ ☐

Read selected material to:

    identify the main idea or theme (stated or implied). .... ☐ ☐ ☐ ☐ ☐

    identify story details..................................... ☐ ☐ ☐ ☐ ☐

CHILD'S NAME — CHILD'S NAME — CHILD'S NAME — CHILD'S NAME — CHILD'S NAME

EVALUATION CHECK LIST FOR EIGHTH GRADE

LANGUAGE ARTS

	CHILD'S NAME	CHILD'S NAME	CHILD'S NAME	CHILD'S NAME	CHILD'S NAME
sequence events from a selection.	❑	❑	❑	❑	❑
select from possible conclusions based on inferences or statements of evidence.	❑	❑	❑	❑	❑
make inferences based on statements of evidence.	❑	❑	❑	❑	❑
identify cause and effect relationships.	❑	❑	❑	❑	❑
distinguish fact from opinion.	❑	❑	❑	❑	❑
identify author's purpose.	❑	❑	❑	❑	❑
make critical evaluations (point of view).	❑	❑	❑	❑	❑
identify first-and third-person narrative.	❑	❑	❑	❑	❑
identify foreshadowing.	❑	❑	❑	❑	❑
Distinguish and interpret examples of figurative language.	❑	❑	❑	❑	❑
Identify forms of literature such as fables, tall tales, novels, short stories, essays, drama and poetry.	❑	❑	❑	❑	❑
Recognize sensory language.	❑	❑	❑	❑	❑
Describe plot development in a selection.	❑	❑	❑	❑	❑
Summarize a selection.	❑	❑	❑	❑	❑

Who hath measured the waters in the hollow of his hand,
and meted out heaven with the span, and
comprehended the dust of the earth in a measure, and
weighed the mountains in scales, and the hills in a balance?

Isaiah 40:12

MATHEMATICS

CONCEPTS OF NUMBERS • COMPUTATION OF WHOLE NUMBERS •

GEOMETRY • MEASUREMENT • FRACTIONS • DECIMALS • INTEGERS •

PERCENTS •

CHARTS, GRAPHS, AND TABLES • PROBLEM SOLVING

MATHEMATICS CONTENTS CONTINUED

EVALUATION CHECK LIST FOR KINDERGARTEN

MATHEMATICS

Kindergarten students should be able to do the following:

CONCEPTS OF NUMBERS

Determine which is larger/smaller, longer/shorter, taller/shorter, etc., when given two similar objects. .... ☐ ☐ ☐ ☐ ☐

Demonstrate terms of relative position (above, under, right, behind, etc.). .... ☐ ☐ ☐ ☐ ☐

Identify, match, and reproduce shapes with given shapes (circle, square, triangle, and rectangle). .... ☐ ☐ ☐ ☐ ☐

Match terms with given shapes. .... ☐ ☐ ☐ ☐ ☐

Identify equivalent sets (1-10) by one to one correspondence. .... ☐ ☐ ☐ ☐ ☐

Identify sets of 1-5 on sight .... ☐ ☐ ☐ ☐ ☐

Show and state that when objects are taken from a set, the set becomes smaller............... ☐ ☐ ☐ ☐ ☐

Show and state that when objects are added to a set, the set becomes larger. .... ☐ ☐ ☐ ☐ ☐

Count to 10; identify numerals 0-10. .... ☐ ☐ ☐ ☐ ☐

Tell which of two numbers is less or which is greater up to 10. .... ☐ ☐ ☐ ☐ ☐

MEASUREMENT

Identify a penny and a nickel. .... ☐ ☐ ☐ ☐ ☐

Recognize clocks and watches as instruments for measuring time. .... ☐ ☐ ☐ ☐ ☐

Recognize the thermometer as a device to measure temperatures. .... ☐ ☐ ☐ ☐ ☐

Evaluation Check List for First Grade

MATHEMATICS

First-grade students should be able to do the following:

CHILD'S NAME CHILD'S NAME CHILD'S NAME CHILD'S NAME CHILD'S NAME

RECOGNIZE NAMES OF NUMBERS

Identify word names of numbers 0-20.............. ❑ ❑ ❑ ❑ ❑

Identify word names by tens from 10 to 96....... ❑ ❑ ❑ ❑ ❑

Identify word names 0-10. .... ❑ ❑ ❑ ❑ ❑

Identify ordinal numbers through 12th. .... ❑ ❑ ❑ ❑ ❑

COUNTING

Count and write by ones, fives, and tens to 100... ❑ ❑ ❑ ❑ ❑

Sequence or order numbers, 0-99; identify
    which comes before, between, or after. .... ❑ ❑ ❑ ❑ ❑

Show which of two numbers, 0-50, is less or
    greater. .... ❑ ❑ ❑ ❑ ❑

OPERATIONS

Recognize and use symbols: Plus (+), minus (-),
    equals (=). .... ❑ ❑ ❑ ❑ ❑

Recognize the following mathematical terms:
    add, subtract, longer, shorter, more than,
    less than, equal, largest, smallest, before,
    between, after, addend, and sum. .... ❑ ❑ ❑ ❑ ❑

PLACE VALUE

Identify the place value and total value of each
    digit for numbers 0-99. .... ❑ ❑ ❑ ❑ ❑

Recognize place value for ones, tens, and hun-
    dreds. .... ❑ ❑ ❑ ❑ ❑

Compare whole numbers through 99. .... ❑ ❑ ❑ ❑ ❑

EVALUATION CHECK LIST FOR FIRST GRADE
MATHEMATICS

CHILD'S NAME   CHILD'S NAME   CHILD'S NAME   CHILD'S NAME   CHILD'S NAME

ADDITION AND SUBTRACTION

Recall basic addition and subtraction facts with sums and differences of ten or less. ...... ☐ ☐ ☐ ☐ ☐

Add two one-digit numbers, horizontally or vertically, with no regrouping (facts to 10)... ☐ ☐ ☐ ☐ ☐

Add three one-digit numbers, horizontally or vertically, with no regrouping. .... ☐ ☐ ☐ ☐ ☐

Add two two-digit numbers without regrouping. ☐ ☐ ☐ ☐ ☐

Subtract two one-digit numbers, horizontally or vertically, with no renaming (facts to 10, minuend from 1-9, and subtrahend from 0-9). .... ☐ ☐ ☐ ☐ ☐

Subtract a one-digit number from a two-digit number without regrouping. .... ☐ ☐ ☐ ☐ ☐

Demonstrate an understanding of the commutative property of addition (3 + 4 = 4 + 3, etc.).

Find the missing addend (facts to 10). .... ☐ ☐ ☐ ☐ ☐

Demonstrate the understanding that when zero is added to or subtracted from any number, the sum or remainder is always the beginning number. .... ☐ ☐ ☐ ☐ ☐

Identify number sentences, involving addition or subtraction with a sum from 1 thru 9, by using illustrations and word problems......... ☐ ☐ ☐ ☐ ☐

GEOMETRY

Recognize the triangle, square, rectangle, and circle. .... ☐ ☐ ☐ ☐ ☐

Match terms with given shapes. .... ☐ ☐ ☐ ☐ ☐

Identify the longer and the shorter of two objects. .... ☐ ☐ ☐ ☐ ☐

Evaluation Check List for First Grade

MATHEMATICS

Identify equivalent and nonequivalent sets by using illustrations. .... ❑ ❑ ❑ ❑ ❑

MEASUREMENT

Estimate the amount a container will hold. .... ❑ ❑ ❑ ❑ ❑

Identify the following coins: penny, nickel, dime, quarter, in terms of pennies (cents). .. ❑ ❑ ❑ ❑ ❑

Tell time to the nearest half-hour, using a standard clock. .... ❑ ❑ ❑ ❑ ❑

Identify the hotter/colder temperature on a thermometer by selecting the higher/lower column of two thermometers........................ ❑ ❑ ❑ ❑ ❑

Name periods of time in sequence. .... ❑ ❑ ❑ ❑ ❑

Mark specified days and dates on a calendar... ❑ ❑ ❑ ❑ ❑

Compare liquid capacities using customary (cup, pint, and quart) or metric (liter) measures.. ❑ ❑ ❑ ❑ ❑

Use a ruler to measure a line segment to the nearest whole unit [customary (inch) or metric (centimeter)]. .... ❑ ❑ ❑ ❑ ❑

FRACTIONS

Identify a shape divided into equal parts. .... ❑ ❑ ❑ ❑ ❑

Distinguish shapes divided into halves. .... ❑ ❑ ❑ ❑ ❑

Determine when one-fourth of an object is shaded.. ❑ ❑ ❑ ❑ ❑

CHARTS, GRAPHS AND TABLES

Interpret a simple bar graph of pictured objects in vertical format. .... ❑ ❑ ❑ ❑ ❑

Identify how much more one frequency is than another pertaining to a simple graph............ ❑ ❑ ❑ ❑ ❑

EVALUATION CHECK LIST FOR SECOND GRADE

MATHEMATICS

Second-grade students should be able to do the following:

Recognizing Names of Numbers...................... ❑ ❑ ❑ ❑ ❑

Identify word names of numbers 0-20.............. ❑ ❑ ❑ ❑ ❑

Identify word names by 10s from 10 to 90. ...... ❑ ❑ ❑ ❑ ❑

Identify word names 0-10. .... ❑ ❑ ❑ ❑ ❑

Identify odd or even numbers randomly select-
ed from 1-20. .... ❑ ❑ ❑ ❑ ❑

COUNTING

Count, recognize and write to 100 by twos,
fives or tens from any point. .... ❑ ❑ ❑ ❑ ❑

Count by threes to 99....................................... ❑ ❑ ❑ ❑ ❑

Count and write to 200 by ones from any point... ❑ ❑ ❑ ❑ ❑

Count and write to 900 by hundreds. .... ❑ ❑ ❑ ❑ ❑

Compare and determine sequence of numbers to
999; identify which comes before, between, or
after. .... ❑ ❑ ❑ ❑ ❑

OPERATIONS

Determine the appropriate sign to be used in a
number sentence.. ❑ ❑ ❑ ❑ ❑

Estimate the sum of two two-digit numbers
given in horizontal form. Demonstrate
knowledge that multiplication is repeated
addition (for example, $2+2+2+2=8$). ...... ❑ ❑ ❑ ❑ ❑

PLACE VALUE

Identify place value and total value for num-
bers 0-999. .... ❑ ❑ ❑ ❑ ❑

EVALUATION CHECK LIST FOR SECOND GRADE
MATHEMATICS

	CHILD'S NAME	CHILD'S NAME	CHILD'S NAME	CHILD'S NAME	CHILD'S NAME
Match cardinals to corresponding ordinal numbers through 20.	❏	❏	❏	❏	❏
Demonstrate an understanding of math terms and symbols: plus (+), minus (-), equals (=), greater than (>), less than (<), minuend, subtrahend, and difference.	❏	❏	❏	❏	❏
Demonstrate knowledge and understanding of place value of three-digit numerals using concrete objects or pictures (ones, tens, hundreds).	❏	❏	❏	❏	❏

ADDITION AND SUBTRACTION

Demonstrate recall of basic addition and subtraction facts up to the sum of 18.	❏	❏	❏	❏	❏
Demonstrate a knowledge of the commutative property of addition.	❏	❏	❏	❏	❏
Add three one-digit numbers with a sum of 0-18.	❏	❏	❏	❏	❏
Add up to two two-digit numbers, horizontally and vertically, with or without regrouping.	❏	❏	❏	❏	❏
Add three two-digit numbers, vertically, without regrouping.	❏	❏	❏	❏	❏
Subtract up to two two-digit numbers, horizontally and vertical, with or without regrouping.	❏	❏	❏	❏	❏
Subtract a two-digit number from a three-digit number without regrouping.	❏	❏	❏	❏	❏

MULTIPLICATION AND DIVISION

Identify "x" for multiplication.	❏	❏	❏	❏	❏
Name the products for multiplication facts with products less than 25.	❏	❏	❏	❏	❏

EVALUATION CHECK LIST FOR SECOND GRADE

MATHEMATICS

Name the product for a basic multiplication problem presented in horizontal form. .... ❏ ❏ ❏ ❏ ❏

Name the product for a basic multiplication problem presented in vertical form. .... ❏ ❏ ❏ ❏ ❏

Be able to name the quotient for basic division facts with dividends less than 25. .... ❏ ❏ ❏ ❏ ❏

GEOMETRY

Identify, name, and match triangle, square, rectangle, and circle. .... ❏ ❏ ❏ ❏ ❏

Identify specified plane figures. .... ❏ ❏ ❏ ❏ ❏

Determine the perimeter of a rectangle given all four sides. .... ❏ ❏ ❏ ❏ ❏

MEASUREMENTS

Indicate time up to the quarter hour. .... ❏ ❏ ❏ ❏ ❏

Be able to distinguish the time difference given two different clocks. .... ❏ ❏ ❏ ❏ ❏

Determine the value of a collection of coins, including pennies (cents), nickels, dimes, quarters, and half-dollars in terms of pennies (cents). .... ❏ ❏ ❏ ❏ ❏

Determine money value from a collection of coins and bills to $1.00. .... ❏ ❏ ❏ ❏ ❏

Identify day of month and day of week on a calendar. .... ❏ ❏ ❏ ❏ ❏

Measure lengths using a nonstandard measure of ten units. .... ❏ ❏ ❏ ❏ ❏

Identify the hotter/colder temperature by selecting the higher/lower column of two thermometers. .... ❏ ❏ ❏ ❏ ❏

Evaluation Check List for Second Grade

MATHEMATICS

Fractions

Identify fractional parts of a region $\frac{1}{2}$, $\frac{1}{4}$, $\frac{1}{10}$. ☐ ☐ ☐ ☐ ☐

Match word names to fractions (halves, fourths, thirds, and tenths) and match fractions to word names. .... ☐ ☐ ☐ ☐ ☐

Charts, Graphs, and Tables

Interpret and solve problems with bar graphs.
Use a table to determine how much more one frequency is than another. .... ☐ ☐ ☐ ☐ ☐

Problem Solving

Interpret pictographs and solve problems with pictographs (exclude partial figures). .... ☐ ☐ ☐ ☐ ☐

Complete number sentences with a missing addend, sums 10-18. .... ☐ ☐ ☐ ☐ ☐

Solve one-step word problems involving addition and subtraction up to two-digit numbers, with or without regrouping. .... ☐ ☐ ☐ ☐ ☐

Solve one-step word problems involving money up to $1.00. .... ☐ ☐ ☐ ☐ ☐

(Column headings, repeated: CHILD'S NAME, CHILD'S NAME, CHILD'S NAME, CHILD'S NAME, CHILD'S NAME)

EVALUATION CHECK LIST FOR THIRD GRADE

MATHEMATICS

Third-grade students should be able to do the following:

RECOGNIZE NAMES FOR NUMBERS

Identify the name of a three-digit number. ...... ❑ ❑ ❑ ❑ ❑

Identify the name of a four-digit number. .... ❑ ❑ ❑ ❑ ❑

Identify the name of a five-digit number. .... ❑ ❑ ❑ ❑ ❑

Identify word names for numbers through 9,999. .... ❑ ❑ ❑ ❑ ❑

Identify ordinals to twentieth. .... ❑ ❑ ❑ ❑ ❑

Identify any even and odd numbers to 99......... ❑ ❑ ❑ ❑ ❑

COUNTING

Order numbers through 9,999 in short sequence. ❑ ❑ ❑ ❑ ❑

Count by twos, threes, fives, and tens to 100, starting at any point .... ❑ ❑ ❑ ❑ ❑

Identify a number greater than a given number in the thousands. .... ❑ ❑ ❑ ❑ ❑

OPERATIONS

Estimate the sum of two two-digit numbers. .. ❑ ❑ ❑ ❑ ❑

Identify and use the symbols: >, <, =. .... ❑ ❑ ❑ ❑ ❑

PLACE VALUE

Round two-digit numerals to the nearest ten. ❑ ❑ ❑ ❑ ❑

Identify place value up to four digits and expanded form up to three digits. .... ❑ ❑ ❑ ❑ ❑

Compare whole numbers up to four digits. ...... ❑ ❑ ❑ ❑ ❑

Express a number as a number of tens and ones when the number of ones is greater than nine. .... ❑ ❑ ❑ ❑ ❑

EVALUATION CHECK LIST FOR THIRD GRADE

MATHEMATICS

	CHILD'S NAME	CHILD'S NAME	CHILD'S NAME	CHILD'S NAME	CHILD'S NAME
Round a number in hundredths to the nearest ten.	❑	❑	❑	❑	❑

ADDITION AND SUBTRACTION

	CHILD'S NAME	CHILD'S NAME	CHILD'S NAME	CHILD'S NAME	CHILD'S NAME
Add multi-digit numbers (up to three-digits)...	❑	❑	❑	❑	❑
Add a four-digit number and a three-digit number.	❑	❑	❑	❑	❑
Subtract up to two three-digit numbers.	❑	❑	❑	❑	❑
Subtract a one-digit number from a two-digit number, renaming tens to ones.	❑	❑	❑	❑	❑
Subtract a two-digit number from a three-digit number, renaming hundreds to tens.	❑	❑	❑	❑	❑
Subtract a three-digit number from a three-digit number.	❑	❑	❑	❑	❑

MULTIPLICATION AND DIVISION

	CHILD'S NAME	CHILD'S NAME	CHILD'S NAME	CHILD'S NAME	CHILD'S NAME
Name the product for a multiplication fact given in horizontal form.	❑	❑	❑	❑	❑
Name the product for a multiplication fact given in vertical form.	❑	❑	❑	❑	❑
Demonstrate an understanding of the terms multiplicand, multiplier, and product.	❑	❑	❑	❑	❑
Complete a function table using multiplication facts.	❑	❑	❑	❑	❑
Recall multiplication tables through fives.	❑	❑	❑	❑	❑
Multiply one-digit numbers.	❑	❑	❑	❑	❑
Multiply a two-digit number by a one-digit number.	❑	❑	❑	❑	❑
Use division facts (1-5) out of sequence.	❑	❑	❑	❑	❑

EVALUATION CHECK LIST FOR THIRD GRADE

MATHEMATICS

Column headers: CHILD'S NAME (×5)

GEOMETRY

Identify points, lines, and line segments. .... ❑ ❑ ❑ ❑ ❑

Relate spatial relationships to symmetry. ...... ❑ ❑ ❑ ❑ ❑

Find area of a square counting square units. .. ❑ ❑ ❑ ❑ ❑

Understand a triangle has three equal sides... ❑ ❑ ❑ ❑ ❑

MEASUREMENT

Read and write money amounts using dollar symbols, decimal notation, and cent symbols. ❑ ❑ ❑ ❑ ❑

Indicate time up to the nearest five-minute interval. .... ❑ ❑ ❑ ❑ ❑

Read temperature on a weather thermometer to the nearest 10 degrees. .... ❑ ❑ ❑ ❑ ❑

Make change for a dollar.................................. ❑ ❑ ❑ ❑ ❑

Determine money value for a collection of coins and bills to $10.00. .... ❑ ❑ ❑ ❑ ❑

Select the most appropriate unit of length, mass, and capacity. .... ❑ ❑ ❑ ❑ ❑

Measure to nearest inch or centimeter............. ❑ ❑ ❑ ❑ ❑

FRACTIONS

Identify fractional parts of a region (denominators through 10) using >, <, =......................... ❑ ❑ ❑ ❑ ❑

Compare two fractions representing shaded regions or sets. .... ❑ ❑ ❑ ❑ ❑

Identify fractions such as $\frac{31}{43}$, $\frac{41}{44}$, and $\frac{101}{410}$ as equal to 1. .... ❑ ❑ ❑ ❑ ❑

DECIMALS

Match decimal numbers from 0.1 to 0.9 to shaded regions.. ❑ ❑ ❑ ❑ ❑

EVALUATION CHECK LIST FOR THIRD GRADE

MATHEMATICS

PROBLEM SOLVING

CHILD'S NAME CHILD'S NAME CHILD'S NAME CHILD'S NAME CHILD'S NAME

Find the missing subtrahend or factor. .... ❏ ❏ ❏ ❏ ❏

Identify information not needed to solve a problem.. ❏ ❏ ❏ ❏ ❏

Solve one-step word problems involving addition and subtraction of numbers up to three digits. .... ❏ ❏ ❏ ❏ ❏

Solve one-step word problems involving multiplication of a one- or two-digit number by a one-digit number....................................... ❏ ❏ ❏ ❏ ❏

GRAPHS, CHARTS, AND TABLES

Construct a bar graph or picture graph. .... ❏ ❏ ❏ ❏ ❏

Interpret picture and bar graphs .... ❏ ❏ ❏ ❏ ❏

Solve problems with graphs (picture, bar, or table-partial pictures should only be in $-^{11}\!/_{42}$ figures). .... ❏ ❏ ❏ ❏ ❏

EVALUATION CHECK LIST FOR FOURTH GRADE
MATHEMATICS

Fourth-grade students should be able to do the following:

RECOGNIZE NAMES FOR NUMBERS

Read and write numbers through 999,999....... ❑ ❑ ❑ ❑ ❑

Identify word names for numbers through 999,999. .... ❑ ❑ ❑ ❑ ❑

COMPARE AND ORDER NUMBERS

Order or compare numbers to 99,999. .... ❑ ❑ ❑ ❑ ❑

Recognize and continue number patterns. ...... ❑ ❑ ❑ ❑ ❑

Write ordinals to twentieth. .... ❑ ❑ ❑ ❑ ❑

Recognize and indicate the value of the following

Roman numeral symbols: I, V, X, L, C. .... ❑ ❑ ❑ ❑ ❑

Identify even and odd numbers through 999... ❑ ❑ ❑ ❑ ❑

Identify the least of four numbers in the ten

thousands.. ❑ ❑ ❑ ❑ ❑

Order five numbers in the hundreds................ ❑ ❑ ❑ ❑ ❑

PLACE VALUE

Identify place value and numbers in expanded

form through 99,999. .... ❑ ❑ ❑ ❑ ❑

Round two-, three-, and four-digit numbers to

the nearest ten and hundred. .... ❑ ❑ ❑ ❑ ❑

Identify a number expressed in expanded

form, numbered in the thousands................ ❑ ❑ ❑ ❑ ❑

Name the number for a number of thousands,

hundredths, tens, and ones. .... ❑ ❑ ❑ ❑ ❑

ADDITION AND SUBTRACTION

Add numbers up to four digits (column should

be only up to three addends). .... ❑ ❑ ❑ ❑ ❑

EVALUATION CHECK LIST FOR FOURTH GRADE

MATHEMATICS

	CHILD'S NAME	CHILD'S NAME	CHILD'S NAME	CHILD'S NAME	CHILD'S NAME
Add two five-digit numbers.	☐	☐	☐	☐	☐
Subtract numbers up to four digits.	☐	☐	☐	☐	☐
Add a column of three- and four-digit numbers.	☐	☐	☐	☐	☐
Name the missing addend in an addition sentence.	☐	☐	☐	☐	☐
	☐	☐	☐	☐	☐

MULTIPLICATION AND DIVISION

Recall from memory, in and out of sequence multiplication and division facts through 9.	☐	☐	☐	☐	☐
Multiply up to a four-digit number by a one-digit number.	☐	☐	☐	☐	☐
Divide one- and two-digit numbers by a one-digit number with and without a remainder.	☐	☐	☐	☐	☐
Demonstrate an understanding of the terms *divisor, dividend, quotient,* and *remainder.*	☐	☐	☐	☐	☐

GEOMETRY

Identify points, lines, rays, and line segments.	☐	☐	☐	☐	☐
Locate points on a grid by counting to right and up.	☐	☐	☐	☐	☐
Identify right angles.	☐	☐	☐	☐	☐
Find the perimeter of a polygon with four sides or less. Measure the area of a figure by counting square units.	☐	☐	☐	☐	☐

MEASUREMENT

Indicate time to the nearest minute on a standard clock.	☐	☐	☐	☐	☐
Identify time relationships (minute/hour, hour/day, a.m./p.m., day/week).	☐	☐	☐	☐	☐
Indicate temperature to the nearest degree on					

Evaluation Check List for Fourth Grade

MATHEMATICS

	CHILD'S NAME	CHILD'S NAME	CHILD'S NAME	CHILD'S NAME	CHILD'S NAME
a Celsius or Fahrenheit thermometer.	☐	☐	☐	☐	☐
Measure length, weight (mass), and liquid capacity in customary or metric units.	☐	☐	☐	☐	☐
Determine money value from a collection of coins and bills to $100.00.	☐	☐	☐	☐	☐

FRACTIONS

Identify the numerator and denominator of a fraction.	☐	☐	☐	☐	☐
Identify and compare fractions with like denominators...	☐	☐	☐	☐	☐
Add fractions having like denominators without regrouping, using denominators through 10.	☐	☐	☐	☐	☐
Subtract fractions having like denominators without regrouping, using denominators through 10.	☐	☐	☐	☐	☐
Add a whole number and a mixed fractional number..	☐	☐	☐	☐	☐
Subtract a whole number from a mixed fractional number.	☐	☐	☐	☐	☐

DECIMALS

Identify the place value and total value of a digit in a decimal numeral up to hundredths place.	☐	☐	☐	☐	☐
Identify the place value and total value of a mixed decimal (to hundredths).	☐	☐	☐	☐	☐
Determine the decimal equivalent of a fraction with a denominator of 10 or 100.	☐	☐	☐	☐	☐
Identify information needed to solve a word problem..	☐	☐	☐	☐	☐

Evaluation Check List for Fourth Grade

Mathematics

	CHILD'S NAME	CHILD'S NAME	CHILD'S NAME	CHILD'S NAME	CHILD'S NAME

Problem Solving

Solve one-step word problems involving addition, subtractions, multiplication, and basic division facts. .... ❏ ❏ ❏ ❏ ❏

Solve money problems using addition and subtractions up to $99. .... ❏ ❏ ❏ ❏ ❏

Solve a rate problem. .... ❏ ❏ ❏ ❏ ❏

Determine probability given the proper facts. ... ❏ ❏ ❏ ❏ ❏

Charts, Graphs, and Tables

Interpret simple charts, graphs, and tables. ..... ❏ ❏ ❏ ❏ ❏

Use information from tables, charts, and graphs to solve problems involving the four basic operations on whole numbers. .... ❏ ❏ ❏ ❏ ❏

Identify categories with most or least frequency using tables, charts, or graphs. .... ❏ ❏ ❏ ❏ ❏

EVALUATION CHECK LIST FOR FIFTH GRADE

MATHEMATICS

Fifth-grade students should be able to do the following:

RECOGNIZE NAMES OF NUMBERS

Read and write numerals through 9,999,999. .... ❑ ❑ ❑ ❑ ❑

Identify word names for numbers through 9,999,999. .... ❑ ❑ ❑ ❑ ❑

Identify numbers in expanded form through 999,999. .... ❑ ❑ ❑ ❑ ❑

Recognize, read and write Roman numerals to 1,000. .... ❑ ❑ ❑ ❑ ❑

Recognize prime numbers less than 20. .... ❑ ❑ ❑ ❑ ❑

PLACE VALUE

Identify place value for up to seven-digit numerals. .... ❑ ❑ ❑ ❑ ❑

Round four- and five-digit numerals to the nearest thousand, hundredth or tenth......... ❑ ❑ ❑ ❑ ❑

ADDITION AND SUBTRACTION

Add multi-digit numbers (up to five addends).
Subtract multi-digit numbers. .... ❑ ❑ ❑ ❑ ❑

Identify the common factors of two whole numbers, each of which is less than 100............... ❑ ❑ ❑ ❑ ❑

Identify the greatest common factor of two whole numbers, each of which is less than 100. .... ❑ ❑ ❑ ❑ ❑

MULTIPLICATION AND DIVISION

Identify common multiples of two whole numbers. ❑ ❑ ❑ ❑ ❑

Identify the least common multiple of two whole numbers. .... ❑ ❑ ❑ ❑ ❑

EVALUATION CHECK LIST FOR FIFTH GRADE

MATHEMATICS

Multiply two- and three-digit numbers with and without a zero. .... ❑ ❑ ❑ ❑ ❑

Divide a two-digit number by a two-digit number with or without a remainder. .... ❑ ❑ ❑ ❑ ❑

Divide a three-digit number by a one-digit number with or without a remainder. .... ❑ ❑ ❑ ❑ ❑

Determine the mean of five one- or two-digit numbers without a remainder. .... ❑ ❑ ❑ ❑ ❑

GEOMETRY

Determine the area of a square, rectangle, and triangle using a formula. .... ❑ ❑ ❑ ❑ ❑

Draw circles and label diameter, circumference, radius, and center. .... ❑ ❑ ❑ ❑ ❑

Identify acute, right, obtuse, and straight angles. ❑ ❑ ❑ ❑ ❑

Recognize and name congruent triangles from a set of triangles and congruent rectangles from a set of rectangles. .... ❑ ❑ ❑ ❑ ❑

MEASUREMENT

Identify standard temperatures on a thermometer. .... ❑ ❑ ❑ ❑ ❑

Identify time relationships (minutes in an hour, hours in a day, a.m., or p.m., ... days in a week, etc) and perform conversions between units of time. .... ❑ ❑ ❑ ❑ ❑

Identify metric and customary relationships (m./cm., kg./g, km./m, lb./oz., ft./in., yd./ft., and yd./in.). .... ❑ ❑ ❑ ❑ ❑

Measure to the nearest millimeter or quarter inch. .... ❑ ❑ ❑ ❑ ❑

EVALUATION CHECK LIST FOR FIFTH GRADE

MATHEMATICS

CHILD'S NAME   CHILD'S NAME   CHILD'S NAME   CHILD'S NAME   CHILD'S NAME

Solve addition, subtraction, multiplication and division problems involving monetary units. ... ☐ ☐ ☐ ☐ ☐

Identify the change due in bills and coins when bills are used for payment. .... ☐ ☐ ☐ ☐ ☐

FRACTIONS

Read simple word problems, including those with whole numbers, fractions, or decimals, and use the appropriate operation to calculate the answer. .... ☐ ☐ ☐ ☐ ☐

Identify fractions in lowest terms using the greatest common factor. .... ☐ ☐ ☐ ☐ ☐

Compare fractions having unlike denominators by finding the common denominator. ... ☐ ☐ ☐ ☐ ☐

Identify a mixed number as an improper fraction and vice versa............................... ☐ ☐ ☐ ☐ ☐

Change improper fractions to mixed numbers and vice versa, reducing fractions to lowest terms. .... ☐ ☐ ☐ ☐ ☐

Add fraction having like denominators with regrouping. .... ☐ ☐ ☐ ☐ ☐

Subtract fractions having like denominators with regrouping................................. ☐ ☐ ☐ ☐ ☐

Add fractions having unlike denominators without regrouping..................................... ☐ ☐ ☐ ☐ ☐

Rename mixed fractional numbers................. ☐ ☐ ☐ ☐ ☐

Add and subtract mixed numbers.................... ☐ ☐ ☐ ☐ ☐

DECIMALS

Identify decimal numbers to thousandths. ...... ☐ ☐ ☐ ☐ ☐

Identify decimal place value to thousandths. ... ☐ ☐ ☐ ☐ ☐

EVALUATION CHECK LIST FOR FIFTH GRADE

MATHEMATICS

	CHILD'S NAME	CHILD'S NAME	CHILD'S NAME	CHILD'S NAME	CHILD'S NAME
Write the word name for a decimal number to thousandths. Identify the greater or lesser of two decimal numbers to thousandths.	❑	❑	❑	❑	❑
Add decimal numbers (including mixed number) to thousandths.	❑	❑	❑	❑	❑
Subtract decimal numbers (including mixed numbers) to thousandths.	❑	❑	❑	❑	❑
Round decimal numbers to the nearest whole number or tenth.	❑	❑	❑	❑	❑
Add and subtract using decimals, money, and cent symbols correctly.	❑	❑	❑	❑	❑

CHARTS, GRAPHS, AND TABLES

Read and interpret a picture graph with partial figures.	❑	❑	❑	❑	❑
Read and interpret simple circle graphs.	❑	❑	❑	❑	❑
Read and interpret bar graphs using estimation.	❑	❑	❑	❑	❑

PROBLEM SOLVING

Solve word problems involving perimeter of three- and four-sided figures.	❑	❑	❑	❑	❑
Perform operations based on the use of parentheses, (distributive property).	❑	❑	❑	❑	❑
Solve one- and two-step word problems involving any combination of basic operation on whole numbers.	❑	❑	❑	❑	❑
Complete a number sentence with a missing number using one of the four basic operations on whole numbers.	❑	❑	❑	❑	❑
Solve problems using whole number data from charts, tables, graphs, and maps.	❑	❑	❑	❑	❑

EVALUATION CHECK LIST FOR SIXTH GRADE

MATHEMATICS

Sixth-grade students should be able to do the following:

WHOLE NUMBERS

Recall and write numerals through 999,999,999,999. .... ❑ ❑ ❑ ❑ ❑

Identify word names through 999,999,999. .... ❑ ❑ ❑ ❑ ❑

Round off numbers to the nearest ten-thousand, thousand, hundred, or ten. .... ❑ ❑ ❑ ❑ ❑

Identify prime numbers and composite numbers less than 100. .... ❑ ❑ ❑ ❑ ❑

Recognize the base and the exponent of an expression and calculate its value................ ❑ ❑ ❑ ❑ ❑

Recognize the Roman numeral symbols I, V, X, L, C, D, and M, indicate their value and Roman numerals up to 2,000........................ ❑ ❑ ❑ ❑ ❑

MEASUREMENT

Determine temperature changes on both Celsius and Fahrenheit thermometers without negative numbers. .... ❑ ❑ ❑ ❑ ❑

Identify the change in bills and coins due when bills and coins are used in payment. .... ❑ ❑ ❑ ❑ ❑

Perform conversions between linear units with the metric and customary systems. .... ❑ ❑ ❑ ❑ ❑

Perform conversions within the metric or customary system of measuring mass or weight.. ❑ ❑ ❑ ❑ ❑

Add and subtract linear units of measurement using renaming (metric or customary)......... ❑ ❑ ❑ ❑ ❑

Perform conversions between units of time. .... ❑ ❑ ❑ ❑ ❑

EVALUATION CHECK LIST FOR SIXTH GRADE

MATHEMATICS

	CHILD'S NAME	CHILD'S NAME	CHILD'S NAME	CHILD'S NAME	CHILD'S NAME
Perform conversions between units of capacity within the metric and customary systems...	☐	☐	☐	☐	☐
Recognize and identify perpendicular lines, polygons by name, and chord, center, diameter, radius, and arc of a circle.	☐	☐	☐	☐	☐

GEOMETRY

Measure simple angles to the nearest degree.					
Determine the area of a triangle and a parallelogram using the formula.	☐	☐	☐	☐	☐
Determine the volume of a rectangular solid...	☐	☐	☐	☐	☐

MULTIPLICATION AND DIVISION

Identify the greatest common factor of two whole numbers.	☐	☐	☐	☐	☐
Multiply two four-digit numbers.	☐	☐	☐	☐	☐
Divide a four-digit number by a two- or three-digit number.	☐	☐	☐	☐	☐
Divide two two-digit numbers with remainder.	☐	☐	☐	☐	☐
Identify the least common multiple of two whole numbers.	☐	☐	☐	☐	☐
Add fractions having unlike denominators with regrouping.	☐	☐	☐	☐	☐

FRACTIONS

Subtract fractions having unlike denominators with regrouping.	☐	☐	☐	☐	☐
Add mixed numbers having like denominators with and without regrouping.	☐	☐	☐	☐	☐
Add mixed numbers having unlike denominators with regrouping.	☐	☐	☐	☐	☐

EVALUATION CHECK LIST FOR SIXTH GRADE

MATHEMATICS

	CHILD'S NAME	CHILD'S NAME	CHILD'S NAME	CHILD'S NAME	CHILD'S NAME
Subtract mixed numbers having like denominators with and without regrouping.	☐	☐	☐	☐	☐
Subtract mixed numbers having unlike denominators with regrouping.	☐	☐	☐	☐	☐
Add or subtract whole numbers and mixed numbers.	☐	☐	☐	☐	☐
Multiply a proper fraction by a proper fraction, using denominators through 10.	☐	☐	☐	☐	☐
Divide a fraction by a fraction.	☐	☐	☐	☐	☐
Write the reciprocal of a rational number.	☐	☐	☐	☐	☐
Multiply or divide a whole number by a fraction.	☐	☐	☐	☐	☐

DECIMALS

Order decimal numbers to ten-thousandths. ..	☐	☐	☐	☐	☐
Write the decimal word name to the ten-thousandths.	☐	☐	☐	☐	☐
Round decimal numbers to the nearest whole number, tenth hundredth, or thousandth.	☐	☐	☐	☐	☐
Add or subtract two decimal numbers through ten-thousandths.	☐	☐	☐	☐	☐
Multiply two mixed decimal numbers with factors to thousandths.	☐	☐	☐	☐	☐
Divide a decimal by a whole number and vice versa.	☐	☐	☐	☐	☐
Divide two decimals without repeating decimals in the quotients.	☐	☐	☐	☐	☐
Change proper fractions to decimals, then to percents.	☐	☐	☐	☐	☐
Compute a given percent of a whole number. ...	☐	☐	☐	☐	☐

EVALUATION CHECK LIST FOR SIXTH GRADE

MATHEMATICS

Determine the mean of ten one- or two-digit numbers with a remainder. .... ☐ ☐ ☐ ☐ ☐

PROBLEM SOLVING

Solve practical problems involving the mean. .... ☐ ☐ ☐ ☐ ☐

Write a mathematical expression using variables. .... ☐ ☐ ☐ ☐ ☐

Evaluate one-step mathematical expressions. .. ☐ ☐ ☐ ☐ ☐

Solve one-step word problems involving any combination of basic operations on whole numbers, decimals, or fractions. .... ☐ ☐ ☐ ☐ ☐

Solve two-step word problems involving any combination of basic operations on whole numbers, decimals, or fractions. .... ☐ ☐ ☐ ☐ ☐

CHARTS, TABLES, GRAPHS

Read and interpret bar, line, and partial pictographs. .... ☐ ☐ ☐ ☐ ☐

Read and interpret charts and schedules. .... ☐ ☐ ☐ ☐ ☐

Interpret data in percent form from a circle graph. .... ☐ ☐ ☐ ☐ ☐

Determine the range of data in a frequency table. .... ☐ ☐ ☐ ☐ ☐

Determine the probability of an event occurring. .... ☐ ☐ ☐ ☐ ☐

Write and solve a proportion, given a word problem. .... ☐ ☐ ☐ ☐ ☐

Identify a ratio comparing the number of objects in two sets using three forms. .... ☐ ☐ ☐ ☐ ☐

Identify equivalent ratios for a given ratio. ...... ☐ ☐ ☐ ☐ ☐

Determine the missing number in a proportion. ☐ ☐ ☐ ☐ ☐

Evaluation Check List for Sixth Grade

MATHEMATICS

	CHILD'S NAME	CHILD'S NAME	CHILD'S NAME	CHILD'S NAME	CHILD'S NAME
Convert fractions with denominators of 100 to percent and vice versa.	☐	☐	☐	☐	☐
Convert a decimal (no more than two significant digits) to a percent and vice versa.	☐	☐	☐	☐	☐
Recognize a negative integer on a number line...	☐	☐	☐	☐	☐
Multiply and divide using dollar and cent symbols correctly.	☐	☐	☐	☐	☐

EVALUATION CHECK LIST FOR SEVENTH GRADE

MATHEMATICS

Seventh-grade students should be able to do the following:

WHOLE NUMBERS

Round numbers to the nearest ten-thousand, thousand, hundred, or ten. .... ❑ ❑ ❑ ❑ ❑

Identify numbers divisible by 2, 3, 4, 5, 6, 9 and 10 using divisibility rules. .... ❑ ❑ ❑ ❑ ❑

Determine the square of any number less than 100. .... ❑ ❑ ❑ ❑ ❑

Identify the positive square root of a perfect square less than 150. .... ❑ ❑ ❑ ❑ ❑

Identify the base and the exponent of an expression and calculate its value......... ❑ ❑ ❑ ❑ ❑

Identify numbers and their expanded form through 10 to the third power. .... ❑ ❑ ❑ ❑ ❑

Identify the prime factors of any number through 100. .... ❑ ❑ ❑ ❑ ❑

INTEGERS

Compare integers. .... ❑ ❑ ❑ ❑ ❑

Order integers on a number line from least to greatest... ❑ ❑ ❑ ❑ ❑

Identify the greater and lesser of two integers. .... ❑ ❑ ❑ ❑ ❑

Determine the absolute value of an integer. .... ❑ ❑ ❑ ❑ ❑

Add integers having like signs. .... ❑ ❑ ❑ ❑ ❑

Add integers having unlike signs. .... ❑ ❑ ❑ ❑ ❑

Subtract integers having like signs................. ❑ ❑ ❑ ❑ ❑

Subtract integers having unlike signs. .... ❑ ❑ ❑ ❑ ❑

EVALUATION CHECK LIST FOR SEVENTH GRADE
MATHEMATICS

MEASUREMENT

Determine the time in one time zone when given time in another zone (contiguous United States time zones). .... ❏ ❏ ❏ ❏ ❏

GEOMETRY

Bisect a line segment using a compass and straight edge. .... ❏ ❏ ❏ ❏ ❏

Draw an angle with a given measure. .... ❏ ❏ ❏ ❏ ❏

Bisect an angle using a compass and a straight-edge. .... ❏ ❏ ❏ ❏ ❏

Determine the circumference of a circle using the formula. .... ❏ ❏ ❏ ❏ ❏

Classify triangles according to angle size. .... ❏ ❏ ❏ ❏ ❏

Classify triangles by the lengths of sides. .... ❏ ❏ ❏ ❏ ❏

MULTIPLICATION AND DIVISION

Divide a three- or four-digit number by a two- or three-digit number with a remainder. ..... ❏ ❏ ❏ ❏ ❏

Multiply a four-digit number by three- or four-digit numbers. .... ❏ ❏ ❏ ❏ ❏

FRACTIONS

Add three mixed numbers having unlike denominators with regrouping. .... ❏ ❏ ❏ ❏ ❏

Subtract mixed numbers having unlike denominators with regrouping. .... ❏ ❏ ❏ ❏ ❏

Subtract a fraction or a mixed number from a whole number. .... ❏ ❏ ❏ ❏ ❏

Multiply three factors in any combination of fractions, mixed fractional numbers and

	CHILD'S NAME	CHILD'S NAME	CHILD'S NAME	CHILD'S NAME	CHILD'S NAME
whole numbers.	❑	❑	❑	❑	❑
Write the reciprocal of a mixed fractional number.	❑	❑	❑	❑	❑
Determine, using division, the decimal number equivalent of a fraction or a mixed number.	❑	❑	❑	❑	❑
Divide a whole number, fraction, or mixed number by a mixed number.	❑	❑	❑	❑	❑
Determine if a fraction converts to a terminating or repeating decimal.	❑	❑	❑	❑	❑

DECIMALS

Read and write decimal numbers to the millionths place.	❑	❑	❑	❑	❑
Write decimal numbers in expanded form to millionths place.	❑	❑	❑	❑	❑
Divide a whole number or decimal by a decimal with a repeating decimal in tile quotient.	❑	❑	❑	❑	❑
Divide a whole number or a decimal by a decimal and round the quotient to tile hundredths place.	❑	❑	❑	❑	❑
Calculate the decimal number that is the equivalent of a fraction or a mixed number.	❑	❑	❑	❑	❑
Read and interpret dual bar graphs and dual broken-line graphs.	❑	❑	❑	❑	❑
Identify the quadrants and signs of a coordinate plane.	❑	❑	❑	❑	❑
Locate a point using ordered pairs of integers on the coordinate plane.	❑	❑	❑	❑	❑
Evaluate mathematical expressions with two operations (whole numbers).	❑	❑	❑	❑	❑

EVALUATION CHECK LIST FOR SEVENTH GRADE
MATHEMATICS

PROBLEM SOLVING

Solve one-step equations with one variable using addition and subtraction of whole numbers. .... □ □ □ □ □

Solve word problems with metric and customary measurements............................... □ □ □ □ □

Solve word problems using multiplication and division of monetary amounts. .... □ □ □ □ □

Given a word problem identify and solve a proportion. .... □ □ □ □ □

Define a probability of 1 and a probability of 0... □ □ □ □ □

Determine the possible outcomes in a situation with two variables. .... □ □ □ □ □

Determine the missing number in a proportion.. □ □ □ □ □

PERCENT

Find the percent of a number. .... □ □ □ □ □

Identify the percent equivalent of a fraction. .... □ □ □ □ □

Identify the fractional equivalent of a percent. .... □ □ □ □ □

Solve percentage statements in proportional form. .... □ □ □ □ □

EVALUATION CHECK LIST FOR EIGHTH GRADE

MATHEMATICS

Eighth-grade students should be able to do the following:

	CHILD'S NAME	CHILD'S NAME	CHILD'S NAME	CHILD'S NAME	CHILD'S NAME
WHOLE NUMBERS					
Recognize numbers in expanded form using exponents through 10 to the 10th power (10_{10}).	❑	❑	❑	❑	❑
Evaluate expressions using the order of operations.	❑	❑	❑	❑	❑
Evaluate expressions which include exponents.	❑	❑	❑	❑	❑
GEOMETRY					
Find the perimeter and area of polygons.	❑	❑	❑	❑	❑
Determine the area of a circle using the formula.	❑	❑	❑	❑	❑
Determine the circumference of a circle using the formula.	❑	❑	❑	❑	❑
Determine the area of a trapezoid using the formula.	❑	❑	❑	❑	❑
Determine the volume of a rectangular solid and a cylinder.	❑	❑	❑	❑	❑
Calculate the volume of a sphere.	❑	❑	❑	❑	❑
Use the Pythagorean Theorem.	❑	❑	❑	❑	❑
Identify central and inscribed angles of a circle.	❑	❑	❑	❑	❑
Identify the properties of congruent triangles.	❑	❑	❑	❑	❑
Identify the properties of similar triangles.	❑	❑	❑	❑	❑
Identify corresponding angles.	❑	❑	❑	❑	❑
Identify vertical angles.	❑	❑	❑	❑	❑

EVALUATION CHECK LIST FOR EIGHTH GRADE

MATHEMATICS

OPERATIONS

Perform basic operations with whole numbers, decimals, and integers (with like and unlike signs). .... ☐ ☐ ☐ ☐ ☐

Perform basic operations with fractions, whole numbers and mixed numbers. .... ☐ ☐ ☐ ☐ ☐

Identify rational numbers using the number line. .... ☐ ☐ ☐ ☐ ☐

Use the commutative and associative properties of addition with rational numbers. .... ☐ ☐ ☐ ☐ ☐

Identify examples of the commutative and associative properties of multiplication with rational numbers. .... ☐ ☐ ☐ ☐ ☐

Demonstrate application of the distributive property over a number. .... ☐ ☐ ☐ ☐ ☐

FRACTIONS

Write the fractional equivalent of a repeating decimal. .... ☐ ☐ ☐ ☐ ☐

Convert a number in standard form to scientific notation and vice versa. .... ☐ ☐ ☐ ☐ ☐

Identify the simplified form of a complex fraction. .... ☐ ☐ ☐ ☐ ☐

PROBLEM SOLVING

Solve one- and two-step equations using whole numbers. .... ☐ ☐ ☐ ☐ ☐

Solve one-step equations using fractions. .... ☐ ☐ ☐ ☐ ☐

Solve distance problems using the formula. .... ☐ ☐ ☐ ☐ ☐

Solve word problems using metric and customary measurements. .... ☐ ☐ ☐ ☐ ☐

EVALUATION CHECK LIST FOR EIGHTH GRADE

MATHEMATICS

	CHILD'S NAME	CHILD'S NAME	CHILD'S NAME	CHILD'S NAME	CHILD'S NAME
Solve one- and two-step word problems using whole numbers, decimals, or fractions.	❏	❏	❏	❏	❏
Determine the missing value in a simple interest formula.	❏	❏	❏	❏	❏
Determine possible outcomes in a situation with two variables.	❏	❏	❏	❏	❏
Identify the mean.	❏	❏	❏	❏	❏
Identify the mode.	❏	❏	❏	❏	❏
Identify the median of a series of two-digit numbers.	❏	❏	❏	❏	❏
Calculate fraction, decimal, and percent equivalence.	❏	❏	❏	❏	❏
Determine the percent of increase and/or decrease.	❏	❏	❏	❏	❏
Determine the unit cost of items to compare prices.	❏	❏	❏	❏	❏

PERCENT

Determine simple interest for one year.	❏	❏	❏	❏	❏
Determine the discount on a sale item.	❏	❏	❏	❏	❏
Determine the commission on a sale.	❏	❏	❏	❏	❏
Locate a point using ordered pairs of integers on the coordinate plane.	❏	❏	❏	❏	❏
Locate the quadrant in which an ordered pair of integers is located.	❏	❏	❏	❏	❏

CHARTS, GRAPHS, AND TABLES

Interpret graphs, tables, scales, and charts by making identification, comparisons and calculations.	❏	❏	❏	❏	❏

When he made a decree for the rain, and a way for the lighting of the the thunder:
Then did he see it, yea, and searched it out. And unto man he said, Behold, the fear of the Lord,
that is wisdom; and to depart from evil is understanding.
Job 28:25-28

SCIENCE

EARTH AND SPACE · BIOLOGICAL SCIENCES: ANIMALS/PLANTS · PHYSICAL SCIENCE · SCIENCE PROCESSING SKILLS

EVALUATION CHECK LIST FOR KINDERGARTEN

SCIENCE

Kindergarten students should be able to do the following:

EARTH AND SPACE

Realize weather conditions change from day to
day...

Realize rocks are part of the earth's composition. ☐ ☐ ☐ ☐ ☐

☐ ☐ ☐ ☐ ☐

Develop an appreciation for the earth's environment and the necessity for keeping it clean. ☐ ☐ ☐ ☐ ☐

BIOLOGICAL SCIENCE

Understand animals reproduce by having
young. .... ☐ ☐ ☐ ☐ ☐

Recognize animals live in a variety of habitats
and change with the different seasons. ...... ☐ ☐ ☐ ☐ ☐

Understand plants as living things that grow
and change. .... ☐ ☐ ☐ ☐ ☐

Recognize human beings have similarities and
differences. .... ☐ ☐ ☐ ☐ ☐

Understand human beings experience their
world through the use of the senses........... ☐ ☐ ☐ ☐ ☐

PHYSICAL SCIENCE

Understand electricity is not only useful but
can be dangerous... ☐ ☐ ☐ ☐ ☐

Learn the importance of observing safety rules
when using electricity.................................. ☐ ☐ ☐ ☐ ☐

Learn magnets can both attract and repel. ...... ☐ ☐ ☐ ☐ ☐

Recognize there are different kinds and
sources of sound................................. ☐ ☐ ☐ ☐ ☐

Evaluation Check List for First Grade

SCIENCE

First-grade students should be able to do the following:

EARTH AND SPACE

Understand earth is our home planet. .... ☐ ☐ ☐ ☐ ☐

Know the common astronomical bodies (clouds, sun, stars, etc.). .... ☐ ☐ ☐ ☐ ☐

Understand the planets rotate. .... ☐ ☐ ☐ ☐ ☐

Understand fossils provide information about the past. .... ☐ ☐ ☐ ☐ ☐

Understand water evaporates. .... ☐ ☐ ☐ ☐ ☐

BIOLOGICAL SCIENCE

Understand the general functions of the:

heart. .... ☐ ☐ ☐ ☐ ☐

lungs. .... ☐ ☐ ☐ ☐ ☐

brain. .... ☐ ☐ ☐ ☐ ☐

stomach. .... ☐ ☐ ☐ ☐ ☐

Understand proper nutrition and caring for the body. .... ☐ ☐ ☐ ☐ ☐

Be able to tell which food group a food item fits into. .... ☐ ☐ ☐ ☐ ☐

Understand food processing makes a difference in nutrition. .... ☐ ☐ ☐ ☐ ☐

BIOLOGICAL SCIENCE: ANIMALS

Understand the difference between living and non-living things. .... ☐ ☐ ☐ ☐ ☐

Understand animals are living things with specific needs and characteristics. .... ☐ ☐ ☐ ☐ ☐

Understand reproductive differences in animals. ☐ ☐ ☐ ☐ ☐

EVALUATION CHECK LIST FOR FIRST GRADE

SCIENCE

The columns are headed: CHILD'S NAME (×5)

Identify an animal that sleeps through the winter. .... ☐ ☐ ☐ ☐ ☐

BIOLOGICAL SCIENCE: PLANTS

Understand plants are living things with specific needs and characteristics. .... ☐ ☐ ☐ ☐ ☐

Realize all living things grow and develop. ...... ☐ ☐ ☐ ☐ ☐

Identify a living thing can grow from a seed..... ☐ ☐ ☐ ☐ ☐

Understand plants are living things with specific needs and characteristics. .... ☐ ☐ ☐ ☐ ☐

Understand how parts of a plant function. ...... ☐ ☐ ☐ ☐ ☐

PHYSICAL SCIENCE

Understand different states of matter (solid, liquid, gas). .... ☐ ☐ ☐ ☐ ☐

Understand heat, light, and energy come from the sun. .... ☐ ☐ ☐ ☐ ☐

Recognize scientists work by using experiments. .... ☐ ☐ ☐ ☐ ☐

Recognize machines are not only useful to man but can be dangerous to use. .... ☐ ☐ ☐ ☐ ☐

Understand the concept of weight. .... ☐ ☐ ☐ ☐ ☐

Understand the use for common household appliances. .... ☐ ☐ ☐ ☐ ☐

Understand matter exists in various states and has identifiable properties. .... ☐ ☐ ☐ ☐ ☐

SCIENCE PROCESSING SKILLS

Analyze a simple bar graph. .... ☐ ☐ ☐ ☐ ☐

Predict results of water evaporation. .... ☐ ☐ ☐ ☐ ☐

Determine the sequence of events in space. .... ☐ ☐ ☐ ☐ ☐

EVALUATION CHECK LIST FOR SECOND GRADE

SCIENCE

Second-grade students should be able to do the following:

EARTH AND SPACE

Understand different bodies of water provide important resources. .... ☐ ☐ ☐ ☐ ☐

Understand the effects of gravity. .... ☐ ☐ ☐ ☐ ☐

Recognize weather is the result of changing atmospheric conditions. .... ☐ ☐ ☐ ☐ ☐

Understand man's environment is affected by the activities of the earth's inhabitants. ...... ☐ ☐ ☐ ☐ ☐

Understand the effects of the following:

earthquake.. ☐ ☐ ☐ ☐ ☐

hurricane. .... ☐ ☐ ☐ ☐ ☐

tornado. .... ☐ ☐ ☐ ☐ ☐

flood... ☐ ☐ ☐ ☐ ☐

Be able to recognize the names of planets. ...... ☐ ☐ ☐ ☐ ☐

BIOLOGICAL SCIENCE: ANIMALS

Realize animals differ in various ways and all living things experience life cycles. .... ☐ ☐ ☐ ☐ ☐

Understand animals have like offspring. .... ☐ ☐ ☐ ☐ ☐

Realize animals live in different environments. ☐ ☐ ☐ ☐ ☐

Be able to classify common animals (reptile, bird, mammal, etc.) .... ☐ ☐ ☐ ☐ ☐

Understand the growth and development of different animal stages.................................. ☐ ☐ ☐ ☐ ☐

BIOLOGICAL SCIENCE: PLANTS

Determine what is required for seed development... ☐ ☐ ☐ ☐ ☐

Understand plants are living things with specific needs and characteristics. ....

EVALUATION CHECK LIST FOR SECOND GRADE

SCIENCE

Understand how parts of plants function.........   ❑ ❑ ❑ ❑ ❑

CHILD'S NAME   CHILD'S NAME   CHILD'S NAME   CHILD'S NAME   CHILD'S NAME

PHYSICAL SCIENCE

Understand sound is produced by vibrations and is transmitted through matter in all directions. ....   ❑ ❑ ❑ ❑ ❑

Compare energy sources with energy uses (sun, heat, etc.) ....   ❑ ❑ ❑ ❑ ❑

Understand different states of matter (solid, liquid, gas). ....   ❑ ❑ ❑ ❑ ❑

Recognize heat and light as related forms of energy that come from various sources. ......   ❑ ❑ ❑ ❑ ❑

Understand heat energy affects matter in various ways. ....   ❑ ❑ ❑ ❑ ❑

Recognize energy exists in many types and must be conserved..........................   ❑ ❑ ❑ ❑ ❑

Understand electricity is not only useful, but can be dangerous...........................   ❑ ❑ ❑ ❑ ❑

Learn the importance of observing safety rules when using electricity...............................   ❑ ❑ ❑ ❑ ❑

SCIENCE PROCESSING SKILLS

Analyze data charts, graphs, and tables...........   ❑ ❑ ❑ ❑ ❑

Given a dangerous situation, predict the proper action. ....   ❑ ❑ ❑ ❑ ❑

Be able to classify into which food group a food item fits..   ❑ ❑ ❑ ❑ ❑

Use observation skills to classify an object. ......   ❑ ❑ ❑ ❑ ❑

Use observation skills to estimate measurement. ....   ❑ ❑ ❑ ❑ ❑

EVALUATION CHECK LIST FOR THIRD GRADE

SCIENCE

Third-grade students should be able to do the following:

EARTH AND SPACE

Realize the solar system is composed of many objects which revolve around a star. .... ☐ ☐ ☐ ☐ ☐

Understand rocks and soil move through a continuous cycle. .... ☐ ☐ ☐ ☐ ☐

Understand day and night result from the rotation of the earth. .... ☐ ☐ ☐ ☐ ☐

Understand earth's temperature differs with sun ray angle. .... ☐ ☐ ☐ ☐ ☐

Understand fossils. .... ☐ ☐ ☐ ☐ ☐

Recognize living things are affected by changes in the environment. .... ☐ ☐ ☐ ☐ ☐

Understand the evaporation process. .... ☐ ☐ ☐ ☐ ☐

Understand precipitation. .... ☐ ☐ ☐ ☐ ☐

Predict the effects of pollution. .... ☐ ☐ ☐ ☐ ☐

BIOLOGICAL SCIENCE

Be able to match skeletal parts to body sections. ☐ ☐ ☐ ☐ ☐

Understand body organs and their functions. ☐ ☐ ☐ ☐ ☐

Understand the four food groups. .... ☐ ☐ ☐ ☐ ☐

Recognize the various body systems that support and protect the human body. .... ☐ ☐ ☐ ☐ ☐

Understand the habitat is the environment in which particular organisms live. .... ☐ ☐ ☐ ☐ ☐

BIOLOGICAL SCIENCE: ANIMALS

Identify common features of animals to determine class. .... ☐ ☐ ☐ ☐ ☐

EVALUATION CHECK LIST FOR THIRD GRADE
SCIENCE

Understand basic animal needs for adult and
baby animals. .... ❑ ❑ ❑ ❑ ❑

Classify common animals (bird, mammal, rep-
tile, etc.). .... ❑ ❑ ❑ ❑ ❑

BIOLOGICAL SCIENCE: PLANTS

Realize plants reproduce and grow in various
ways. .... ❑ ❑ ❑ ❑ ❑

Identify common plant forms. .... ❑ ❑ ❑ ❑ ❑

Understand composition of plants. .... ❑ ❑ ❑ ❑ ❑

PHYSICAL SCIENCE

Understand classifying. .... ❑ ❑ ❑ ❑ ❑

Understand the force of gravity. .... ❑ ❑ ❑ ❑ ❑

Be able to classify a simple machine. .... ❑ ❑ ❑ ❑ ❑

Be able to measure the length of an object in
centimeters. .... ❑ ❑ ❑ ❑ ❑

Understand uses of machines to make work
easier. .... ❑ ❑ ❑ ❑ ❑

Realize all matter is made up of atoms in con-
stant motion. .... ❑ ❑ ❑ ❑ ❑

Understand different states of matter. .... ❑ ❑ ❑ ❑ ❑

SCIENCE PROCESSING SKILLS

Be able to interpret charts and graphs. .... ❑ ❑ ❑ ❑ ❑

Be able to explain a food chain sequence. .... ❑ ❑ ❑ ❑ ❑

Be able to classify objects into their proper groups. ❑ ❑ ❑ ❑ ❑

Use observation skills to predict outcomes of
experiments. .... ❑ ❑ ❑ ❑ ❑

Be able to classify forms of energy. .... ❑ ❑ ❑ ❑ ❑

CHILD'S NAME CHILD'S NAME CHILD'S NAME CHILD'S NAME CHILD'S NAME

EVALUATION CHECK LIST FOR FOURTH GRADE

SCIENCE

CHILD'S NAME   CHILD'S NAME   CHILD'S NAME   CHILD'S NAME   CHILD'S NAME

Fourth-grade students should be able to do the following:

EARTH AND SPACE

Understand the human body is composed of sensory organs which detect heat, light, and sound. .... ❑ ❑ ❑ ❑ ❑

Understand a solar eclipse. .... ❑ ❑ ❑ ❑ ❑

Realize proper growth and development are dependent on many factors working together. ❑ ❑ ❑ ❑ ❑

Realize differing atmospheric conditions. .... ❑ ❑ ❑ ❑ ❑

Realize the importance of oceans to life on earth. .... ❑ ❑ ❑ ❑ ❑

Realize chemicals may be harmful to the environment. .... ❑ ❑ ❑ ❑ ❑

Understand environmental problems may vary from one community to another. .... ❑ ❑ ❑ ❑ ❑

Realize each individual impacts the environment. .... ❑ ❑ ❑ ❑ ❑

Determine past environment based on specific information. .... ❑ ❑ ❑ ❑ ❑

Understand why we have four seasons on earth. .... ❑ ❑ ❑ ❑ ❑

Forecast the form of precipitation at certain temperatures. .... ❑ ❑ ❑ ❑ ❑

Know what scientists study to learn about the past. .... ❑ ❑ ❑ ❑ ❑

BIOLOGICAL SCIENCE

Identify the effect of the sun on humans. .... ❑ ❑ ❑ ❑ ❑

Identify major food groups. .... ❑ ❑ ❑ ❑ ❑

EVALUATION CHECK LIST FOR FOURTH GRADE
SCIENCE

Identify the major organs in the human body. ☐ ☐ ☐ ☐ ☐

BIOLOGICAL SCIENCE: ANIMALS

Understand major animal groups. .... ☐ ☐ ☐ ☐ ☐

Recognize the differences among animals. ...... ☐ ☐ ☐ ☐ ☐

Predict the habitation of a given animal. .... ☐ ☐ ☐ ☐ ☐

Understand the food chain. .... ☐ ☐ ☐ ☐ ☐

Know how a given animal gives birth (live or
    eggs). .... ☐ ☐ ☐ ☐ ☐

Understand how animals move (fly, crawl,
    walk). .... ☐ ☐ ☐ ☐ ☐

Understand how an animal adapts to its envi-
    ronment. .... ☐ ☐ ☐ ☐ ☐

Use observation skills to classify an animal. ..... ☐ ☐ ☐ ☐ ☐

BIOLOGICAL SCIENCE: PLANTS

Understand the functioning of a plant. .... ☐ ☐ ☐ ☐ ☐

Understand the functions of plant parts. .... ☐ ☐ ☐ ☐ ☐

Understand the importance of plant repro-
    duction. .... ☐ ☐ ☐ ☐ ☐

PHYSICAL SCIENCE

Classify different forms of energy. .... ☐ ☐ ☐ ☐ ☐

Interpret measurements of mass. .... ☐ ☐ ☐ ☐ ☐

Recognize magnets are fundamental parts of
    generators and are required to produce cur-
    rent electricity. .... ☐ ☐ ☐ ☐ ☐

Realize current electricity may travel along
    one or more paths. .... ☐ ☐ ☐ ☐ ☐

Realize all matter conducts electricity. .... ☐ ☐ ☐ ☐ ☐

Understand sound travels by molecular motion. ☐ ☐ ☐ ☐ ☐

CHILD'S NAME · CHILD'S NAME · CHILD'S NAME · CHILD'S NAME · CHILD'S NAME

EVALUATION CHECK LIST FOR FOURTH GRADE

SCIENCE

CHILD'S NAME CHILD'S NAME CHILD'S NAME CHILD'S NAME CHILD'S NAME

Realize heat and light are obtained from various sources. .... ❑ ❑ ❑ ❑ ❑

SCIENCE PROCESSING SKILLS

Use research skills to explain why certain shapes have different shadows. .... ❑ ❑ ❑ ❑ ❑

Interpret graphs, tables, and charts. .... ❑ ❑ ❑ ❑ ❑

Analyze an experiment and predict the outcome. .... ❑ ❑ ❑ ❑ ❑

Evaluate the suitability of an environment for certain animals. .... ❑ ❑ ❑ ❑ ❑

Analyze a simple circuit. .... ❑ ❑ ❑ ❑ ❑

A downloadable version of this book.is available for purchase at **http://Homeschool-Books.com**.
With it you can search for text and and print the pages from your computer.

253

EVALUATION CHECK LIST FOR FIFTH GRADE

SCIENCE

Fifth-grade students should be able to do the following:

EARTH AND SPACE

Be able to explain what plant lives well in a certain environment.	☐	☐	☐	☐	☐
Identify an egg-laying animal.	☐	☐	☐	☐	☐
Explain the effect sun has on humans.	☐	☐	☐	☐	☐
Understand common forms of major animal groups.	☐	☐	☐	☐	☐
Understand the four food groups and their nutritional values.	☐	☐	☐	☐	☐
Identify major body organs and their functions.	☐	☐	☐	☐	☐
Realize plants have complex structures with specialized functions.	☐	☐	☐	☐	☐
Recognize there are two basic types of seed plants.	☐	☐	☐	☐	☐
Realize humans have specialized systems responsible for body functioning.	☐	☐	☐	☐	☐
Realize each body system is subject to disease.	☐	☐	☐	☐	☐
Realize microscopic organisms are essential to life.	☐	☐	☐	☐	☐
Explain how the earth rotates.	☐	☐	☐	☐	☐
Understand how fossils form.	☐	☐	☐	☐	☐
Understand the effect of gravity.	☐	☐	☐	☐	☐
Understand the cause of seasonal change.	☐	☐	☐	☐	☐
Predict the form of precipitation at different temperatures.	☐	☐	☐	☐	☐
Understand the functions of plant parts.	☐	☐	☐	☐	☐
Classify animals into major groups.	☐	☐	☐	☐	☐
Understand seed germination.	☐	☐	☐	☐	☐

EVALUATION CHECK LIST FOR FIFTH GRADE

SCIENCE

	CHILD'S NAME	CHILD'S NAME	CHILD'S NAME	CHILD'S NAME	CHILD'S NAME
Understand the topography of the ocean floor is in constant change.	☐	☐	☐	☐	☐
Realize energy consumption impacts the environment.	☐	☐	☐	☐	☐
Realize each local community has important plants and animals.	☐	☐	☐	☐	☐

PHYSICAL SCIENCE

Realize use of machines increases productivity.	☐	☐	☐	☐	☐
Realize machines can be used to alter a force.	☐	☐	☐	☐	☐
Tell temperature on a thermometer.	☐	☐	☐	☐	☐
Be able to classify different forms of energy.	☐	☐	☐	☐	☐
Understand a simple electrical unit.	☐	☐	☐	☐	☐
Understand matter consists of atoms.	☐	☐	☐	☐	☐
Understand energy exists in many forms.	☐	☐	☐	☐	☐
Understand the properties of matter can be identified and measured.	☐	☐	☐	☐	☐
Classify a simple machine.	☐	☐	☐	☐	☐
Realize motion of objects is affected by friction.	☐	☐	☐	☐	☐

SCIENCE PROCESSING SKILLS

Interpret graphs and charts.	☐	☐	☐	☐	☐
Predict the outcome of an experiment.	☐	☐	☐	☐	☐

EVALUATION CHECK LIST FOR SIXTH GRADE

SCIENCE

Sixth-grade students should be able to do the following:

EARTH AND SPACE

Realize the universe has various components. ☐ ☐ ☐ ☐ ☐

Recognize changes are constantly occurring in and on the earth. .... ☐ ☐ ☐ ☐ ☐

Understand communities address their energy needs in differing ways. .... ☐ ☐ ☐ ☐ ☐

Recognize factors influencing the stability of ecosystems. .... ☐ ☐ ☐ ☐ ☐

BIOLOGICAL SCIENCE

Recognize traits are passed from parents to offspring. .... ☐ ☐ ☐ ☐ ☐

Understand why we have safety rules. .... ☐ ☐ ☐ ☐ ☐

Identify the source of a disease........................ ☐ ☐ ☐ ☐ ☐

Identify the function of major body organs....... ☐ ☐ ☐ ☐ ☐

Understand energy used in muscles. .... ☐ ☐ ☐ ☐ ☐

BIOLOGICAL SCIENCE: ANIMALS

Understand animal adaptation to the environment. .... ☐ ☐ ☐ ☐ ☐

Identify characteristics of animals. .... ☐ ☐ ☐ ☐ ☐

Understand the food chain. .... ☐ ☐ ☐ ☐ ☐

Use observation skills to determine if an animal is suited to an environment. .... ☐ ☐ ☐ ☐ ☐

BIOLOGICAL SCIENCE: PLANTS

Understand photosynthesis and cellular respiration are life-sustaining plant processes. ☐ ☐ ☐ ☐ ☐

EVALUATION CHECK LIST FOR SIXTH GRADE

SCIENCE

Understand the life cycle of plants. .... □ □ □ □ □

Using observation methods, evaluate plant
  growth in different environments................ □ □ □ □ □

Identify plant parts. .... □ □ □ □ □

PHYSICAL SCIENCE

Recognize magnets as either natural or man-
  made. .... □ □ □ □ □

Identify various sources of energy that can be
  utilized in the production of electricity......... □ □ □ □ □

Understand electricity involves the movement
  of electrons. .... □ □ □ □ □

Understand electricity can be harmful. .... □ □ □ □ □

Understand sound is produced by vibrating
  matter and is transmitted in all directions. □ □ □ □ □

SCIENCE PROCESSING SKILLS

Read charts, graphs, and tables to gather
  information. .... □ □ □ □ □

Use a model of the food chain to predict the
  results of the chain. .... □ □ □ □ □

Analyze an experiment and predict the results. □ □ □ □ □

CHILD'S NAME   CHILD'S NAME   CHILD'S NAME   CHILD'S NAME   CHILD'S NAME

EVALUATION CHECK LIST FOR SEVENTH GRADE

SCIENCE

Seventh-grade students should be able to do the following:

EARTH AND SPACE

Realize the earth's weather is an interaction of many parts of the environment.	❑	❑	❑	❑	❑
Recognize the force of gravity.	❑	❑	❑	❑	❑
Anticipate the findings of a change in gravitational pull.	❑	❑	❑	❑	❑
Know the importance of the ocean, its life forms, its physical features and resources.	❑	❑	❑	❑	❑
Understand ecosystems are dependent on interrelationships within the environment.	❑	❑	❑	❑	❑
Recognize a property of a common rock type.	❑	❑	❑	❑	❑
Predict the forecast of a solar eclipse.	❑	❑	❑	❑	❑
Determine causes of air pollution.	❑	❑	❑	❑	❑
Understand the rotation of the earth.	❑	❑	❑	❑	❑

BIOLOGICAL SCIENCE

Know the human body is composed of different biological systems that are interrelated.	❑	❑	❑	❑	❑
Know the human body is dependent upon good nutrition.	❑	❑	❑	❑	❑
Know the cell is the basic unit of living things.	❑	❑	❑	❑	❑
Know the importance of body organs based on their functions.	❑	❑	❑	❑	❑
Classify foods based on nutritional value.	❑	❑	❑	❑	❑
Using observation skills, match a group of skeleton bones to the body section.	❑	❑	❑	❑	❑
Identify major body systems.	❑	❑	❑	❑	❑
Associate structure and function of cells.	❑	❑	❑	❑	❑

EVALUATION CHECK LIST FOR SEVENTH GRADE

SCIENCE

BIOLOGICAL SCIENCE: ANIMALS

Sequence food chains............................... ❑ ❑ ❑ ❑ ❑

Understand a model of a food web. .... ❑ ❑ ❑ ❑ ❑

Compare and classify common animals. .... ❑ ❑ ❑ ❑ ❑

Realize animals and plants are classified according to various structures. .... ❑ ❑ ❑ ❑ ❑

Given an animal, evaluate the proper ability to adapt to an environment. .... ❑ ❑ ❑ ❑ ❑

BIOLOGICAL SCIENCE: PLANTS

Understand the coloring pigment in a plant. .. ❑ ❑ ❑ ❑ ❑

Identify plant parts and functions.................... ❑ ❑ ❑ ❑ ❑

PHYSICAL SCIENCE

Understand simple and compound machines make work easier. .... ❑ ❑ ❑ ❑ ❑

Understand matter and energy in the universe are governed by physical laws............. ❑ ❑ ❑ ❑ ❑

SCIENCE PROCESSING SKILLS

Be able to interpret charts, graphs and tables.

Be able to identify a compound. .... ❑ ❑ ❑ ❑ ❑

Draw conclusions when given an experiment.

Understand simple machines. .... ❑ ❑ ❑ ❑ ❑

Show an understanding of a chemical formula

Estimate the measurement of an item............ ❑ ❑ ❑ ❑ ❑

EVALUATION CHECK LIST FOR EIGHTH GRADE

SCIENCE

Eighth-grade students should be able to do the following:

EARTH AND SPACE

Realize the knowledge of the universe is expanding.. ❑ ❑ ❑ ❑ ❑

Realize the earth is constantly changing. .... ❑ ❑ ❑ ❑ ❑

Know civilization is dependent upon both renewable and non-renewable resources. .. ❑ ❑ ❑ ❑ ❑

Realize people influence the quality of the environment. .... ❑ ❑ ❑ ❑ ❑

Determine the differences in climates (tropical, polar, marine, desert, etc.)...................... ❑ ❑ ❑ ❑ ❑

Understand the earth's motions. .... ❑ ❑ ❑ ❑ ❑

Recognize the effect of different layers of our atmosphere. .... ❑ ❑ ❑ ❑ ❑

BIOLOGICAL SCIENCE

Realize the continuation of a species is maintained through heredity............................... ❑ ❑ ❑ ❑ ❑

BIOLOGICAL SCIENCE: ANIMALS

Understand the different roles in the ecosystem. ❑ ❑ ❑ ❑ ❑

Formulate a conclusion based on the understanding of reproduction and mutation rates. ❑ ❑ ❑ ❑ ❑

BIOLOGICAL SCIENCE: PLANTS

Understand the functions of plant parts. .... ❑ ❑ ❑ ❑ ❑

Formulate a consequence based on the understanding of plant structure. .... ❑ ❑ ❑ ❑ ❑

EVALUATION CHECK LIST FOR EIGHTH GRADE

SCIENCE

PHYSICAL SCIENCE

Realize electricity and magnetism are related forms of energy. .... ❑ ❑ ❑ ❑ ❑

Understand sound, heat, and light are integral parts of the environment. .... ❑ ❑ ❑ ❑ ❑

Understand observation and experimentation are the bases of scientific reasoning. .... ❑ ❑ ❑ ❑ ❑

Understand all matter has a definite structure which determines physical and chemical properties. .... ❑ ❑ ❑ ❑ ❑

Understand what produces a chemical change.. ❑ ❑ ❑ ❑ ❑

SCIENCE PROCESSING SKILLS

Use observation skills to determine the use of a simple machine. .... ❑ ❑ ❑ ❑ ❑

Be able to interpret charts, graphs, and tables. ❑ ❑ ❑ ❑ ❑

Be able to identify a compound. .... ❑ ❑ ❑ ❑ ❑

Draw conclusions when given an experiment. ❑ ❑ ❑ ❑ ❑

Show an understanding of a chemical formula. ❑ ❑ ❑ ❑ ❑

Estimate the measurement of an item. .... ❑ ❑ ❑ ❑ ❑

262

Go ye therefore, and teach all nations, baptizing them in the name of the Father,
and of the Son, and of the Holy Ghost: Teaching them to observe all things whatsoever
I have commanded you: and, lo, I am with you alway,
even unto the end of the world. Amen.

Matthew 28:19-20

SOCIAL SCIENCES

GEOGRAPHY · HISTORY · POLITICAL SCIENCE
· ECONOMICS · PSYCHOLOGY/SOCIOLOGY

Evaluation Check List for Kindergarten

Social Science

Kindergarten students should be able to do the following:

	CHILD'S NAME	CHILD'S NAME	CHILD'S NAME	CHILD'S NAME	CHILD'S NAME

GEOGRAPHY

Recognize a map.	☐	☐	☐	☐	☐
Recognize a globe.	☐	☐	☐	☐	☐

HISTORY

Understand different forms of transportation through history.	☐	☐	☐	☐	☐
Understand individuals have a personal history (family tree).	☐	☐	☐	☐	☐
Understand things change over time.	☐	☐	☐	☐	☐

POLITICAL SCIENCE

Recognize the need for rules at home and school.	☐	☐	☐	☐	☐
Understand the need for cultural rules and laws.	☐	☐	☐	☐	☐
Know rules of safety.	☐	☐	☐	☐	☐
Understand the need for environmental rules.	☐	☐	☐	☐	☐
Develop an understanding of space and spatial relationships.	☐	☐	☐	☐	☐
Understand environments and recognize their differences.	☐	☐	☐	☐	☐
Recognize the need for guidance from others...	☐	☐	☐	☐	☐
Understand the concept of being a citizen.	☐	☐	☐	☐	☐
Recognize different methods of meeting needs and wants.	☐	☐	☐	☐	☐
Understand the importance of jobs.	☐	☐	☐	☐	☐

PSYCHOLOGY/SOCIOLOGY

Understand the worth of each individual and self.	☐	☐	☐	☐	☐

EVALUATION CHECK LIST FOR KINDERGARTEN

SOCIAL SCIENCE

	CHILD'S NAME	CHILD'S NAME	CHILD'S NAME	CHILD'S NAME	CHILD'S NAME
Understand the similarities and differences among individuals.	❑	❑	❑	❑	❑
Know the roles of family members.	❑	❑	❑	❑	❑
Understand the behavior of individuals is changed by relationships with others.	❑	❑	❑	❑	❑
Understand the concept of culture and its effect on individuals.	❑	❑	❑	❑	❑
Know the contributions of different cultures.	❑	❑	❑	❑	❑
Understand many jobs require people working together.	❑	❑	❑	❑	❑
Understand the position of an individual to his family and the world.	❑	❑	❑	❑	❑

EVALUATION CHECK LIST FOR FIRST GRADE

SOCIAL SCIENCE

First-grade students should be able to do the following:

CHILD'S NAME   CHILD'S NAME   CHILD'S NAME   CHILD'S NAME   CHILD'S NAME

GEOGRAPHY

Recognize how geography affected early settlements. .... ❑ ❑ ❑ ❑ ❑

Know the location of land masses and bodies of water. .... ❑ ❑ ❑ ❑ ❑

Know the geographic location of the United States and your state on a globe or a map. .... ❑ ❑ ❑ ❑ ❑

Know directions on a globe or a map. .... ❑ ❑ ❑ ❑ ❑

Understand the difference between land and water on a map and globe. .... ❑ ❑ ❑ ❑ ❑

Realize there are seven main bodies of land on earth. .... ❑ ❑ ❑ ❑ ❑

Recognize map symbols and graph symbols. .. ❑ ❑ ❑ ❑ ❑

Be able to recognize major characteristics of each continent. .... ❑ ❑ ❑ ❑ ❑

HISTORY

Know about the pilgrims. .... ❑ ❑ ❑ ❑ ❑

Grasp the concept that people were here on earth long ago. .... ❑ ❑ ❑ ❑ ❑

Recognize people have different religious beliefs .... ❑ ❑ ❑ ❑ ❑

Understand how communication has developed and improved through history. .... ❑ ❑ ❑ ❑ ❑

Understand American history as it relates to the holidays; why we celebrate the Fourth of July, etc. .... ❑ ❑ ❑ ❑ ❑

EVALUATION CHECK LIST FOR FIRST GRADE

SOCIAL SCIENCE

CHILD'S NAME   CHILD'S NAME   CHILD'S NAME   CHILD'S NAME   CHILD'S NAME

Be able to sequence historical periods by clothing of different time periods or means of transportation............................... ❏ ❏ ❏ ❏ ❏

Recognize the transformation countries have made from first settlement to the present. .... ❏ ❏ ❏ ❏ ❏

Develop a respect for and appreciation of other cultures in relation to families, homes and schools. .... ❏ ❏ ❏ ❏ ❏

Have an understanding of the development of the American flag. .... ❏ ❏ ❏ ❏ ❏

POLITICAL SCIENCE

Understand the development of neighborhoods and how they differ. .... ❏ ❏ ❏ ❏ ❏

Determine that individuals have rights. .... ❏ ❏ ❏ ❏ ❏

Understand neighborhood responsibilities and needs. .... ❏ ❏ ❏ ❏ ❏

Identify occupation in the community. .... ❏ ❏ ❏ ❏ ❏

Recognize the importance of both the individual and families as parts of neighborhoods. .... ❏ ❏ ❏ ❏ ❏

Understand environmental effects on homes. ❏ ❏ ❏ ❏ ❏

Understand the role of culture to a neighborhood. .... ❏ ❏ ❏ ❏ ❏

Understand the effect of environment upon jobs. ❏ ❏ ❏ ❏ ❏

Recognize the services provided by workers. .. ❏ ❏ ❏ ❏ ❏

PSYCHOLOGY/SOCIOLOGY

Understand the individual's responsibilities to a group as a citizen. .... ❏ ❏ ❏ ❏ ❏

EVALUATION CHECK LIST FOR FIRST GRADE

SOCIAL SCIENCE

	CHILD'S NAME	CHILD'S NAME	CHILD'S NAME	CHILD'S NAME	CHILD'S NAME
Understand why groups are formed.	❑	❑	❑	❑	❑
Understand the rules of communication.	❑	❑	❑	❑	❑
Recognize the uses of communication.	❑	❑	❑	❑	❑
Understand the role of language in communication.	❑	❑	❑	❑	❑
Recognize the importance of communication to people all over the world.	❑	❑	❑	❑	❑

EVALUATION CHECK LIST FOR SECOND GRADE

SOCIAL SCIENCE

Second-grade students should be able to do the following:

GEOGRAPHY

Understand the concept of physical location. ☐ ☐ ☐ ☐ ☐

Know the need for certain geographical
 laws. .... ☐ ☐ ☐ ☐ ☐

Know the location of specific areas on maps. ☐ ☐ ☐ ☐ ☐

HISTORY

Know the major exports of the country. .... ☐ ☐ ☐ ☐ ☐

Understand the necessity of imports. .... ☐ ☐ ☐ ☐ ☐

Identify national holidays. .... ☐ ☐ ☐ ☐ ☐

Sequence historical events by identifying communication, transportation, or clothing. ...... ☐ ☐ ☐ ☐ ☐

Identify major events in American history. ...... ☐ ☐ ☐ ☐ ☐

POLITICAL SCIENCE

Understand the voting process. .... ☐ ☐ ☐ ☐ ☐

Understand how communities change with
 time. .... ☐ ☐ ☐ ☐ ☐

Understand community interdependence. ☐ ☐ ☐ ☐ ☐

Understand how communities form and adapt
 to their environment. .... ☐ ☐ ☐ ☐ ☐

Grasp the concept of cultural loyalty. .... ☐ ☐ ☐ ☐ ☐

Recognize the need for community govern-
 ment. .... ☐ ☐ ☐ ☐ ☐

Recognize different roles of community mem-
 bers in different cultures. .... ☐ ☐ ☐ ☐ ☐

Understand the role of culture in community
 rights and responsibilities. .... ☐ ☐ ☐ ☐ ☐

EVALUATION CHECK LIST FOR SECOND GRADE

SOCIAL SCIENCE

	CHILD'S NAME	CHILD'S NAME	CHILD'S NAME	CHILD'S NAME	CHILD'S NAME
Know that communities produce goods and services.	☐	☐	☐	☐	☐
Understand jobs that provide community services.	☐	☐	☐	☐	☐
Recognize available careers and their dependent factors.	☐	☐	☐	☐	☐

PSYCHOLOGY/SOCIOLOGY

	CHILD'S NAME	CHILD'S NAME	CHILD'S NAME	CHILD'S NAME	CHILD'S NAME
Understand the rights and responsibilities of individuals and community members.	☐	☐	☐	☐	☐
Understand the position of an individual in his community.	☐	☐	☐	☐	☐
Recognize the influence of other cultures in our lives.	☐	☐	☐	☐	☐

EVALUATION CHECK LIST FOR THIRD GRADE

SOCIAL SCIENCE

Third-grade students should be able to do the following:

GEOGRAPHY

Know specific places within the local community............................... ❑ ❑ ❑ ❑ ❑

Recognize the influence of land forms, climate, and natural resources in community location and growth. .... ❑ ❑ ❑ ❑ ❑

Recognize geographical and agricultural regions of the United States. .... ❑ ❑ ❑ ❑ ❑

Understand changes made by technological advances............................... ❑ ❑ ❑ ❑ ❑

Identify a continent on a map or globe. .... ❑ ❑ ❑ ❑ ❑

Identify the capitol of the United States. .... ❑ ❑ ❑ ❑ ❑

Identify main bodies of water........................... ❑ ❑ ❑ ❑ ❑

Apply map skills to determine a specific location. .... ❑ ❑ ❑ ❑ ❑

Use physical and political maps....................... ❑ ❑ ❑ ❑ ❑

Understand technological effects upon environment. .... ❑ ❑ ❑ ❑ ❑

Recognize the supply limits of natural resources. .... ❑ ❑ ❑ ❑ ❑

Understand the need for conservation. .... ❑ ❑ ❑ ❑ ❑

Recognize the family's cultural contribution to a community. .... ❑ ❑ ❑ ❑ ❑

HISTORY

Identify activities of the pioneers...................... ❑ ❑ ❑ ❑ ❑

Understand how and why communities have developed and changed. .... ❑ ❑ ❑ ❑ ❑

EVALUATION CHECK LIST FOR THIRD GRADE

SOCIAL SCIENCE

	CHILD'S NAME	CHILD'S NAME	CHILD'S NAME	CHILD'S NAME	CHILD'S NAME
Recognize the effects of mechanization and industrialization upon agricultural and urban communities.	❑	❑	❑	❑	❑
Identify a president of the United States.	❑	❑	❑	❑	❑
Associate a holiday with the event or season.	❑	❑	❑	❑	❑
Recognize the need for environmental protection.	❑	❑	❑	❑	❑
Recognize the factors leading to economic growth.	❑	❑	❑	❑	❑
Understand the role of culture in behavior, growth, and change in a community.	❑	❑	❑	❑	❑
Recognize the elements leading to future community changes.	❑	❑	❑	❑	❑
Understand the interdependence of the world's people.	❑	❑	❑	❑	❑
Understand the effects of technological changes upon the world's people.	❑	❑	❑	❑	❑

POLITICAL SCIENCE

Understand the laws, values, issues and concerns of communities.	❑	❑	❑	❑	❑
Understand the effect of population upon a community.	❑	❑	❑	❑	❑
Understand the relationship of local governments to the state and nation.	❑	❑	❑	❑	❑
Understand the need for international laws.	❑	❑	❑	❑	❑
Understand the Pledge of Allegiance.	❑	❑	❑	❑	❑
Understand the voting process.	❑	❑	❑	❑	❑
Know the length of term for the President.	❑	❑	❑	❑	❑
Be able to tell whether a service is provided by public or private domain.	❑	❑	❑	❑	❑

EVALUATION CHECK LIST FOR THIRD GRADE

SOCIAL SCIENCE

CHILD'S NAME · CHILD'S NAME · CHILD'S NAME · CHILD'S NAME · CHILD'S NAME

ECONOMICS

Understand supply and demand. .... ❑ ❑ ❑ ❑ ❑

Identify different occupations. .... ❑ ❑ ❑ ❑ ❑

Understand how one buys on credit............. ❑ ❑ ❑ ❑ ❑

Understand manufacturing. .... ❑ ❑ ❑ ❑ ❑

PSYCHOLOGY/SOCIOLOGY

Understand different forms of communi-
cation. .... ❑ ❑ ❑ ❑ ❑

Understand why and how individuals obtain
values... ❑ ❑ ❑ ❑ ❑

Understand individuals' basic needs............ ❑ ❑ ❑ ❑ ❑

EVALUATION CHECK LIST FOR FOURTH GRADE

SOCIAL SCIENCE

Fourth-grade students should be able to do the following:

GEOGRAPHY

Know the characteristics of natural land forms and how they are represented on different maps. .... ❑ ❑ ❑ ❑ ❑

Recognize regions, land forms, climate, vegetation, and natural resources of your state. .... ❑ ❑ ❑ ❑ ❑

Use longitudinal and latitudinal lines to locate natural regions on maps.............................. ❑ ❑ ❑ ❑ ❑

Know the relationship between the characteristics of a natural region and its history. ...... ❑ ❑ ❑ ❑ ❑

Name the capitol of the United States. .... ❑ ❑ ❑ ❑ ❑

Determine factors that influence certain crops. ❑ ❑ ❑ ❑ ❑

Distinguish between natural and political boundaries. .... ❑ ❑ ❑ ❑ ❑

Recognize differences in natural regions with respect to production, career opportunities, and technical opportunities. .... ❑ ❑ ❑ ❑ ❑

Recognize the importance of natural regions in development of cultural diversities, and regional growth. .... ❑ ❑ ❑ ❑ ❑

Know directional map lines (North, South, East, West).. ❑ ❑ ❑ ❑ ❑

HISTORY

Relate holidays with seasons. .... ❑ ❑ ❑ ❑ ❑

Recognize the importance of cultural values and priorities in shaping the future......... ❑ ❑ ❑ ❑ ❑

EVALUATION CHECK LIST FOR FOURTH GRADE

SOCIAL SCIENCE

Know the important events in the history of your state and important factors which have affected this history. .... ❑ ❑ ❑ ❑ ❑

Know the individuals and groups who have had a major impact on your state. .... ❑ ❑ ❑ ❑ ❑

Identify a President of the United States. .... ❑ ❑ ❑ ❑ ❑

Understand the way pioneers lived. .... ❑ ❑ ❑ ❑ ❑

Understand the changes in transportation. .... ❑ ❑ ❑ ❑ ❑

Know individuals who have had a major impact on other societies. .... ❑ ❑ ❑ ❑ ❑

POLITICAL SCIENCE

Understand the Pledge of Allegiance. .... ❑ ❑ ❑ ❑ ❑

Know the causes of pollution. .... ❑ ❑ ❑ ❑ ❑

Know the length of a presidential term. .... ❑ ❑ ❑ ❑ ❑

Recognize the similarities and differences among cultures. .... ❑ ❑ ❑ ❑ ❑

Understand how migration affects cultural diversity. .... ❑ ❑ ❑ ❑ ❑

Understand the population distribution of your state and the cultural diversity represented. .... ❑ ❑ ❑ ❑ ❑

Understand your state has a constitution..... ❑ ❑ ❑ ❑ ❑

Understand the three branches of your state government. .... ❑ ❑ ❑ ❑ ❑

Know the major industrial and agricultural products of the state. .... ❑ ❑ ❑ ❑ ❑

Understand the role of taxation. .... ❑ ❑ ❑ ❑ ❑

Recognize different job opportunities in your state. .... ❑ ❑ ❑ ❑ ❑

Understand how your state interacts with

EVALUATION CHECK LIST FOR FOURTH GRADE

SOCIAL SCIENCE

other states, our national government, and
other nations. .... ❏ ❏ ❏ ❏ ❏

Understand differences in roles within
groups. .... ❏ ❏ ❏ ❏ ❏

Know the importance of major social and
political organizations. .... ❏ ❏ ❏ ❏ ❏

Understand the role of technology in your
state's future. .... ❏ ❏ ❏ ❏ ❏

PSYCHOLOGY/SOCIOLOGY

Recognize the importance of physical location
to a person's role in society. .... ❏ ❏ ❏ ❏ ❏

Recognize the individual's role in the cultural
group. .... ❏ ❏ ❏ ❏ ❏

Recognize the individual's role at the local,
state, national, and international levels. .... ❏ ❏ ❏ ❏ ❏

Recognize the importance of culture to one's
individual identity. .... ❏ ❏ ❏ ❏ ❏

Identify different modes of communication. .... ❏ ❏ ❏ ❏ ❏

EVALUATION CHECK LIST FOR FIFTH GRADE

SOCIAL SCIENCE

Fifth-grade students should be able to do the following:

GEOGRAPHY

Locate the United States using a global grid. .. ❑ ❑ ❑ ❑ ❑

Know the size, shape, and boundaries of the United States. .... ❑ ❑ ❑ ❑ ❑

Know land forms, climate, and natural resources of the United States. .... ❑ ❑ ❑ ❑ ❑

Apply map skills to determine various information. .... ❑ ❑ ❑ ❑ ❑

Relate an area with a given climate. .... ❑ ❑ ❑ ❑ ❑

Recognize names of major countries. .... ❑ ❑ ❑ ❑ ❑

Identify major bodies of water. .... ❑ ❑ ❑ ❑ ❑

Understand how land form characteristics influenced cultures in colonization. .... ❑ ❑ ❑ ❑ ❑

HISTORY

Know the symbolic meaning of the American flag. .... ❑ ❑ ❑ ❑ ❑

Know the reasons for exploration of the United States. .... ❑ ❑ ❑ ❑ ❑

Understand the relationship of the British with the United States. .... ❑ ❑ ❑ ❑ ❑

Understand the changes in the government during the nation's development. .... ❑ ❑ ❑ ❑ ❑

Understand the people who lived in the United States prior to exploration and colonization. .... ❑ ❑ ❑ ❑ ❑

Understand the importance of migration and immigration upon the culture of the

Evaluation Check List for Fifth Grade

Social Science

	Child's Name	Child's Name	Child's Name	Child's Name	Child's Name
United States.	❑	❑	❑	❑	❑
Arrange major historical events in historical order.	❑	❑	❑	❑	❑
Understand how the thirteen colonies developed.	❑	❑	❑	❑	❑
Know how the pilgrims lived.	❑	❑	❑	❑	❑
Analyze a time line.	❑	❑	❑	❑	❑
Know the major events in the nation's history which brought diverse cultures to the United States.	❑	❑	❑	❑	❑
Economics					
Understand the importance of the nation's economy to the world.	❑	❑	❑	❑	❑
Understand the effect of industrialization and urbanization upon careers.	❑	❑	❑	❑	❑
Understand the meaning of import and export.	❑	❑	❑	❑	❑
Realize why advertising is used.	❑	❑	❑	❑	❑
Recognize the need for changes to meet the future needs of society.	❑	❑	❑	❑	❑
Understand the economic development of the United States.	❑	❑	❑	❑	❑
Understand supply and demand.	❑	❑	❑	❑	❑
Political Science					
Understand the evolution of democracy and the legal system in the United States.	❑	❑	❑	❑	❑
Understand the individual's role in government.	❑	❑	❑	❑	❑
Know how the American government was					

EVALUATION CHECK LIST FOR FIFTH GRADE

CHILD'S NAME   CHILD'S NAME   CHILD'S NAME   CHILD'S NAME   CHILD'S NAME

formed and its function according to the constitution. .... ❏ ❏ ❏ ❏ ❏

Understand the system of checks and balances. .... ❏ ❏ ❏ ❏ ❏

Understand how the constitution can be changed. .... ❏ ❏ ❏ ❏ ❏

Have an understanding of most laws in the United States. .... ❏ ❏ ❏ ❏ ❏

Recognize the importance of the American constitution to other nations. .... ❏ ❏ ❏ ❏ ❏

Understand being a citizen of a democracy. .. ❏ ❏ ❏ ❏ ❏

Know the rights and responsibilities provided in the Bill of Rights. .... ❏ ❏ ❏ ❏ ❏

Understand how career choices influence the economy. .... ❏ ❏ ❏ ❏ ❏

Recognize cultural contributions to American society. .... ❏ ❏ ❏ ❏ ❏

Recognize the contributions made by Blacks in American history. .... ❏ ❏ ❏ ❏ ❏

Understand the role of minority groups as they are incorporated into society. .... ❏ ❏ ❏ ❏ ❏

Understand the right of a person accused of a crime in the United States. .... ❏ ❏ ❏ ❏ ❏

Recognize the influence of other cultures upon our political system. .... ❏ ❏ ❏ ❏ ❏

Understand the principles of a constitutional government. .... ❏ ❏ ❏ ❏ ❏

Understand the major differences in the various cultural groups. .... ❏ ❏ ❏ ❏ ❏

Recognize the contribution of new cultures to the nation. .... ❏ ❏ ❏ ❏ ❏

Evaluation Check List for Fifth Grade

Social Science

	CHILD'S NAME	CHILD'S NAME	CHILD'S NAME	CHILD'S NAME	CHILD'S NAME
Understand the interrelationship and interdependency of cultural groups in the nation. ..	❑	❑	❑	❑	❑

Psychology/Sociology

	CHILD'S NAME	CHILD'S NAME	CHILD'S NAME	CHILD'S NAME	CHILD'S NAME
Understand the individual's role and responsibility as a member of American society. ..	❑	❑	❑	❑	❑
Understand basic human needs.	❑	❑	❑	❑	❑
Determine how two people from different countries differ.	❑	❑	❑	❑	❑
Understand different means of communication.	❑	❑	❑	❑	❑

EVALUATION CHECK LIST FOR SIXTH GRADE

SOCIAL SCIENCE

Sixth-grade students should be able to do the following:

CHILD'S NAME | CHILD'S NAME | CHILD'S NAME | CHILD'S NAME | CHILD'S NAME

GEOGRAPHY

Locate geographic centers of early civilization. ❑ ❑ ❑ ❑ ❑

Understand the importance of land forms, climate, resources, and heritage upon early civilizations. .... ❑ ❑ ❑ ❑ ❑

Name and find the different continents. .... ❑ ❑ ❑ ❑ ❑

Identify physical features of a continent.......... ❑ ❑ ❑ ❑ ❑

Locate the United States using a global grid. .. ❑ ❑ ❑ ❑ ❑

Know the size, shape, and boundaries of the United States. .... ❑ ❑ ❑ ❑ ❑

Know land forms, climate, and natural resources of the United States. .... ❑ ❑ ❑ ❑ ❑

Apply maps skills to determine various information. .... ❑ ❑ ❑ ❑ ❑

Find the equator. .... ❑ ❑ ❑ ❑ ❑

Relate an area with a given climate.......... ❑ ❑ ❑ ❑ ❑

Recognize names of major countries. .... ❑ ❑ ❑ ❑ ❑

Identify major bodies of water. .... ❑ ❑ ❑ ❑ ❑

Understand how land form characteristics influenced cultures in colonization. .... ❑ ❑ ❑ ❑ ❑

HISTORY

Understand the factors which influenced the development of early civilizations. .... ❑ ❑ ❑ ❑ ❑

Recognize important leaders and events in the growth of ancient Greece and Rome. .... ❑ ❑ ❑ ❑ ❑

Understand the rise and decline of ancient civilizations. .... ❑ ❑ ❑ ❑ ❑

EVALUATION CHECK LIST FOR SIXTH GRADE

SOCIAL SCIENCE

	CHILD'S NAME	CHILD'S NAME	CHILD'S NAME	CHILD'S NAME	CHILD'S NAME
Know major explorers and explorations of the world.	☐	☐	☐	☐	☐
Understand the causes of the Civil War.	☐	☐	☐	☐	☐
Understand the purpose of the Declaration of Independence.	☐	☐	☐	☐	☐
Know a country that helped America gain its independence.	☐	☐	☐	☐	☐
Identify a President during the Civil War.	☐	☐	☐	☐	☐
Understand the sequence of technological advancements in history.	☐	☐	☐	☐	☐

POLITICAL SCIENCE

	CHILD'S NAME	CHILD'S NAME	CHILD'S NAME	CHILD'S NAME	CHILD'S NAME
Recognize ideas concerning citizenship, government, and cultural groups in ancient civilizations.	☐	☐	☐	☐	☐
Understand the importance of trade, food production, weapons, and tools to early civilization.	☐	☐	☐	☐	☐
Recognize sources of conflict among cultural groups.	☐	☐	☐	☐	☐
Understand the influence of geographic factors upon world cultures.	☐	☐	☐	☐	☐
Understand the increasing complexity of societies.	☐	☐	☐	☐	☐
Understand the historical development of social and political organizations.	☐	☐	☐	☐	☐
Understand the historical impact of various forms of government.	☐	☐	☐	☐	☐
Know how tribal groups and caste systems affect cultures.	☐	☐	☐	☐	☐

EVALUATION CHECK LIST FOR SIXTH GRADE

SOCIAL SCIENCE

CHILD'S NAME · CHILD'S NAME · CHILD'S NAME · CHILD'S NAME · CHILD'S NAME

ECONOMICS

Recognize the influence of capitalism upon economic growth. .... ❑ ❑ ❑ ❑ ❑

Understand the role of the natural environment in limiting, protecting, providing political power, and meeting needs......... ❑ ❑ ❑ ❑ ❑

Know the impact of technological changes in societies. .... ❑ ❑ ❑ ❑ ❑

Know the effects of colonization, technology, and urbanization upon the economy of the nation. .... ❑ ❑ ❑ ❑ ❑

Know the effects of pollution for industrialized nations. .... ❑ ❑ ❑ ❑ ❑

Understand the effects of the types of government upon the citizens. .... ❑ ❑ ❑ ❑ ❑

Recognize the factors leading to a standard of living.. ❑ ❑ ❑ ❑ ❑

Understand the Common Market.................... ❑ ❑ ❑ ❑ ❑

Understand the impact of global concerns. ...... ❑ ❑ ❑ ❑ ❑

PSYCHOLOGY/SOCIOLOGY

Recognize the importance of heritage to citizens. .... ❑ ❑ ❑ ❑ ❑

Recognize the increased interest in human rights.. ❑ ❑ ❑ ❑ ❑

Understand roles and rights of citizens......... ❑ ❑ ❑ ❑ ❑

Understand the basic needs of a human. ...... ❑ ❑ ❑ ❑ ❑

EVALUATION CHECK LIST FOR SEVENTH GRADE

SOCIAL SCIENCE

Seventh-grade students should be able to do the following:

(See the State History at the end of this section)

GEOGRAPHY

	☐	☐	☐	☐	☐
Understand the definition, purpose, and tools of geography.	☐	☐	☐	☐	☐
Understand the earth, its structure, and elements.	☐	☐	☐	☐	☐

Know the different characteristics and influences of physical features, natural resources, and climates on the peoples of:

North America	☐	☐	☐	☐	☐
Latin America	☐	☐	☐	☐	☐
Africa	☐	☐	☐	☐	☐
Asia	☐	☐	☐	☐	☐
Europe and Russia	☐	☐	☐	☐	☐
Know the different characteristics of oceans, and understand what natural resources can be found there.	☐	☐	☐	☐	☐
Compare different regions with different topography.	☐	☐	☐	☐	☐

HISTORY

Identify a ruler of a given country.	☐	☐	☐	☐	☐
Recognize the sequence of technology developments.	☐	☐	☐	☐	☐
Recognize the sequence of events in space exploration.	☐	☐	☐	☐	☐
Detect the purpose of the Boston Tea Party.	☐	☐	☐	☐	☐

EVALUATION CHECK LIST FOR SEVENTH GRADE

SOCIAL SCIENCE

Understand the industrial revolution. .... ❏ ❏ ❏ ❏ ❏

Identify accomplishments of famous Americans. .... ❏ ❏ ❏ ❏ ❏

Explain the reasoning for the stars on the U. S. Flag. .... ❏ ❏ ❏ ❏ ❏

Identify the location of the Renaissance. .. ❏ ❏ ❏ ❏ ❏

POLITICAL SCIENCE *(People as a Group)*.

Understand the term *Freedom of Press.* .... ❏ ❏ ❏ ❏ ❏

Understand the basic principles of the Bill of Rights. .... ❏ ❏ ❏ ❏ ❏

Explain the voting process. .... ❏ ❏ ❏ ❏ ❏

Understand the American political system. .. ❏ ❏ ❏ ❏ ❏

Explain the responsibility of local government. .... ❏ ❏ ❏ ❏ ❏

ECONOMICS

Understand inflation. .... ❏ ❏ ❏ ❏ ❏

Define supply and demand. .... ❏ ❏ ❏ ❏ ❏

Determine what increases production in different industries. .... ❏ ❏ ❏ ❏ ❏

Identify communism. .... ❏ ❏ ❏ ❏ ❏

PSYCHOLOGY/SOCIOLOGY

Understand individuals' rights. .... ❏ ❏ ❏ ❏ ❏

Explain learned behavior. .... ❏ ❏ ❏ ❏ ❏

Define sociology. .... ❏ ❏ ❏ ❏ ❏

Predict behavior in different situations. .... ❏ ❏ ❏ ❏ ❏

Understand different forms of communication. .... ❏ ❏ ❏ ❏ ❏

EVALUATION CHECK LIST FOR EIGHTH GRADE

SOCIAL SCIENCE

Eighth-grade students should be able to do the following:

(See the State History Section at the end of this chapter)

	CHILD'S NAME	CHILD'S NAME	CHILD'S NAME	CHILD'S NAME	CHILD'S NAME

GEOGRAPHY

Recognize the geographic regions, climate patterns and natural resources of North America. .... ❑ ❑ ❑ ❑ ❑

Understand how factors affect a country's climate. .... ❑ ❑ ❑ ❑ ❑

Understand and read map symbols and legends. .... ❑ ❑ ❑ ❑ ❑

HISTORY

Understand the major social, economic, and political reasons for European exploration and colonization of the New World. .... ❑ ❑ ❑ ❑ ❑

Know the events that led to English domination of North America. .... ❑ ❑ ❑ ❑ ❑

Understand the governments, economies, and different lifestyles of the thirteen American colonies. .... ❑ ❑ ❑ ❑ ❑

Know the causes, major events, and personalities of the American Revolution. .... ❑ ❑ ❑ ❑ ❑

Know the weakness of the Articles of Confederation and that the United States Constitution created a stronger central government while protecting the rights of citizens. .... ❑ ❑ ❑ ❑ ❑

Understand the problems and accomplishments of the young American republic.......... ❑ ❑ ❑ ❑ ❑

EVALUATION CHECK LIST FOR EIGHTH GRADE

SOCIAL SCIENCE

Understand the expansion and development of the United States during the different presidential terms. .... ❑ ❑ ❑ ❑ ❑

Know the sectional differences that evolved as the America frontier expanded and the country developed culturally and economically. .... ❑ ❑ ❑ ❑ ❑

Know the causes, course, and consequences of the Civil War. .... ❑ ❑ ❑ ❑ ❑

Understand the causes and accomplishments of the Progressive Era............................. ❑ ❑ ❑ ❑ ❑

Know the events that led to American entry into World War I and the subsequent role played by American military forces. .... ❑ ❑ ❑ ❑ ❑

Understand America's return to isolationism and the disillusionment of the Roaring Twenties. .... ❑ ❑ ❑ ❑ ❑

Know causes of the Great Depression and the major efforts of the New Deal. .... ❑ ❑ ❑ ❑ ❑

Understand the causes and worldwide scope of American involvement in World War II. ❑ ❑ ❑ ❑ ❑

Understand the causes and events of the Cold War and its impact on American policies at home and abroad. .... ❑ ❑ ❑ ❑ ❑

Recognize a time period by a given mode of transportation. .... ❑ ❑ ❑ ❑ ❑

POLITICAL SCIENCE

Understand the changes in American society brought about by the Industrial Revolution. .... ❑ ❑ ❑ ❑ ❑

EVALUATION CHECK LIST FOR EIGHTH GRADE

SOCIAL SCIENCE

Understand the concept of imperialism and the establishment of the United States as a world power. .... ☐ ☐ ☐ ☐ ☐

Understand the changes in American society brought about by the Civil Rights movement, technological advances, and economic and political challenges from other nations. ☐ ☐ ☐ ☐ ☐

Identify political parties in the United States. ☐ ☐ ☐ ☐ ☐

Understand the powers of the President. .... ☐ ☐ ☐ ☐ ☐

Understand the voting process. .... ☐ ☐ ☐ ☐ ☐

Identify political leaders in different levels of government. .... ☐ ☐ ☐ ☐ ☐

Understand the difference between rights and responsibilities of a United States citizen. .. ☐ ☐ ☐ ☐ ☐

ECONOMICS

Apply an understanding of the association of supply and demand...................................... ☐ ☐ ☐ ☐ ☐

Understand what affects job satisfaction. .... ☐ ☐ ☐ ☐ ☐

Predict the results on a country if its exports were no longer available.............................. ☐ ☐ ☐ ☐ ☐

Understand inflation...................................... ☐ ☐ ☐ ☐ ☐

Understand the depression. .... ☐ ☐ ☐ ☐ ☐

PSYCHOLOGY/SOCIOLOGY

Define psychology. .... ☐ ☐ ☐ ☐ ☐

Determine what consequences different acts will have for an individual. .... ☐ ☐ ☐ ☐ ☐

Realize the changing role of women in society. ☐ ☐ ☐ ☐ ☐

Understand what subjects need to be studied for different professions. .... ☐ ☐ ☐ ☐ ☐

STATE HISTORY

Seat of State Government ·
Developments: Historic/Cultural/Economic

State governments require, usually by the end of seventh grade, that a child
will have learned certain basic knowledge about the state.
Check with the educational offices in your state about its requirement.

The following Evaluation Check List is the requirement for a child in the
State of Tennessee. It reflects the acceptable level by the end of the seventh year of schooling.

EVALUATION CHECK LIST FOR SEVENTH & EIGHTH GRADES

STATE HISTORY

Know your state capitol .... ▢ ▢ ▢ ▢ ▢

Understand the diversity of your state's physical geography and its impact on the state's historic, economic, and cultural development. .... ▢ ▢ ▢ ▢ ▢

Know the major developments in the area that became your state prior to and during European exploration......................... ▢ ▢ ▢ ▢ ▢

Know the events that led to statehood for your state.. ▢ ▢ ▢ ▢ ▢

Understand your state Constitution and its relationship to the United States constitution and national government. .... ▢ ▢ ▢ ▢ ▢

Recognize your state's leadership role in the expansion of the young republic. .... ▢ ▢ ▢ ▢ ▢

Understand political, economic, and social developments in the antebellum period on your state... ▢ ▢ ▢ ▢ ▢

Know the causes of the Civil War as reflected by your state's sectional differences, if applicable. .... ▢ ▢ ▢ ▢ ▢

Understand the role of your state during the Civil War, if applicable. .... ▢ ▢ ▢ ▢ ▢

Understand the political, social, and economic changes brought to your state through the Reconstruction. .... ▢ ▢ ▢ ▢ ▢

Understand the problems and progress that characterized your state at the turn-of-the-century. .... ▢ ▢ ▢ ▢ ▢

Recognize the impact of the Great Depression and World War II on your state and

EVALUATION CHECK LIST FOR SEVENTH & EIGHTH GRADES

STATE HISTORY

	CHILD'S NAME	CHILD'S NAME	CHILD'S NAME	CHILD'S NAME	CHILD'S NAME
the nation.	☐	☐	☐	☐	☐
Understand the political and social changes that came to your state in the post-World War II years.	☐	☐	☐	☐	☐
Recognize the growing diversity of your state's economy and its impact on national and world markets.	☐	☐	☐	☐	☐
Understand the organization and structure of state and local government.	☐	☐	☐	☐	☐

SECTION V
APPENDICES

GLOSSARY I
BIBLICAL EDUCATIONAL TERMS

From *International Standard Bible Encylopedia, Electronic Database* by Biblesoft.

A rich variety of words is employed in the Bible to describe the teaching process. The terms do not so much indicate an office and an official as a function and a service, although both ideas are often expressed or implied.

OLD TESTAMENT TERMS

discernment: *bin,* to separate: The word meaning "to separate," "to distinguish," is often used in a causative sense to signify "to teach." The idea of teaching was not an aggregation of facts bodily transferred, like merchandise. Real learning followed genuine teaching. This word suggests a sound psychological basis for a good pedagogy. The function of teaching might be exercised with reference to the solution of difficult problems, the interpretation of God's will, or the manner of a godly life (Dan. 8:16,26; Neh. 8:7-9; Ps. 119:34).

discipline: *lamadh,* to beat: A very common word for "to teach"; it may have meant "to beat with a rod," "to chastise," and may have originally referred to the striking and goading of beasts, by which they were curbed and trained. By a noble evolution, the term came to describe the process of disciplining and training men in war, religion and life (Isa. 2:3; Hos. 10:11; Micah 4:2). As teaching is both a condition and an accompaniment of disciplining, the word often means simply "to teach," "to inform" (2 Chr. 17:7; Ps. 71:17; Prov. 5:13). The glory of teaching was its harmony with the will of God, its source

in God's authority, and its purpose to secure spiritual obedience (Deut. 4:5,14; 31:12-13).

illumination: *zahar,* to shine: This verbal root signifies "to shine," and when applied to the intellectual sphere indicates the function of teaching to be one of illumination. Ignorance is darkness, knowledge is light. Moses was to teach the people statutes and laws, or to enlighten them on the principles and precepts of God's revelation (Exo. 18:20). The service rendered by the teachers-- priests, Levites and fathers-- sent forth by Jehoshaphat, was one of illumination in the twofold sense of instruction and admonition (2 Chr. 19:8-10).

inspiration: *nabha´,* to boil up: The most significant word for "prophet" is derived from the verb which means "to boil up or forth like a fountain," and consequently to pour forth words under the impelling power of the Spirit of God. The Hebrews used the passive forms of the verb because they considered the thoughts and words of the prophets due not to personal ability but to divine influence. The utterances of the prophets were characterized by instruction, admonition, persuasion and prediction (Deut. 18:15-22; Ezek. 33:1-20).

knowledge: *yadha´,* to see (compare *oida*): This verb literally means "to see" and consequently "to perceive," "to know," "to come to know," and "cause to know or teach." It describes the act of knowing as both progressive and completed. The causative conception signifies achievement in the sphere of instruction. It is used of the interpretation and application by Moses of the principles of the law of God (Exo. 18:16,20), of the elucidation of life's problems by the sages (Prov. 9:9; 22:19), and of constant Providential guidance in the way of life (Ps. 16:11).

law: *yarah,* to cast, teach, instruct, inform: The teaching idea from which the law was derived is expressed by a verb which means "to throw," "to cast as an arrow or lot." It is also used of thrusting the hand forth to point out or show clearly (Gen. 46:28; Exo. 15:25). The original idea is easily changed into an educational conception, since the teacher puts forth new ideas and facts as a sower casts seed into the ground. But the process of teaching was not considered external and mechanical but internal and vital (Exo. 35:34-35; 2 Chr. 6:27). The nominal form is the usual word for law, human and divine, general and specific (Deut. 4:8; Ps. 19:8; Prov. 1:8). The following are suggestive phrases: "the book of the law" (Deut. 28:61; 2 Kings 22:8); "the book of the law of Moses" (Josh 8:31; 2 Kin 14:6); "the book of the law of God" (Josh. 24:26); "the book of the law of Yahweh" (2 Chr. 17:9). Thus even in the days of Joshua there was in the possession of the religious teachers a book of the Law of the Lord as given by Moses. This recorded revelation and legislation continued to be the divine norm and ultimate authority for priest, king and people (2 Chr. 23:11; Neh. 8:1-3).

nourishment: *ra`ah,* to feed a flock: The name "shepherd," so precious in both the Old Testament and the New Testament, comes from a verb meaning "to feed," hence, to protect and care for out of a sense of devotion, ownership and responsibility. It is employed with reference to civil rulers in their positions of trust (2 Sam. 5:2; Jer. 23:2); with reference to teachers of virtue and wisdom (Prov. 10:21; Eccl. 12:11); and pre-eminently with reference to God as the great Shepherd of His chosen people (Ps. 23:1; Hos. 4:16). (Ezek. 34) presents an arraignment of the unfaithful shepherds or civil rulers; (Ps. 23) reveals Yahweh as the Shepherd of true believers, and (Jn. 10) shows how religious teachers are shepherds under Jesus the Good Shepherd.

vision: *ra´-ah,* to see: The literal meaning of this verb is "to see," and the nominal form is the ancient name for prophet or authoritative teacher who was expected to have a clear vision of spiritual realities, the will of God, the need of man and the way of life (1 Sam. 9:9; 1 Chr. 9:22; 2 Chr. 16:7) f; (Isa. 30:10).

wisdom: *sakhal,* to be wise: The verb from which the various nominal forms for "wisdom" are derived means "to look at," "to behold," "to view," and in the causative stem describes the process by which one is enabled to see for himself what had never before entered his physical or intellectual field of consciousness. The noun indicates a wise person or sage whose mission is to instruct others in the ways of the Lord (Prov. 16:23; 21:11); and often in the Wisdom literature). In Dan. 12:3 we read: "They that are wise (margin, "the teachers") shall shine as the brightness of the firmament."

NEW TESTAMENT TERMS

Further light is thrown upon religious teaching in Bible times by a brief view of the leading educational terms found in the New Testament.

acquisition: *manthano,* to learn: The central thought of teaching is causing one to learn. Teaching and learning are not scholastic but dynamic, and imply personal relationship and activity in the acquisition of knowledge (Mt. 11:29; 28:19; Acts 14:21). There were three concentric circles of disciples in the time of our Lord: learners, pupils, superficial followers, the multitude (Jn. 6:66); the body of believers who accepted Jesus as their Master (Mt. 10:42); and the Twelve Disciples whom Jesus also called apostles (Mt. 10:2).

authority: *prophetes,* one who speaks for: A prophet was a man who spoke forth a message from God to the people. He might deal with past failures and achievements, present privileges and responsibilities, or future doom and glory. He received his message and authority from God (Deut. 18:15-22; Isa. 6). The word refers to Old Testament teachers (Mt. 5:12), to John the Baptist (Mt. 21:26), to Jesus the Messiah (Acts 3:25), and to special speakers in the Apostolic age (Mt. 10:41; Acts 13:1; 1 Cor. 14:29,37).

care: *poimen,* a shepherd: The word for shepherd signifies one who tends a flock, and by analogy a person who gives mental and spiritual nourishment, and guards and supports those under his care (Mt. 9:36; Jn. 10:2,16; 1 Pet. 2:25; Eph. 4:11). Love is a fundamental prerequisite to the exercise of the shepherding function (Jn. 21:15-18). The duties are to be discharged with great diligence and in humble recognition of the gifts and appointment of the Holy Spirit (Acts 20:28).

elucidation: *diermeneuo,* to interpret: In the walk to Emmaus, Christ explained to the perplexed disciples the Old Testament Scriptures in reference to Himself. The work of interpreter is to make truth clear and to effect the edification of the hearer (Lk. 24:27; 1 Cor. 12:30; 14:5,13,27).

exposition: *ektithemi,* to place out: The verb literally means "to set or place out," and signifies to bring out the latent and secret ideas of a literary passage or a system of thought and life. Thus Peter interpreted his vision, Aquila and Priscilla unfolded truth to Apollos, and Paul expounded the gospel in Rome (Acts 11:4; 18:26; 28:23). True teaching is an educational exposition.

instruction: *didasko,* to teach: The usual word for "teach" in the New Testament signifies either to hold a discourse with others in order to instruct them, or to deliver a didactic discourse where there may not be direct personal and verbal participation. In the former sense it describes the interlocutory method, the interplay of the ideas and words between pupils and teachers, and in the latter use it refers to the more formal monologues designed especially to give information (Mt. 4:23); chapters 5-7; (13:36) f; (Jn. 6:59; 1 Cor. 4:17; 1 Tim. 2:12). A teacher is one who performs the function or fills the office of instruction. Ability and fitness for the work are required (Rom. 2:20; Heb. 5:12). The title refers to Jewish teachers (Jn. 1:38), to John the Baptist (Lk. 3:12), to Jesus (Jn. 3:2; 8:4), and often, to Paul (1 Tim. 2:7; 2 Tim. 1:11), and to instructors in the early church (Acts 13:1; Rom. 12:7; 1 Cor. 12:28). Teaching, like preaching, was an integral part of the work of an apostle (Mt. 28:19; Mk. 16:15; Eph. 4:1).

presentation: *paratithemi,* to place beside: The presentative idea involved in the teaching process is intimately associated with the principle of adaptation. When it is stated that Christ put forth parables unto the people, the sacred writer employs the figure of placing alongside of, or near one, hence, before him in an accessible position. The food or teaching should be sound, or hygienic, and adapted to the capacity and development of the recipient (Mt. 13:24; Mk. 8:6; Acts 16:34; 1 Cor. 10:27; 2 Tim. 4:3; Heb. 5:12-14).

supervision: *episkopos,* an overseer: The bishop or overseer was to feed and protect the blood-bought church of God (Acts 20:28). Among the various qualifications of the religious overseers was an aptitude for teaching (1 Tim. 3:2; Tit. 1:9). The Lord is pre-eminently shepherd and bishop (1 Pet. 2:25).

GLOSSARY II
MODERN EDUCATIONAL TERMS

achievement test. an objective examination that measures educationally relevant skills or knowledge about such subjects as reading, spelling, or mathematics.

addend. A number added to another number. In the problem "40 + 73 = ?" the addend is 73.

age norms. values representing typical or average performance of people of age groups.

antebellum. A period before the United States Civil War.

antonym. A word that means the opposite of another word.

average. a statistic that indicates the central tendency or most typical score of a group of scores. Most often, average refers to the sum of a set of scores divided by the number of scores in the set.

battery. a group of carefully selected tests that are administered to a given population, the results of which are of value individually, in combination, and totally.

ceiling. the upper limit of ability that can be measured by a particular test.

clause. A group of words that contain a subject and a verb or verb phrase and forms part of a compound or complex sentence.

congruent. *Geometry,* exactly coinciding: Congruent triangles have the same size and shape. *Algebra,* producing the same remainder when divided by a given number.

contraction. One word made up of two words that have been shortened. It's—it is, hasn't—has not.

Criterion-Referenced Test. A measurement of achievement of specific criteria or skills in terms of absolute levels of mastery. The focus is on performance of an individual as measured against a standard

diacritical. A mark placed over, under, or attached to a letter to indicate pronunciation, stress accent or other value.

diagnostic test. An intensive, in-depth evaluation process with a relatively detailed and narrow coverage of a specific area. The purpose of this test is to determine the specific learning needs of individual students (rather than comparing students to other students, as the standardized tests) and to be able to meet those needs through regular or remedial classroom instruction.

digraph. Two letters used together to spell a single sound. Example: *ea* in each, *th* in with, *sh* in shop.

diphthong. A vowel made up of two vowel sounds pronounced as one syllable. Such as *ou* in house.

Dolch Sight Words. See page 288.

domain-referenced test. A test in which performance is measured against a well-defined set of tasks or body of knowledge (domain). Domain-referenced tests are a specific set of criterion-referenced tests and have a similar purpose.

ecosystem. A system made up of living organisms and its physical environment. A pond, a lake, a forest or an ocean may be an ecosystem. An ecosystem includes such factors as food supply, weather and natural enemies.

factor. Any one of the numbers or expressions which produce a given number of quantity when multiplied together. Example: 2 and 5 are factors of 10.

food chain. A group of organisms so interrelated that each member of the group feeds upon the one below it and, in turn, is eaten by the one above.

food web. 1. A group of interrelated food chains in a certain community. **2.** food cycle.

grade equivalent. The estimated grade level that corresponds to a given score.

heteronym. A word spelled the same as another, but having a different sound and meaning. Example: lead, to conduct and lead, a metal.

homograph. See homonym.

homonym. 1. A word having the same pronunciation and spelling of another word, but different in meaning and origin. Example: bass meaning a fish and bass meaning a male singing voice. **2.** homograph. **3.** homophone.

hyperbole. An exaggerated statement used for effect and not meant to be taken literally. Example: Waves as high as mountains broke over the reef.

inflection. A variation in a word to show case, number, gender, person, tense, mood, voice or comparison. A suffix or other ending used in inflecting: *-est* and *-ed* are common inflections.

informal test. A nonstandardized test that is designed to give an approximate index of an individual's level of ability or learning style; often teacher-constructed.

integer. A whole number (as distinct from fractions). Any positive or negative number including 0.

interrogative. Having the form of asking a question.

inventory. A catalog or list for assessing the absence or presence of certain attitudes, interests, behaviors, or other items regarded as relevant to a given purpose.

item. An individual question or exercise in a test or evaluative instrument.

normal curve equivalent. standard scores with a mean of 50 and a standard deviation of approximately 21.

norm. performance standards that is established by a reference group and that describes average or typical performance. Usually norms are determined by testing a representative group and then calculating the group's test performance.

norm-referenced test. An objective test that is standardized on a group of individuals whose performance is evaluated in relation to the performance of others; contrasted with criterion-referenced test.

objective percent correct. The percent of the items measuring a single objective that a student answers correctly.

ordinal. A number that shows position in a series. First, second, etc.

percent score. The percent of items that are answered correctly.

percentile. The percent of people in the norming sample whose scores were below a given score.

performance Test. Designed to evaluate general intelligence or aptitudes. Consists primarily of motor items or perceptual items because verbal abilities play a minimal role.

polysyllabic. A word with more than three syllables.

predicate. The word or words in a sentence that tell what is said about the subject. In *men work, The men dug wells,* and *The men are soldiers, work, dug wells,* and *are soldiers* are all predicates.

published test. A test that is publicly available because it has been copyrighted and published commercially.

Pythagorean theorem. The theorem that the square of the hypotenuse of a right triangle equals the sum of the squares of the other two sides.

rating scales. Subjective assessments made on predetermined criteria in the form of a scale. Rating scales include numerical scales or descriptive scales. Forced choice rating scales require that the rater determine whether an individual demonstrates more of one trait than another.

raw score. The number of items that are answered correctly.

reliability. The extent of which a test is dependable, stable, and consistent when administered to the same individuals on different occasions. Technically, this is a statistical term that defines the extent to which errors of measurement are absent from a measurement instrument.

schwa. An unstressed vowel sound such as *u* in *circus*. Represented by the symbol of an upside-down *e*.

screening. A fast, efficient measurement for a large population to identify individuals who may deviate in a specified area, such as the incidence of maladjustment or readiness for academic work.

specimen set. A sample set of testing materials that are available from a commercial test publisher.

standard scores--A score that is expressed as a deviation from a population mean.

standardization--Is obtained by administering the test to a given population and then calculating means, standard deviations, standardized scores, and percentiles. Equivalent scores are then produced for comparisons of an individual score to the norm group's performance.

standardized test. A form of measurement that has been normed against a specific population.

stanine. One of the steps in a nine-point scale of standard scores.

synonym. Words of similar meanings. *Small* is the synonym of *little*.

validity. The extent to which a test measures what it was intended to measure. Validity indicates the degree of accuracy of either predictions or inferences based upon a test score.

Dolch Sight Words

a	cam	has	must	see	want
about	could	have	my	seven	warm
after	cute	he	myself	shall	was
again	did	help	never	she	wash
all	do	her	new	show	we
always	does	here	no	sing	well
am	done	him	not	sit	went
an	don't	his	now	six	were
and	down	hold	of	sleep	what
any	draw	hot	off	so	when
are	eat	how	old	some	where
around	eight	hurt	on	soon	which
as	every	I	once	start	white
ask	fall	if	one	thank	who
at	far	in	only	that	why
age	fast	into	open	there	will
be	find	is	or	them	wish
because	first	it	our	then	with
between	five	it's	out	these	work
before	fly	jump	over	they	would
best	for	just	own	think	write
better	found	keep	pick	this	yellow
big	four	kind	play	those	yes
black	from	know	please	three	you
blue	full	laugh	pretty	to	your
birth	funny	let	pull	today	
bring	gay	like	put	together	
brown	get	little	ran	too	
but	give	live	read	try	
buy	go	long	red	two	
by	goes	look	ride	under	
call	going	made	right	up	
came	good	make	round	upon	
can	got	many	run	us	
carry	green	may	said	use	
clean	grow	me	saw	very	
cold	had	much	say	walk	

BIBLIOGRAPHY

Books marked with a ☆ are available through Heart of Wisdom Web Site at HomeschoolUnitStudies.com and most home school supply stores.

Adams, Dan. *The Child Influencers: Restoring the Lost Art of Parenting*. Cuyohoga Falls, OH: Home Team Press, 1990. ☆

Auch, Ron. *The Heart of the King: A Devotional Commentary on Psalm 119*. Green Forest, AZ: New Leaf Press, 1995. ☆

Bacon, Earnest. Spurgeon, *Heir of the Puritans*. Arlington Heights, IL: Christian Liberty Press, 1996.

Bean, E. William. *New Treasures: A Perspective of New Testament Teachings Through Hebraic Eyes*. Oak Creek, WI: Cornerstone Publishing, 1995. ☆

Beckett, John D. *Loving Monday: Succeeding in Business Without Selling Your Soul,* Intervarsity Pr; 1998. ☆

Beechick, Ruth. *The Language Wars: and Other Writings for Homeschoolers*. Pollock Pines, CA: Arrow Press, 1995. ☆

———. *You Can Teach Your Child Successfully*. Pollock Pines, CA: Arrow Press, 1993. ☆

———. *Teaching Primaries: Understanding How They Think and How They Learn*. Denver, CO: Accent Books, 1985. ☆

Bloch, Abraham P. *The Biblical and Historical Background of Jewish Customs and Ceremonies,* New York, NY: . KTAV Publishing House, Inc., 1980. ☆

Blumefield, Samuel. *Is Public Education Necessary?* Old Greenwich, CT: The Devin-Adair Company, 1981.

Bradley, Reb. *Child Training Tips,* Family Ministries, PO Box 1412, Fair Oaks, CA 95628, (916) 965-7873, familyministries.com

Burtness, Bill. *Judah Bible Curriculum: Education for Liberty*. Urbana, IL: Judah Bible Curriculum, 1988.

Cannon, Inge. *Education Plus: Patterning Learning Upon Scripture*. *Education Plus*, 1995.

Cavett, Rick. "Goals, Standards, and All That." *The Mississippi Conservative*. May, 1995.

Clarkson, Clay and Sally. *Educating the Whole Hearted Child: A Handbook for Christian Home Educators*. Walnut Springs, TX: Whole Heart Ministries, 1996.☆

Coder, S. Maxwell. *First Steps To Knowing God's Will: Everything You Need to Live A Christian Life*. Meridian Publication, 1996.

Coke, Karl D., Ph.D. "Restoring The Home As The Center For Spiritual Growth." Charlotte, NC: Family Restoration Fellowship.

David de Sola Pool. *Why I Am a Jew*. Boston: Beacon Press, 1957.

Deparrie, Paul and Mary Pride. *Ancient Empires of the New Age*. Westchester, IL: Crossway Books, 1989.

Deporter, Bobbi and Mike Hernacki. *Quantum Learning: Unleashing the Genius in You*. New York, NY: Dell Publishing, 1992.

Duffy, Cathy. *Government Nannies: The Cradle - To - Grave Agenda of Goals 2000 & Outcome Based Education*. Gresham, OR: Noble Publishing Associates, 1995. ☆

Eakman, B. K. *Educating for the New World Order* Portland, OR: Halcyon House, 1991. ☆

Eaton, Tamera, Christian Homeschool Forum, http://www.gocin.com/home-school/

Edersheim, Alfred. *Sketches of Jewish Social Life*. Peabody, MA: Hendrickson Publishers, 1994. ☆

———. *The Temple: Its Ministry and Services.* Peabody, MA: Hendrickson Publishers, Inc.,1994. ☆

Education Liberator, the monthly publication of the Separation of School & State Alliance. 4578 N. First St., #310, Fresno, CA, 93726; http://www.sepschool.org, 209-292-1776.

Eldridge, Tom. *Safely Home*, Patriarch Magazine, PO Box 50, Willis, VA 24380, http://www.Patriarch.com

Feder, Don. A *Jewish Conservative Looks at Pagan America*. Lafayette, LA: Huntington House Publishers, 1993. ☆

Flannery, Edward H. *The Anguish of the Jews*, New Jersey: Paulist Press., 1985.

Finn, Chester E. Jr. "What To Do about The Schools." *Commentary Magazine*, October, 1994.

Follette, John Wright. *Broken Bread: A Devotional Classic for Developing Christian Character* Springfield, MO: Gospel Publishing House, 1957.

Frangipane, Francis. H*oliness, Truth and the Presence of God: A Powerful, Penetrating Study of the Human Heart and How God Prepares it For His Glory.* Marion, IN: Francis Frangipane, 1986.

Freeman, James M. *Manners And Customs of the Bible: A Complete Guide to the Origin and Significance of Our Time* - Honored Biblical Tradition.

Fugate, J. Richard. *What the Bible says about Child Training*. Tempe, AZ: Aletheia Publishers, Inc., 1980. ☆

Gatto, John Taylor. *Dumbing Us Down: The Hidden Curriculum of Compulsory Schooling*. Philadelphia, PA: New Society Publishers, 1992. ☆

Goodrich, Donna, Mary Lou Klingler and Jan Potter. *100 Plus Motivational Moments for Writers and Speakers.* San Juan Capistrano, CA: Joy Publishing, 1991.

Green, Albert. *Thinking Christianly.* Seattle, WA: Alta Vista College Press, 1990.

Gruber, Dr. Gary. *Dr. Gary Gruber's Essential Guide to Test Taking for Kids Grades 3-4-5*. New York, NY: Quill William Morrow, 1986.

Hawkins, O. S. *In Sheep's Clothing: Jude's Urgent Warning about Apostasy in the Church*. Neptune, NJ: Loizeaux, 1994.

Haycock, Dr. Ruth C. *Encyclopedia of Bible Truths for School Subjects, Association of Christian Schools International*.

Henry, Matthew. *Commentary of the Whole Bible by Matthew Henry.* Grand Rapids, MI: Zondervan Publishing House, 1960.

Howse, Brannon. *An Educational Abduction: Do You Know What Your Child Is Being Taught?* Green Forest, AR: New Leaf Press, 1993.

Houston, J. M., Contributor Pictorial Bible Atlas, 8th Ed. (Grand Rapids, MI: Zondervan, 1981) p. 3

Hubbard, David A. T*he Wisdom of the Old Testament,* Messiah College Occasional Papers, no.3 (Grantham, PA: Messiah College, August, 1982) p. 23.

Independence Institute is a nonprofit, nonpartisan Colorado think tank.

Institute for the Learning Sciences (ILS), http://www.ils.nwu.edu/

International Institute for Christian Studies. WWW. 73754.1132@compuserve.com

International Standard Bible Encyclopedia. Electronic Database by Biblesoft, 1996.

Jacoby, Russell. D*ogmatic Wisdom: How the Culture Wars Divert Education and Distract America*. New York, NY: Doubleday, 1994.

Jeremiah, Dr. David. *The Power of Encouragement*, (1998) Multnomah Publishers Inc.; ISBN: 1576731359

Johnston, Henry P., ed., *The Correspondence and Public Papers of John Jay*, reprint. New York, NY: Burt Franklin, 1970.

Juster, Dan. *Jewish Roots: A Foundation of Biblical Theology*. Shippensburg, PA: Destiny Image, 1995.

Kahn, Gary H. *The Demonic Roots of Globalism: En Route to Spiritual Deception*.

———. *En Route to Global Occupation: A High Ranking Governmental Liaison Exposes the Secret Agenda for World Unification*. Lafayette, LA: Huntington House Publishers, 1991.

Kandel, I. L. *Colliers Encyclopedia CD-ROM. Education*, History of, Vol. 8, 02-28-1996. ☆.F. Collier, A Division of Newfield Publications, 1996.

Kimeldorf, Martin. *Creating Portfolios: For Success in School, Work, and Life*. Minneapolis, MN: Free Spirit Publishing, 1994.

Lahaye, Tim. *The Race for the 21st Century: What Christians must do to Survive*. Nashville, TN: Thomas Nelson, Inc., 1986.

Lapide, Pinchas E. *Hebrew in the Church*, trans. Erroll F. Rhodes. Grand Rapids: William B. Eerdmans Publishing Co., 1984, p. x.

Leitch, Cliff. Wisdom of the Bible Shareware, 1996.

Limburg, James, ed. *Judaism: An Introduction for Christians* Minneapolis, MN: Augsburg Publishing House, 1987.

Luksik, Peg and Pamela Hobbs. *Outcome Based Education: The State's Assault on Our Childrens Values*. Lafayette, LA: Huntington House, 1995.

MacDonald, William ed. *Believers Bible Commentary: A Thorough, Yet Easy To Read Bible Commentary That Turns Complicated Theology Into Practical Understanding*, Nashville, TN: Thomas Nelson Publishers, 1995.

Marx, Karl and Friedrich. Engels. *Basic Writings on Politics and Philosophy*, ed. Lewis S. Feuer. New York: 1959.

Mason, Charlotte, Home Education. London: England, 1925. Wheaton, IL: Reprint by Tyndale House Publishers, Inc., 1954.

———. *Formation of Character*.

———. *Ourselves*.

———. *Parents and Children*.

———. *School Education*.

———. *A Philosophy of Education*.

Mathis, James and Susan. *Foundations of A Christian World View*. Gainesville, FL: Christian World View Publishing, 1993.

McCarthy, Bernice. *The 4Mat System*. Barrington, IL: Excel, Inc., 1987.

McGill-Franzen, A. and R. L. Allington. "Flunk 'em or Get Them Classified: The Contamination of Primary Grade Accountability Data." *Educational Researcher* 22 (1, Jan-Feb): 19-22. (1993). EJ 464 906.

Meisels, S. J. "Doing Harm by Doing Good: Iatrogenic Effects of Early Childhood Enrollment and Promotion Policies." *Early Childhood Research Quarterly*. 2 June 1992, 155-174. EJ 450 523.

——, A. Dorfman, and D. Steele. "Equity and Excellence in Group-Administered and Performance-Based Assessments" in M. T. Nettles, and A. L. Nettles (Eds.) *Equity And Excellence In Educational Testing And Assessment* (Boston: Kluwer Academic Publishers, 1995).

——, J. R. Jablon, D. B. Marsden, M. L. Dichtelmiller, A. B. Dorfman, and D. M. Steele. *The Work Sampling System: An Overview.* Ann Arbor: Rebus Planning Associates, Inc., 1995.

——, Fr. Liaw, A. B. Dorfman, and R. Fails. "The Work Sampling System: Reliability and Validity of a Performance Assessment for Young Children." *Early Childhood Research Quarterly* 10 (Sept. 3, 1995).

——. "Remaking Classroom Assessment with The Work Sampling System." *Young Children*, 5 July 1993, 34-40. EJ 465 921.

Microsoft® Encarta® 97 Encyclopedia. Microsoft Corporation, 1993-1996.

Millar, Keith ed., student at Northwest Nazarene College (Nampa, ID),

Moody, Joshua, "Teaching of the Puritan Thinker." See Henry L. Feingold, *The Jewish Role Shaping America Society*, ed. A James Rudin and Marvin Wilson (Grand Rapids: William B. Eerdmans Publishing Co., 1987), p. 46

Moseley, Dr. Ron. Yeshua: A Guide to The Real Jesus and The Original Church, Hagerstown, MD: EBED Publications, 1996.✩

Mulligan, David. *Far Above Rubies: Wisdom in the Christian Community*. Marshfield, VT: Messenger Publishing, 1994.✩

Murray, Andrew. *How to Raise Your Children for Christ,* (June 1984) Whitaker House, ISBN: 0871232243.

Nash, Ronald H. *The Closing of the American Heart: What's Really Wrong With America's Schools.* Probe Books.

National Home Education Research Institute (NHERI) Brian D. Ray, Ph.D., Western Baptist College, 5000 Deer Park Dr. SE, Salem, Oregon 79301-9392, ph. (503) 375-7019.

Nourse, Ruth. *The Hijacking of American Education*: "Part 2 - War of the Poets: Longfellow vs. Poe."

O'Connor, Elizabeth. Eighth Day of Creation, Waco, TX: Word Books, 1971, p. 18.

Overman, Christian. *Assumptions That Affect Our Lives,* Simi Valley, CA, Micah 6:8; ISBN:1883035503, 1996. ✩

Packer, J. I. *A Quest For Godliness: The Puritan Vision of the Christian Life.* Wheaton, IL: Crossway Books, 1994.

Patriarch Magazine, PO Box 50, Willis, VA 24380, http://www.Patriarch.com

Phillips, John. *Exploring the World of the Jew*. Neptune, NJ: Loizeaux, 1993.

Pride, Mary. *School Proof: How to Help Your Family Beat the System and Learn to Love Learning - The Easy, Natural Way.* Wheaton, IL: Crossway Books, 1988.

Richards, Lawrence O. *The Teacher's Commentary: Explains and Applies the Scriptures in a Way That Will Help You Teach Any Lesson From Genesis to Revelation.* Wheaton, IL: Victor Books, 1987.

Riese, Alan W. and Herbert J. La Salle. *The Story of Western Civilization: Greece and Rome Build Great Civilizations.* Cambridge, MA: Educators Publishing Service, 1990.

Rosovsky, Nitza. *The Jewish Experience at Harvard and Radcliff.* Cambrage: Harvard University Press, 1986,

Sampson, Robin, *A Family Guide to the Biblical Holidays.* Woodbridge, VA. ☆

———. *Far Above Rubies Companion.* Woodbridge, VA:, Heart of Wisdom Pub, 1995. ☆

———. *Far Above Rubies Lesson Plans Volume 1.* Heart of Wisdom, 1996. ☆

Schaeffer, Francis A.*A Christian View of Philosophy and Culture,* vol. 1 of The Complete Works of Francis A Schaeffer, A Christian WorldView. Westchester, IL: Crossway Books, 1982.

———*A Christian View of the Bible as Truth,* vol. 2..

———. *A Christian View of Spirituality,* vol. 3.

———. *A Christian View of the Church,* vol. 4.

———. *A Christian View of the West,* vol. 5.

Schoeder, John F. ed., *Maxims of Washington.* Mt. Vernon: 1942.

Skillen, James W., ed. *The School Choice Controversy: What is Constitutional?* Grand Rapids, MI: Baker Books, 1993.

Slater, Rosalie J. *Teaching and Learning America's Christian History:* The Principle Approach. San Francisco, CA: 1965.

———. *A Family Program For Reading Aloud.* San Francisco, CA: Foundation For American Christian Education, 1991.

Smith (Eds.), *Assessment For Instruction In Early Literacy.* Englewood Cliffs, NJ: Prentice Hall, 7-44.

Stamps, Don. Study notes and articles from *The Full Life Study Bible KJV.* Life Publishers Int 1992.

Thayer, William M. *Gaining Favor With God & Man.* Woodbridge, VA: Heart of Wisdom Pub, 1997. ☆

Tozer, A. W. The Quotable Tozer: Wise Words With a Prophetic Edge. Camp Hill, PA: Christian Publications, 1994.

Van Brummelen, Harro W. *Steppingstones to Curriculum: A Biblical Path.* Seattle: Alta Vista College Press, 1994.

———. *Walking with God in the Classroom: Christian Approaches to Learning & Teaching.* Seattle, WA: Alta Vista College Press, 1988.

———. *Telling the Next Generation: Educational Development in North American Calvinist Christian Schools.* Lanham, Md: University Press of America, 1986.

Ward, Kaari, ed. *Jesus and His Times.* Pleasantville, NY: Readers Digest Association, Inc., 1987.

Waring, Diana. Beyond Survival: A Guide to Abundant-Life Homeschooling. Lynnwood, WA: Emerald Books, 1996. ☆

Wilkins, Steven. America: The First 350 Years. Monroe, LA: Covenant Publications, 1988. ☆

Wilson, Douglas. *Recovering The Lost Tools of Learning: An Approach to Distinctively Christian Education.* Wheaton, IL: Crossway Books, 1991.

SPIRITUAL FRUITS EVALUATION FORM

	Aug	Sept	Oct	Nov	Dec	Jan	Feb	March	April	May	June	July
LOVE (SEEKING THE HIGHEST GOOD FOR OTHERS)												
JOY (GLADNESS BASED ON THE NEARNESS OF GOD)												
PEACE (QUIETNESS OF HEART)												
KINDNESS (DESIRE NOT TO CAUSE ANYONE PAIN)												
GENTLENESS (RESTRAINT, STRENGTH, AND COURAGE, ANGRY WHEN NEEDED AND SUBMISSIVE WHEN NEEDED)												
SELF-CONTROL (MASTERING ONE'S OWN DESIRES AND PASSIONS)												
GOODNESS (ZEAL FOR THE TRUTH AND RIGHTEOUSNESS)												
FAITHFULNESS (FIRM LOYALTY)												
PATIENCE (ENDURANCE, LONGSUFFERING)												

1=Weak in this area
2=Needs Improvement in this area
3=I am proud of my child's efforts in this area

*COMMENTS:*_____

_____

_____

_____

_____

WORK AND STUDY HABITS EVALUATION FORM

	Aug	Sept	Oct	Nov	Dec	Jan	Feb	March	April	May	June	July
LISTENING ABILITY												
SITS ATTENTIVELY												
FOLLOWS DIRECTIONS												
COMPLETES WORK IN GIVEN TIME												
ORGANIZED												
USES TIME WISELY												
NEAT WORK												
WORKS TO POTENTIAL												
ATTEMPTS DIFFICULT WORK												
DOES NOT COMPLAIN												

1=Weak in this area
2=Needs Improvement in this area
3=I am proud of my child's efforts in this area

*COMMENTS:*_____

_____

_____

_____

_____

SHOWS:	Aug	Sept	Oct	Nov	Dec	Jan	Feb	March	April	May	June	July
COURTESY FOR OTHERS												
WILLINGNESS TO HELP												
ATTITUDE TOWARDS CORRECTION												
SELF-CONTROL												
RESPECT FOR OTHER CHILDREN												
RESPECT FOR ADULTS												
HANDLING OF PROBLEMS												
COOPERATION IN A GROUP												

ATTITUDE EVALUATION FORM

1=Weak in this area
2=Needs Improvement in this area
3=I am proud of my child's efforts in this area

COMMENTS:_____

_____

_____

_____

RESPONSIBILITY EVALUATION FORM

	Aug	Sept	Oct	Nov	Dec	Jan	Feb	March	April	May	June	July
DOES NOT COMPLAIN OR GRUMBLE												
STAYS WITHIN CHAIN OF AUTHORITY												
RECEIVES DISCIPLINE WITH PROPER ATTITUDE												
COMPLETES CHORES ON TIME												
COMPLETES SCHOOL WORK ON TIME												
RESPECTS OTHERS' PROPERTY												
WORKS WELL WITH SIBLINGS												
ACCEPTS RESPONSIBILITY FOR BELONGINGS												
RESOLVES CONFLICTS WITH SIBLINGS												
GIVES AND RECEIVES EMPATHY												

1=Weak in this area
2=Needs Improvement in this area
3=I am proud of my child's efforts in this area

*COMMENTS:*_____

_____

_____

_____

_____

CHARACTER TRAITS EVALUATION FORM

	Aug	Sept	Oct	Nov	Dec	Jan	Feb	March	April	May	June	July
FAITH												
LOYALTY												
RESPONSIBILITY												
PUNCTUALITY												
PATIENCE												
SELF-CONTROL												
MODESTY												
SELF-RESPECT												
HONESTY												
TACT												
GIVING												
PERSEVERANCE												
HARD WORK												
PATRIOTISM												
USING TIME WISELY												

1=Weak in this area
2=Needs Improvement in this area
3=I am proud of my child's efforts in this area

These are traits we need every hour. Children will not need algebra or spelling rules at all times, and in all places, but they need these traits.

COMMENTS: